SECOND EDITION

Basketball for Women

Nancy Lieberman

Human Kinetics

Library of Congress Cataloging-in-Publication Data

Lieberman, Nancy, 1958-
Basketball for women / Nancy Lieberman. -- 2nd ed.
p. cm.
Includes index.
ISBN-13: 978-0-7360-9294-4 (soft cover)
ISBN-10: 0-7360-9294-3 (soft cover)
1. Basketball for women. I. Title.
GV886.L44 2011
796.323'8--dc23
2011018480

ISBN-10: 0-7360-9294-3 (print)
ISBN-13: 978-0-7360-9294-4 (print)

The web addresses cited in this text were current as of July 2011, unless otherwise noted.

Acquisitions Editor: Justin Klug; **Managing Editor:** Laura Podeschi; **Assistant Editor:** Elizabeth Evans; **Copyeditor:** Patrick Connolly; **Indexer:** Betty Frizzéll; **Permissions Manager:** Martha Gullo; **Graphic Designer:** Fred Starbird; **Cover Designer:** Keith Blomberg; **Photographer (cover and interior, unless otherwise noted):** Neil Bernstein; **Photo Asset Manager:** Laura Fitch; **Visual Production Assistant:** Joyce Brumfield; **Photo Production Manager:** Jason Allen; **Art Manager:** Kelly Hendren; **Associate Art Manager:** Alan L. Wilborn; **Illustrations:** © Human Kinetics; **Printer:** Sheridan Books

We thank Fieldhouse USA in Frisco, Texas, for assistance in providing the location for the photo shoot for this book.

Human Kinetics books are available at special discounts for bulk purchase. Special editions or book excerpts can also be created to specification. For details, contact the Special Sales Manager at Human Kinetics.

Printed in the United States of America 10 9 8 7 6 5 4 3 2 1

The paper in this book is certified under a sustainable forestry program.

Human Kinetics
Website: www.HumanKinetics.com

United States: Human Kinetics
P.O. Box 5076
Champaign, IL 61825-5076
800-747-4457
e-mail: humank@hkusa.com

Canada: Human Kinetics
475 Devonshire Road Unit 100
Windsor, ON N8Y 2L5
800-465-7301 (in Canada only)
e-mail: info@hkcanada.com

Europe: Human Kinetics
107 Bradford Road
Stanningley
Leeds LS28 6AT, United Kingdom
+44 (0) 113 255 5665
e-mail: hk@hkeurope.com

Australia: Human Kinetics
57A Price Avenue
Lower Mitcham, South Australia 5062
08 8372 0999
e-mail: info@hkaustralia.com

New Zealand: Human Kinetics
P.O. Box 80
Torrens Park, South Australia 5062
0800 222 062
e-mail: info@hknewzealand.com

E5135

My life has been about playing, coaching, and loving this game called basketball. It gives me much joy to share my passion and experiences with the next generation, so we can continue to push the bar for each and every one of you that reads and puts this knowledge to work. My career isn't worth having if I don't share it. This book is for you, and I wish you "Intentional greatness" each step of the way! To all my coaches and basketball friends, thank you for sharing. It's being passed on.

God Bless,

Nancy Lieberman

Contents

Foreword

Women's basketball has made great strides in the last quarter century. More women and girls participate in this sport than ever before. Games are shown on national television. Top 25 polls for colleges and high schools are published regularly in most newspapers around the country. And the old six-player game—played until 1994 in Oklahoma—has given way to a more competitive, up-tempo, full-court brand of ball.

Despite these advances, we've only scratched the surface. Players like Nancy Lieberman, Cheryl Miller, Lynette Woodard, Lisa Leslie, and Sheryl Swoopes have given us a glimpse of what's possible. These players have paved the way and set an example that has helped develop current stars such as Diana Taurasi, Swin Cash, Tamika Catchings, and Candace Parker. Their brilliance is reflected in their total game, not just one facet. They can shoot, pass, handle, and defend. Plus they play smart and are team leaders. The total package.

What we need to elevate our game to new heights is to develop multiple skills in players. This will take an even greater commitment by women and girls who coach and play basketball; more time on the court; better instruction, better practices, better conditioning, more studying; a tough mental approach that distinguishes the serious, competitive athlete from the recreational player.

Basketball for Women, Second Edition, is for players to expand and improve their individual and team performance. The book motivates the serious player to work on all areas of her game, and not to be satisfied with her current level of skill, conditioning, or knowledge. After all, the worst type of player is a complacent player.

Coaches will want every player on their team to have a copy of this book. A roster full of complete players would make our job much easier, right coaches? When I recruit players to the University of Tennessee or am involved in selecting players to participate on all-star teams, I look for more than just physical talent. I look for players with multidimensional games; players who can turn to option B when option A isn't working; players who push themselves to be the best they can be and are never satisfied with their current level of play.

Nancy Lieberman is a perfect author for this book. She has excelled in both her basketball and professional career as a player and a coach. And her book will help you excel, too.

Pat Summitt

Preface

When I look back on the many moments in my career that have led me to where I am today, I first remember that phone call in 1974 that Mildred Asheper, the athletic director at Far Rockaway High School, made to the U.S. Olympic Committee. She talked with Bob Paul. He had received calls like this before: a coach or athletic director telling him that she had an athlete—a high school athlete—who she thought could make the Olympic women's basketball team. I was that athlete, and this time Bob's caller was right. I came home from Montreal in 1976 with a silver medal. Afterward, Bob told me that I was a success story. I was the first high school athlete to make a women's Olympic basketball team.

Basketball has truly been a blessing for me. During my career, I've realized many dreams and learned many lessons. My coaches and teammates were my teachers and role models. They inspired me and guided me when I was developing as a player. This book is my way of sharing what I have learned and motivating the next generation of young players and coaches, providing them with the best and latest instruction available for their growth.

Basketball and competition build confidence, self-esteem, and trust in yourself, your teammates, and your coaches. Basketball teaches you to never be afraid of accepting challenges and to always try, even when it seems as if you can't do something. Failure is noble; it means that you've tried. Accepting the possibility of failure will take away your need to use excuses and explanations. I have a mantra: "No excuses, no explanations." You must have accountability in whatever you choose to do. Excuses are moments to nowhere!

Think about your basketball skills. Are you a solid performer? Do you want to achieve greatness? Are you doing what it takes to excel? Hard work, discipline, and training can be fun for every player, parent, or coach who reads this book. It's easy to work hard on the days you feel good and have extra energy. But on the days you are mentally and physically tired, you must also find discipline and focus to practice and perform at a higher level.

That's the attitude it takes for you to get to the next level. You need to have the whole package—attitude, ability, desire, and effort. All great women basketball players share this goal to be the best. Diana Taurasi of the WNBA's Phoenix Mercury is one of the most gifted scorers in the world. As she has matured and grown in her game, she has learned to play solid defense and has developed the mind-set to compete each day, in practice and in games. Tamika Catchings, a three-time Olympian and winner at every level of her career, has worked on her ballhandling and outside shot to complement her already awesome athletic ability and work ethic. Angel McCoughtry of the Atlanta Dream was at one time thought to be just a great individual star.

This is no longer true! She is a leader and shows it by example—hard work, mental toughness, and unselfishness.

Today's athletes have it all: both amazing role models and countless opportunities to watch the game, from college to the WNBA to the Olympics, using various technologies. You are the next generation, and it's your job to set the bar even higher than it is today. You can be a part of the elite group mentioned previously, but it will take hard work and a love for the game. Give yourself every opportunity to find out just how good you can be. Put yourself in a position for good things to happen. You are the only one who knows how hard you're willing to work and how far you want to go. Be efficient and gamelike in your approach to practice. Approach your development systematically. Great players never become great in one season. It takes years of effort, determination, and practice. Identify your weaknesses as well as your strengths, then make your weaknesses strengths and make your strengths your ace in the hole—your go-to moves.

Watch players you like and admire. Imitate their moves and techniques. Watch as many games as you can. Go to women's and men's college and high school games with your parents, coach, or friends. Other players are out on the floor—faking, shaking, talking, driving, stopping, and popping—and someday that can be you!

Treat your development seriously. One of the greatest ingredients you will ever have is called repetition. By working on your skills in all areas and concentrating on the details over and over again, you will see constant changes and improvements in your game. You will maximize your game according to the amount of time you are willing to invest. Don't limit what you can be.

Your love of the game is very personal. This is why I keep saying that making it to the next level is about attitude, accountability, and responsibility. It's yours, and you own it.

I wish you intentional greatness.

God bless,

Nancy Lieberman

Key to Diagrams

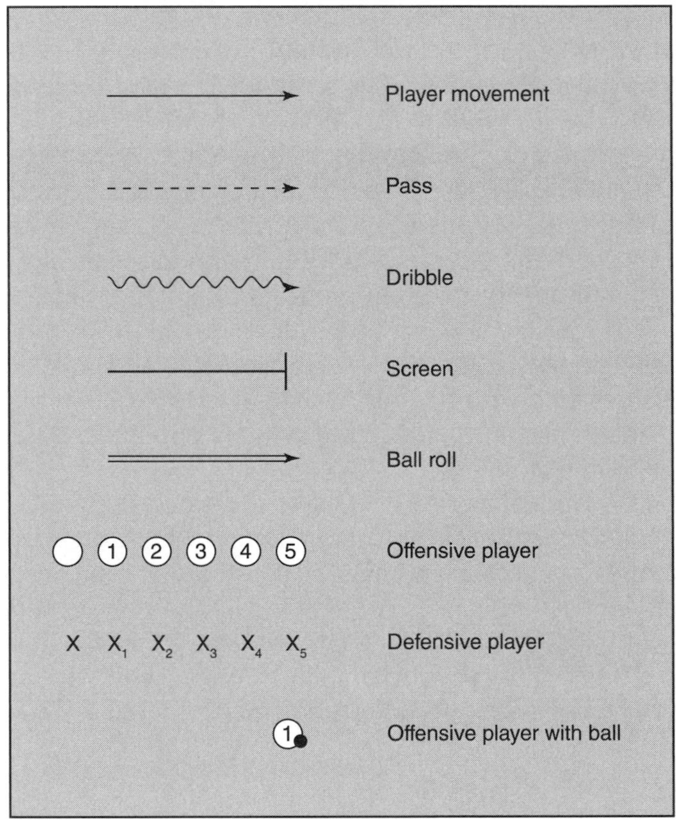

chapter

1

Taking Your Game to the Next Level

Taking your game to the next level of performance takes patience and focus. You should feel comfortable with yourself and your choices. Being feminine is completely fine. You don't have to give up your femininity or try to hide being a woman in order to succeed on the basketball court. Some women believe that in order to be taken seriously on the court, they can't be attractive. That theory has been blown out of the water. We have to be proud of who and what we are.

At the same time, we need to be aggressive and physical, and we must not be afraid to mix it up on the court. Sound confusing? It's all part of the identity crisis that women have had to face since they began playing basketball over 100 years ago. We've been told to be dainty and docile, not aggressive and athletic. Senda Berenson, the daughter of a Russian peddler who prized education, faced this dilemma when she first took a liking to a new indoor game that inventor James Naismith called basketball. Berenson, frail as a child, enrolled at the Boston Normal School of Gymnastics to improve her strength. She thrived, and she was later selected to fill a vacancy at Smith College as its gymnastics teacher. At Smith, Berenson experimented with the curriculum and ended up changing the course of women's athletics. Naismith's basketball intrigued her, but she did not want to be accused of promoting exercise that could be considered unfeminine. Berenson resolved the problem of society's stereotypes about women through compromise. She divided the basketball court into three sections and modified the rules. That way, physical contact between players was minimized.

A ROLE IN HISTORY

Since the inaugural season of the WNBA in 1997, women's basketball has been helped on all levels, and our game has expanded. Women's basketball is more up-tempo than it once was. Players push the ball up and down the

Title IX

Women's basketball received a boost in 1972 from Title IX, the gender equity law that prohibits discrimination based on gender in educational programs and activities at the collegiate level. With regard to athletic programs, Title IX addresses three basic equal opportunity program requirements: participation opportunities, scholarship dollars, and other athletic program benefits.

Schools are obligated to provide athletic opportunities for men and women in proportion to their enrollment in the general student body. If a college has 55 percent male undergraduates and 45 percent female undergraduates, athletic participation should reflect this mix. This does not mean that a school must provide an equal number of teams. Rather, the number of athletes should reflect this ratio.

In addition, scholarship dollars must be provided to male and female athletes proportional to their athletic participation. If a school is spending $400,000 per year for athletic scholarships and half of these athletes are women, then half the amount should be funding athletic scholarships for women. Equal opportunity also applies to program benefits—equipment, uniforms, and supplies. An institution must spend whatever is required to provide female basketball players with the same quality uniforms and equipment provided to male basketball players.

The game took another direction in 1982 when women's basketball became part of the NCAA. The women's game receives more exposure, funding, opportunities, and credibility as part of the NCAA. The game received still another boost through its partnership with CBS, which began airing regular-season games on television. In addition, more national awards are given to players who excel on the court and in the classroom. Finally, the NCAA established its women's basketball tournament, which began with 36 teams, later expanded to 48, and now invites 64 squads—the same as the men's tournament.

Comparisons Between Men's and Women's Basketball

Not long ago, people in women's basketball often had to deal with fans who compared the game to men's basketball. Such comparisons were certainly not negative, although women's basketball will continue to forge its own identity. Because of the physical differences between men and women (and the height of the rim), most women have not mastered the dunk or the ability, as they say, to play above the rim. Men's basketball has taken years to achieve the status it now enjoys. As female basketball players become better athletes, our game will take on these and other new elements.

Today's players face highly skilled competition. To improve, you must be eager to learn, listen, and apply new knowledge and skills to your game. You need to have solid fundamentals, good communication skills, mental preparedness, a solid work ethic, and physical ability.

nen's basketball has been fortunate to have its superstars: White, es, Dawn Staley, Anne Donovan, Katrina McClain, and many others. en players get bigger and quicker—and as they develop the ability higher and shoot better—it's likely that the day will come when nd players reminisce about yesterday's stars in this manner: "Yeah, r Staley and Swoopes. They were good, but wait until you see the atched today. They're really going to be great."

layers have opportunities to shine on many stages, from collegiate VNBA to the Olympics. Fans across the world are appreciating of women basketball players at all levels. Even though the guys perior physical traits—they are bigger, stronger, and quicker— now respected for similar talents. Men and women alike n up playing hoops from the beginning. Plus, the technology ilities are better for today's athletes. So this offers a lot of g where these young players might go and where the game ough the men's side is 55 years ahead of us in developing their fan base (with generations of loyal fans at both the level), we are slowly developing a devoted fan base of (like myself) who played the game are ticket-buying, TV- d it's only going to get better.

much further ahead of where men's basketball was in d '50s. Time is our biggest ally. The NBA wasn't playing re Garden, the Staples Center, or other major arenas or on n in years 1 to 10, nor did they have the salaries that WNBA draw. These are good times for women's sports on every aby!

e Moments

tball has achieved many milestones in addition to Title IX:

Senda Berenson introduces basketball to Smith College stu- ne first official women's basketball game is played at Smith n 1893.

the first official publication, *Basket Ball for Women*, is pub- y the Spalding Athletic Library, with Senda Berenson as its

two-court, six-player basketball is introduced.

, the first Kodak All-American Team is named.

78, the Women's Professional League opens in Milwaukee.

982, the Women's Basketball Coaches Association is formed.

984, the United States wins its first Olympic gold medal in women's ernational basketball. The U.S. squad defends its gold in 1988. The oviet Union had dominated women's basketball since 1958.

- In 1985, Kansas' Lynette Woodard becomes the first woman to with the Harlem Globetrotters.
- In 1986, Nancy Lieberman becomes the first woman to play in a m professional league—the United States Basketball League (USBL). plays for the Springfield Fame in 1986 and the Long Island Kni in 1987.
- At the 1990 NCAA tournament in Knoxville, Tennessee, 16,595 f watch the championship game, and 17,601 watch the semifinals. most pleasing aspect is that Tennessee is not even in the tournam
- In 1991, the NAIA championship tournament expands to 32 tea
- In 1991, Lisa Leslie sets a record by scoring 101 points in the first of a high school game.
- In 1992, Kodak sponsors the first All-American game for girls' h school players. Katie Smith and Crystal Robinson are named MV
- In 1993, the Women's Basketball Hall of Fame is established in Jacks Tennessee. The Basketball Hall of Fame in Springfield, Massachuse has enshrined Nera White, Coach Margaret Wade (Delta State), A Meyers, Carol Blazejowski, Lucy Harris-Stewart, Anne Donovan, a Cheryl Miller.
- The 1993 women's Final Four in Atlanta sells out, drawing more th 17,000 fans.
- In 1993, collegiate women's basketball begins having its own p season classic—the State Farm Women's Basketball Hall of Fa Tip-Off Classic. Inaugural participants are Texas Tech, Ohio Sta Tennessee, and Vanderbilt.
- The 1994 NCAA women's Final Four in Richmond, Virginia, sells o a year before the tournament. More than 13,000 fans attend.
- In 1995, Liberty Sports purchases the Women's Basketball Associatio
- The 1996 women's Final Four in Charlotte, North Carolina, sells o More than 23,000 tickets are sold.
- In 1997, the WNBA plays its inaugural season. At age 39, Nan Lieberman becomes the oldest player in the league with the Phoen Mercury.
- In 1998, Tennessee's women's basketball team wraps up a perfect 39 season with their third consecutive national championship.
- In 2005, Pat Summitt wins her 880th game as a coach, giving her th most victories in NCAA basketball history for both men and wome
- In 2008, the WNBA's Detroit Shock sign hall of famer Nancy Liebe man to a seven-day contract. She makes history by playing again the Houston Comets at the age of 50.

- In 2009, the Dallas Mavericks' NBA developmental team in Frisco, Texas, hires hall of famer Nancy Lieberman as the first female head coach in league history.
- In 2010, UConn's women's basketball team wins its 89th consecutive game, the longest winning streak in NCAA basketball history. The streak ends at 90 with a loss to Stanford.

GETTING STARTED

To play any sport at the highest level, you need to have self-esteem and true confidence, which are developed by putting your time in and practicing. In addition, you must have the ability to be focused and to make whatever you are doing a priority.

Not everybody is going to do that. Maybe some players can be good while giving it half their effort. But here's one thing I know about life: If you love something, you'll give it the best you have—your focus, your concentration, your time, your effort, and your energy.

You also need to have a risk–reward mentality. You must be willing to take risks to get to the next level. You can't be afraid to try because you're afraid of failing. Play through mistakes; failure is noble! It means that you gave it your best effort and didn't play it safe.

First and foremost, you must work to achieve individual improvement. You must be better individually to be better in a team concept. How great is that? It's about you and your self-improvement and how much time you are willing to put into it!

Identifying Your Goals

Learning how to set realistic goals and then achieve them is the most important thing you can do as a young player. How do you start? Let's say your goal is to make all-state in your area. You need to honestly assess your level of ability. Think of it as a scouting report. What are your strengths and weaknesses? Are they physical? Mental? Set up a plan and evaluate the following eight areas of your game:

- Shooting
- Passing
- Ballhandling
- Rebounding
- Defense
- Conditioning
- Mental approach
- Coachability

Developing Your Plan

Now that you have identified your goals for improvement and the order in which you will undertake them, you need to develop your plan for overall improvement. Have your coach or mentor work with you. Share your evaluation of your strengths and weaknesses with the coach. Ask the coach to recommend some drills that you can use to work on each of the areas you have listed. Now, take a step back and review. First, you know your problem areas. Second, you are getting information that will enable you to establish a proper plan for improvement. Coaches are a great source of knowledge. They are also objective. You want to have three to five drills to work on in each skill area. This way, you won't be doing the same drill over and over. Diversity will keep challenging you and keep your interest level up. Different drills can achieve the same results.

Next, determine how much time you can devote to your game each day. Remember, you have other commitments during your day to think about—school, family, practice, and so on. Find a good time to fit basketball into your schedule. Make sure it is a time when you can concentrate totally on your game. I always tell my players, "Don't mistake activity for success." Be efficient with your time and intensity; how you work really does matter! Do your skill and drill work with intensity in order to get something out of it. One day, you might want to use your time to work on drills in four of the categories. The next day, you might work on the other four. Maybe you need to work only on ballhandling and shooting. Push yourself to be uncomfortable.

Now that you have developed your plan, you must put it into action.

Taking Action

Basically, taking action is practicing. And practicing might mean watching films, working on your conditioning, or playing one on one. Too many players today only play the game and don't spend enough time breaking their game down to work on individual skills and drills. They think that if they just play, they will get better. This is not true! These players are only reinforcing the bad habits they might have. Taking action can make the difference in your basketball career. You're not just talking about improvement; you are actually working on your skills. It sounds easy, and it can be. That's how the great players became great.

Start by getting to the gym or court early enough to stretch and loosen up. If you are with a partner, make sure she also has an organized plan for her areas of improvement. You want to push each other's intensity. Remember, you can push yourself when practicing on your own, too. Keep in mind what you want to accomplish, and when you get tired, work harder and work through it. This will push you to a higher level and take you where you want to go.

Be Prepared

Make sure you have the number of basketballs you will need. Maybe it's just one. (I always had two balls when doing ballhandling drills so that I could work both hands at the same time.) Get into the drill immediately. Remember, you should make it gamelike. Be quick. Explode. Be focused and concentrate on each skill and the drill you have chosen. Try not to cut corners. Don't make your goal just to get through a drill; master the drill through repetition.

Practice the not-so-glamorous parts of the game. And remember, repetition is key. Practicing your shooting is important, but you must also practice dribbling—using your ballhandling skills to shake a defender or to create separation one on one. In addition, you must practice being a penetrator so that teams will have to run at you or double-team you to get the ball out of your hands. Then, you can make a sweet pass to a teammate. Maybe the clock is winding down and your team is behind by 1. You play great defense and pick up a charge. You put your team in a position to win. That's why you need to become fundamentally sound by practicing each of these different areas of the game. You will have more advantages on the court. The more skills you have, the better your chances of succeeding and, ultimately, of winning.

Players get named to all-state teams by doing the extra things: putting in hours of practice and repetition. Players earn college athletic scholarships by doing more than the average players. Cynthia Cooper, who was the MVP of the WNBA when she played for the Houston Comets, would pay a ball kid to meet her at the arena early, before all her teammates got to the game. She would put up 300 to 400 shots each game day! You must push yourself more than others. You reach another level of performance and reach your goals by dedicating yourself to hard work and practice, by studying the game, and by having fun.

Sacrifice

Taking action also means sacrifice, which means giving up personal glory. It means putting your team's success first. It also means organizing your time to make the most of your day. You can eliminate distractions from your hectic everyday schedule. Stay focused on a few areas: academics, practice, games, and family. Academics are extremely important. To be a good team player, you must be on the team. Stay eligible! Show your teammates that you have balance in life. This will reflect how your teammates look at you. Use your time wisely. There are only so many hours in the day. I'm not saying you should live your whole life around basketball. But if you want to be good or great, you must determine what your priorities will be.

Finding an Edge

When I was playing at Old Dominion University, I was always looking for an edge. I was never satisfied with my play. I always wanted more. In a sense, this may sound as if I were greedy. I was. Being the best was important to me. My teammates were good, very good. I wanted to be better than them and my opponents. If a teammate was a better outside shooter, my goal was to improve my shooting to match hers. If we had a drill, I wanted to be first in line. I wanted to win every wind sprint and suicide. For me, being number two was only acceptable after I gave my best effort to be first.

Maybe it was my drive, my willingness to always compete, and my everyday focus that separated me from others. Growing up in New York, I knew at age 10 that I wanted to be the best basketball player in the world. When I heard this man on TV say he was the "greatest of all time," I immediately said to my mom, "I'm going to be the greatest basketball player of all time!" She said, "Are you crazy, Nancy? Girls don't play sports or basketball." But I told her to get used to it. If Muhammad Ali was the greatest boxer of all time, then I was going to be the greatest basketball player. That was my goal, and I made sacrifices to enhance that dream. I didn't go to parties or watch a lot of television or movies. I was always in the gym or school yard shooting, playing against better players (especially against boys), practicing my ballhandling skills, and thinking about the game. I loved it. And you know what? I never thought of playing basketball 5 or 6 hours a day as a sacrifice. It's what I wanted to do. It has helped me with the work ethic I have today in all areas of my life. My passion for basketball has given me an understanding of how I want to live my life.

Be a Student of the Game

You've probably heard the phrase "You have to be a student of the game." When you are in the classroom, you're there to learn. The same is true when you're on the court. So much valuable information is available. Watch college and high school games. Single out players and study their moves. Tape women's games on television and watch them again and again. Listen to what the commentators are saying about the players when they analyze the action. The commentators may be breaking down a defense or offense that you haven't mastered. Read basketball magazines and watch instructional tapes. There's nothing better than participating in summer camps and clinics to improve your game and to challenge yourself against other players. Doing these things will help you improve. If you're willing to learn, you're going to get better.

To truly be a student of the game, you must have an overall approach to improvement. Of course, getting out and practicing the fundamentals is vital. But so is having knowledge and an understanding of the game.

The information you need is close by. Use your coaches as sources of information. Don't be shy about asking for their time. The game will be much simpler if you understand it. Coaches can objectively evaluate your skill level and your mental approach to games and practices. With the information that the coaches share with you, you can determine where your strengths and weaknesses lie. Once you know these things, a plan for improvement can be put together. Knowing how to listen is important. That allows you to learn. View your coaches or other mentors as people who can help you get better. Take their comments positively. Try not to take any criticism personally. Your coaches are just being truthful and helpful.

And coaches, your responsibility is to be there for your players. Teach them the skills they need in order to improve, but also teach them about the mental aspects of the game. Be available to work with players who hunger for more time and improvement. Take pride in them as they reach another level of performance. As you know, being a coach is a demanding role. Players watch you and emulate your characteristics, mannerisms, and overall philosophy. They're around you a lot. Be a solid role model for your kids. Go the extra step. Take them to clinics and encourage them to work hard but enjoy the game.

Make improvements in your coaching game as well. Go to clinics and talk the game with other coaches. Watch high school and college games. Your overall improvement and learning will enhance your ability to teach your players and to communicate with your team, no matter what level you are coaching.

The relationship between a coach and player is special. The time, respect, trust, and achievement the two share will last a lifetime. Coaches are changing the lives of their players. What could be a greater feeling than knowing you are helping mold a young lady's future?

Listening and Learning

Can you imagine being just 17 years old and having already played for legendary coaches such as hall of famers Cathy Rush, Billie Moore, and Sue Gunter, not to mention outstanding AAU and high school coaches? Each of these coaches presented me with so much information. Sometimes it was confusing, but I didn't let their different styles frustrate me. I tried to be flexible, which was a key learning point. I couldn't be stubborn when it came to improving my skills. If a coach suggested that I try a new technique, I needed to be open to the advice. Refusing to try would have been a major mistake.

Now, it wasn't easy. Yes, I got yelled at, and yes, my ego was sometimes hurt, but I knew I was getting better from the criticism. If the coach isn't yelling at you or telling you what you are doing wrong, you're not in the mix. If you are needed, the coach will yell and coach you up! To tell you the truth, I'm not fond of coaches who yell and scream, but you will come across them. Please don't be sensitive when this happens; get tough and move on! Coaches really do want you to be better, and it's their job to make you uncomfortable and push you to a new level!

Envision Success

Have you ever been on the court by yourself shooting? In your mind, the clock is counting down—5, 4, 3, 2, 1. You shoot and make the shot at the buzzer. You win the game. How many times have you missed that last shot? In your mind, not many. That's your vision. You are seeing yourself in a successful moment. Mentally, you've done it so many times that when you have to respond in a game situation, you've been there before. You can practice having vision. Doing so creates confidence—muscle memory of being successful in your own mind. I'm a big believer in the practice of mentally seeing yourself in a successful situation. Being able to do this is a tremendous advantage. You can develop this ability. All it takes is mental practice. Here are four steps you can use to improve your ability to envision success:

1. On or off the court, think of game or practice situations in which you want to be successful.
2. On or off the court, create mental games for yourself. For example, you're at the foul line with 1 second left, and your team is down by 1 point. The fans are going nuts. You step to the line for two foul shots. You nail the first one and shoot the second one to win the championship for your team. You see it going through the net. You make the shot. It's a great feeling.
3. Use mirror vision. Stand in front of a mirror. Work on whatever skill you need to improve. Maybe it's your shooting form. Shoot a ball and check out your form. Is it what you thought it was? If your form is incorrect, you can now see it and make the correction. For example, is your elbow out, or in the correct L position? The mirror doesn't lie.
4. Dream on. Every night while lying in bed before you go to sleep, envision a part of your game. Maybe it's picking up a charge or grabbing a rebound. Maybe it's shooting. Make 100 shots to perfect your form and follow-through before you go to sleep. Always visualize success. This will help you when you get to the court. Your confidence will soar as you work on your vision of what you can accomplish.

Politics and Vision

The people who came before us allow us to have vision. I would never have thought that one day a woman could be president of the United States had it not been for Geraldine Ferraro, who was the Democratic vice-presidential candidate in 1984. She opened the door for other women to succeed in politics and government. Thanks to Ferraro, women can aspire to lead our country—and someday will. She didn't win the election, but she gave women vision.

More recently, Danica Patrick began racing at Indy and driving NASCAR. We elected an African-American president in Barack Obama. And I was the first woman to become a head coach of a men's team in the NBA developmental league. Anything is possible with faith and hard work!

Practice, Practice, Practice

Practice is the word you will hear most often from coaches. Practice is the place where you can be in control of your actions and your rate of improvement. Practice gives you a chance to work on individual and team skills. It teaches you chemistry and timing, which are so important when playing a team sport.

You can take so much knowledge away from a practice session. You gain answers to many questions: How did I match up against the other players? What were my strong points and weaknesses during practice? Was I competitive? Did I play as if I wanted to be the best? Was I coachable? Was I focused? Did I make myself and my teammates better? What was my level of intensity? These are all questions you should think about when getting ready to practice. Your answers will reflect how you play in games. Here are some things that will help you dominate on the court:

- Think about practice before you get there. Be ready to compete!
- Arrive early enough to relax. Get warmed up properly and stretch so that you are ready to start when practice begins, not 10 or 15 minutes later.
- Work on your weaknesses. Turn them into strengths.
- Be a positive person. Encourage others. Don't get down on your teammates or yourself after a mistake.
- Be a leader. Set an example by having focus, enthusiasm, and intensity in all practices.

- Listen to the coach. Ask questions if you are not sure about a drill or situation.
- If you are practicing by yourself, have a plan for what areas you want to cover. Be efficient. Don't waste time.
- Most important, even in practice, play to win. By doing so, you will raise the playing level of all your teammates.

Motivation

Motivation is the key to any challenge. If you are competitive enough to want to be better, maybe even the best, then you have the ability to be motivated. Motivation is the reason you put more time and effort into your individual game. Motivation is your desire to achieve personal and team success. Pat Summitt is still motivated today even though she is already the all-time winningest women's coach with more than 1,000 career wins. And Diana Taurasi has been motivated enough to win three national titles with UConn, two championships with the WNBA's Phoenix Mercury, and even Olympic gold! Someone, somewhere—it could be you—may be motivated to accomplish even more one day.

Your motivation should be fueled by the goals you set. Here are some examples of goals you might set:

- Work on weaknesses.
- Make the all-state team.
- Win a championship.
- Receive a full scholarship to college.
- Play in the women's Final Four, and win it.
- Play in the Olympics and the WNBA—anything is possible!

Be motivated to practice, work hard, and achieve every goal you set. Motivation comes from seeing other athletes' success. This gives the rest of us something to shoot for. Being motivated for success is a great feeling, even as you work toward your goals.

Positive Influences

As a player, you spend most of your time with coaches. You watch how they talk, walk, and dress. You may even pick up on their mannerisms without knowing it. Coaches are a great source of information. Many times you think you know what the coach wants, but maybe the timing or the options are difficult to understand. Ask questions! It's much like being in the classroom. Listen, ask the teacher questions, and get the explanation. Then, apply it.

We all have our own stories of who guided us at certain times in our careers. I'm a lucky lady. When I was growing up, my AAU coach, La Vosier LaMar, taught me not to fear anyone and to respect everyone. So many others influenced me. Brian Sackrowitz and Larry Morse, my high school coaches, taught the street player in me discipline, teamwork, and, of course, the fundamentals.

Other positive influences can include older players whom you've watched and players you've competed against. In addition, a great number of collegiate and WNBA players are now prominent figures. Study how they handle themselves both on and off the court. Look for individuals who carry themselves with class. It's one thing to be a great basketball player, but it's another thing to embrace good sporting behavior.

Learn from your influences. Just as you have watched players before you, others will watch how you deal with referees and how you show respect for your coaches. They will also observe how you handle defeat. It's easy to behave well when you win. But unpleasant situations are more telling. Are you willing to give other teams and players credit if they beat you? Always remember that someone somewhere is watching your actions. You don't want to do anything to embarrass yourself, your family, or your school.

The Reports Didn't Lie

Scouting reports can be valuable tools for winning. Hall of famer Marianne Stanley, my coach at Old Dominion University, would order scouting reports about our opponents, but she would also order reports about Old Dominion. This gave us a chance to see how other teams viewed our strengths and weaknesses. She allowed us to read our individual reports. Scouting reports listed my left hand as weak and indicated that opponents should give me the outside shot. This was different from how I viewed my game. I began working on these two areas consistently on my own during practice. By my senior year, my left hand and outside shooting were no longer listed as weaknesses. As a matter of fact, they became strengths. I had new options and was more unpredictable on the court. The more options you have, the more chances you have for success.

At the 1976 Olympics, Billie Moore and Sue Gunter of Louisiana State University shared their wisdom and patience with me. University of Tennessee coach Pat Summitt, who was a teammate on the 1975 and 1976 U.S. teams, taught me toughness, showed me how to be mentally and physically ready, and, more than anything else, pushed me to achieve. Marianne Stanley, my coach at Old Dominion, gave me the thinking part of the game. She also showed me how to make each of my teammates better. She taught me how to be a leader.

I will always have a soft spot in my basketball heart for Coach C. Vivian Stringer (of Rutgers University). She gave me an honest chance to make the 1989 U.S. national team. The United States had just opened the Olympics to professional athletes. I hadn't played for my country since the 1980 Olympic trials. At age 29, I made the team.

Greg Williams (currently the head coach at Rice University) taught me to be a true professional when I was with the Dallas Diamonds in the first two women's pro leagues in the early '80s. I would be committing an injustice if I left out Henry Bibby and Dean "The Dream" Meminger, whom I played for in the United States Basketball League (USBL). They were in a difficult position, having a woman on their teams. They needed to win, play the best players, keep the media and fans happy, and find playing time for me. They accomplished all that, but it was a difficult task. During our time together, Bibby and Meminger learned to handle new situations. I learned more about myself and my game from the limited minutes I received. By playing against the guys every day in practice, I gained valuable insight on how to play the game at a higher level. I was forced to use my fundamentals and not just my athletic ability. I had to be smarter in how I played the game. I also learned to understand coaches better. More than anything, I learned to soak up as much knowledge and information as possible from each coach for whom I've had the pleasure of playing!

Soaking Up Knowledge

When I was at Old Dominion, I'm sure my coach thought I was a nuisance. I didn't care. I was there to learn, and she was one of the best. Look at Coach Stanley's credentials: a three-time All-American who at age 24 became head coach at one of the best women's basketball schools in the country. Coach Stanley had played basketball at Immaculata College in Pennsylvania for Cathy Rush, the John Wooden of women's basketball. I couldn't pass up the opportunity to learn from Coach Stanley. I figured I might not get another chance to learn from such a basketball expert, one who had learned from another legend. I wanted to be like a sponge and soak up all the information she had to share. I asked a lot of questions—probably to the point of being annoying. "What do you see?" "How do you do that?" She always answered, and I always listened. She gave me freedom to make decisions, let me play through my mistakes, and most important, showed confidence and trust in me to lead my team! She was one of the best teachers of the game I have ever encountered.

SUMMARY

Taking your game to the next level means understanding who came before you and who set the standards for you to surpass. Remember these points:

- Women's basketball has a rich history. You can learn from the persistence of the sport pioneers who helped advance the game.
- The keys for success are self-confidence, desire, and discipline.
- You need to put your plan for success into action.
- To succeed, you must be a student of the game. Identify the roles of players and coaches; everyone has an important role.
- You should develop your vision for your game. See yourself succeeding.
- To improve your game, you must practice, practice, practice.
- Your motivation will determine how far you will go.

chapter

2

Developing a Winning Attitude

Some people have a great level of skill, while some people have will—that is, they are mentally tough. If you have both, you have every chance to succeed. Everyone has a different take on what winning is and what it means. I really believe in John Wooden's thoughts on leadership. His well-known pyramid of success specifies that people need to be industrious and have friendship, loyalty, cooperation, and enthusiasm. You must have these building blocks in order to develop a winning attitude. To play, you're going to need teammates. And to work as a team, you must be loyal to one another. Being loyal means cooperating with your teammates; it can't just be your way. Finally, cooperation leads to a more cohesive team, which breeds enthusiasm.

You must also have enthusiasm for the game of basketball itself. Part of having a winning attitude means always striving for more. To me, success is a mind-set. Visualize where you want to be, and then do whatever you have to do to get there. I have a handwritten letter that a friend gave to me. The letter—dated March 18, 1986—is from Pete Maravich to Larry King after Larry had Pete on his show. Here's the best part of the letter:

> "One of the great keys to my success was an ingredient called repetition. By working on particular areas of basketball, shooting, ballhandling, dribbling, passing, spinning, and others and concentrating on the details over and over again, I saw this constant change taking place in the improvement of my game. I often share with young people that they will maximize their God-given talent according to the amount of time they are willing to invest in it. At least, I have experienced that. I have witnessed the same in many aspiring young people. You also have reached the top of your field. Not by luck or coincidence, but by Godly talent, hard work, and repetition. And I'm sure by other factors as well."

This is exactly what players should be thinking about. *How do I maximize my God-given talent? How do I become great?* Pete hit it right on the head. Repetition. Over and over and over again. Even when people believe that they have gotten to the top of the mountain, if they stop working, they are not going to improve.

In the '80s, many people considered me to be the best basketball player in the world. Even then, when I walked onto the basketball court, I never thought of myself as having made it. I was always still hunting, going after something. I never wanted to be satisfied that I made it to the top.

THE MENTAL GAME

The mental part of basketball can separate you from others. If you can clearly see situations on and off the court, you will be able to make proper decisions based on what you think and what you actually do when you are playing. The mental aspect of the game allows you to be aware of what is happening. When you know that you can outsmart an opponent with strategy or deception, this gives you a great edge. Here are the four elements to the mental portion of the game:

- Thinking the game
- Having confidence
- Knowing skills and strategies
- Using creativity (feeling the game)

Each component can be used to your advantage. All it takes is effort. Remember, the most talented athlete isn't always the best player or the winner. Sometimes, the player who thinks a better game comes out on top.

Thinking the Game

Play games with yourself. Take a piece of paper and draw a miniature court. Run your offense or defense as you think it's meant to be run. By putting it on paper and drawing the screens, cuts, and dribbles, you start to look at timing, and you mentally go through your options. For example, in this process, you might think, *OK, we're stuck. Let's reverse the movement and check the weak-side options. Let's say the defender overplayed the wing. I could fade to the corner for the shot. It might be open.* This process also works with defenses. In that case, you might think, *If I rotate up on the trap, what passing lanes are open? If it's in the corner, I'd better get off the ball and rotate to protect the basket.*

When referring to thinking the game, I'm not saying that you should stop, think about what to do, and then do it. You will not have success if you have to totally stop and think the game. To think the game, you must have the ability to react spontaneously on the court—and to do so better and more quickly than your opponents or teammates. You have studied the offenses and defenses, and you can read situations as they develop.

You can think the game by knowing your options on the court, by having the ability to see where players are, and by doing what you can to create situations within your team's game plan.

Thinking is knowing what's going on (seeing what's going on around you). This includes knowing how much time is on the clock—both the game clock and the shot clock. You may need to decide whether you should call a time-out. Was it a smart time-out to burn? Can you play with three fouls? It all comes down to what you do repeatedly. Are your choices sound?

You can learn the thinking part of the game. You will usually learn this from your mistakes. That's how you find out if your choices on the court are correct. Thinking goes hand in hand with solid fundamentals. If you master both, you'll be able to determine (through thinking) what you need to do and then execute it.

Having Confidence

Confidence means knowing that you will be successful. Success and hard work breed confidence. The more you experience being successful, the better you are going to feel about yourself and your skills. If you have made jumper after jumper from the corner in practice, you will remember that success when it's time to take that shot in a game.

A serious athlete must have confidence and must know that she can win. In the early 1980s, Martina Navratilova was already one of the greatest tennis players in the history of the game and had won two Wimbledon titles, yet she still didn't believe she was a winner. She didn't believe that she could win consistently. At that time, Martina didn't train for success consistently. When she changed her training habits in 1981 and began believing that she could win consistently, she went into every match believing that she couldn't lose. That's the attitude you have to take with you on the basketball court. If you think you can defeat your opponent, you already have an edge.

Confidence allows you to control your success and setbacks. If you know what you're capable of accomplishing on the court, you're going to be self-assured when it's time to test your skills. Let's say you can bench-press 135 pounds 10 times in a row. If you're asked to lift that 135 pounds—or even a little bit more—you're going to be confident that you can accomplish the task. It's the same on the basketball court. If you constantly hit your free-throw shots in practice, you can be confident that you're going to hit them in a game.

Confidence allows you to walk onto the court, size up your opponent, and tell yourself that there's no way you're going to lose to this person or team. You're going to play to the best of your ability, and your opponent is going to have to outplay you in order to win. You need to prepare properly and take care of all the elements you can control. You can't worry about those elements that are outside of your control.

I love watching players in warm-ups. I can usually tell who the studs are! It's the way they walk and carry themselves. If you are a player who is being recruited, you must be sure to warm up hard; college coaches will come early to see your work ethic and preparation habits. What people think of you is in your hands; I just love that—it's in your hands!

Building Confidence

You began building your confidence the first time you picked up a basketball. This might have been with your parents or with some friends. You checked out the game. You may have thought, *I like this game. I think I'll give it a try.*

As your basketball career progressed, you began to get an idea of what you do well. At the same time, you probably discovered what areas needed some work. If you targeted those weaknesses and worked until they were eliminated, you accomplished two important things. First, you mastered your weaknesses and became a better all-around player. Second, you saw what you could accomplish with a little work and determination. That builds confidence.

Your progress will help your confidence soar. You will be a more well-rounded player. You will know it and so will your opponents. You will be much more difficult to guard. You'll be able to take defenders inside or outside, shoot over them, or drive around them. If that doesn't get your confidence going, nothing will.

Another way to build your confidence is to find and develop your specialty, or go-to move. Everyone knows about Diana Taurasi's three-point shot; she is a master of the quick shot, separating herself from the defense. People also recognize Kobe Bryant's fade shot. Whenever the Los Angeles Lakers need a basket, they turn to Bryant. You need to determine what part of your game is strongest and then polish and accentuate that skill. That way, you always have an ace to turn to in a tight situation. This doesn't mean you can neglect the rest of your game or the other players around you, but when it's money time, that's when the great players shine. Reputation and street credibility are built on big-time fearless performances in big moments!

Working for a Shot

When my collegiate basketball career ended, despite what I had already accomplished, I was not a great outside shooter. Perimeter defenders often backed off me a few steps, knowing that I was likely to pass or drive rather than shoot a jumper. I had succeeded as a penetrator and opportunity-type player. Many of my easy baskets were off steals and turnovers. Those days, I realized, were coming to an end.

In 1980, I signed a contract to play in the Women's Professional Basketball League. I knew that my game had to go to another level and that I needed to add the outside shot in order to be more effective. My head coach, Greg Williams of the Dallas Diamonds, told me quite bluntly, "Nancy, you need an outside game."

That summer was one of the most challenging, yet rewarding, periods of my life. My former college teammate Rhonda Rompola and I played every day. Without exception, I took 400 to 500 shots a day. In college, we didn't yet have the three-point shot. Now, in the women's league, we would. I needed to be ready to add the three-point shot to my game. So every day when I was practicing my shooting, I made sure that 150 of those shots were from three-point range.

That first year in the women's league was a good one for me. I averaged 30 points a game. I shot 56 percent from the floor and 40 percent from three-point range. I had the confidence to pull up and shoot from the outside, and the threat of my outside shot set up my slashing to the basket. I had another weapon.

When I later played in the men's leagues, my three-point shot and my range were a key to my success.

In 1993, Sheryl Swoopes was the best player in the nation, and she led Texas Tech to the NCAA championship. With all her talent, Sheryl was never a one-dimensional player. But with a game on the line, Swoopes and the Lady Raiders knew that they could rely on her outside shot.

Confidence comes from winning. First, you have to know how to win. We're not talking strictly in terms of points on the scoreboard and who finishes ahead. If you control your emotions during a game, then you're a winner. If you are respectful of the referees throughout a game, you're a winner. If you concentrate on working with your teammates so everyone plays better rather than worrying about your own statistics in a game, then you're definitely a winner.

If you think of success and winning in terms of progress and achievement, you can be a winner every time you take the court. Just make sure that you don't waste your time and you'll always improve.

Finally, a confident basketball player is one who has done her homework. You should want to learn everything you can about the game. You need to know your offensive and defensive strategies by heart. We'll talk more later about how knowledge of skills and strategies sharpens your mental game. For now, remember that you can play your best if you are sure of yourself, are relaxed, and know what you should be doing. There's no excuse for the player who isn't prepared. Knowledge comes from practice. So pay attention. When your coach is talking, listen. Your coach may be sharing valuable information to help you understand a drill or strategy. Even if your coach is speaking to another player, it never hurts to listen.

Incorporating Confidence Into Your Game

Turning yourself into a confident player isn't easy. It all begins with pride. You should be proud of your team and yourself. This has to come from within. Pride comes from constantly challenging yourself and your teammates to get better. That pride and hard work will turn into confidence, and your opponents will sense that you are sure of yourself. Confidence shows in the way you hustle on and off the court. It shows in the way you keep your cool when a referee's call goes the other way.

His Airness Versus Lady Magic

In July 1993, I was a guest of Michael Jordan at his basketball camp for boys and girls, which was held at Elmhurst College near Chicago. During one of Michael's lectures, he talked about one-on-one moves. The next thing I knew, it was me and Mike going one on one with 450 campers watching. My goal was not only to make Michael sweat, but also to make him work. He's a talker. He talks trash. And, he's full of confidence. He was trying to intimidate me, seeing if I would accept the challenge. I was thinking, *No way am I going to roll over and let him have his way.* I wasn't about to let his reputation and his confidence sway my confidence. Obviously, I was overmatched. I did manage to make some moves and slide by for a lefty running shot off the glass. Not only did it put a smile on Michael's face, but the shot drew a cheer from the kids. OK, I lost 10-2, but I was giving it my best—mentally and physically. I think my effort and confidence surprised everyone. It wasn't about the score or about who won and who lost. It was about earning Michael's respect and keeping my own. From years of experience, I had the confidence to play him to the best of my ability. I couldn't ask more of myself.

Confidence, however, doesn't mean cockiness. Some players cross the line and are no longer confident, just cocky. They showboat and pop their jerseys, and they sacrifice the good of their team for their own glory. They seek attention first and worry about others second. It might be easy to show off your skills just for the sake of letting others see what you can do. But that doesn't make it right. Don't dribble behind your back or between your legs just because you feel like doing it or you believe it might impress someone. You need to have a reason. If it's the best option for gaining an edge on your opponent, then go ahead. But if you're doing these things just to show off, it will someday backfire on you—that's not being a good team player. Players who show off live for the moment—what they think is the spectacular. You should strive for long-term consistency and quality. That's what is really spectacular.

A confident player is difficult to stop because she feels good about her game. Confident players carry their teams to victory. You're sure to build your confidence if you focus on improvement and progress. After each game, evaluate your performance. Watch the game film, if possible. Focus on what you did well and not so well. Remember those things and think about them before the next game. Learn from your mistakes. Watch what you did before you made a mistake and try to figure out what you can do to prevent yourself from making the same mistake again. If you notice (on film) that every time you missed a free throw, your elbow was out and it changed the position of your arm, you would know that you have to work on your mechanics. When you do things well, get a mental picture of exactly how you did it and how you felt. If you're a confident player, you'll be able to take a good, hard look at your performance and take steps to make it even better next time.

Knowing Skills and Strategies

When it comes to skills and strategy, basketball players don't have it easy. There's much more to the game than Xs and Os. You have to know when to press and when to trap. You have to know how to break a press and how to work that trap. You have to be aware of spacing on both offense and defense. Football players, in some ways, have it much easier. They specialize. They have to know offensive or defensive strategies and plays, but usually not both. In basketball, you must know both offense and defense if you want to compete. In the early days of basketball, girls played offense or defense in six-on-six competition. They specialized in one portion of the game. With today's up-tempo, transition style of basketball, you need to be proficient at both or you'll be left behind.

When you're young, you are responsible for learning some of the basic skills you need in order to compete. High school and college coaches have less time to teach these days because of all the rule changes restricting practice time (these rule changes allow players to have more time to handle their academic requirements). If the next step for you is to play college basketball, you should play the game as often as you can in order to get your fundamentals down. College coaches don't have as much time these days for players who can't dribble the ball with both hands or who don't box out well. You don't have to be perfect, but you must have the skills that coaches believe they can work with. Years ago, a player who was extremely tall, but clumsy, was considered a project; coaches wouldn't expect this person to contribute to their program right away. These days, with so many talented players in junior high and high school, there's not much time for projects. Scholarships are expensive and valuable for a player's education and development. The best advice I can give you is to learn these skills—the basics—early so you are ready for high school ball. You can then spend time polishing your skills instead of learning them.

Building Knowledge of Skills and Strategies

Understanding of basketball skills and strategies can be developed in many ways. As you experience situations on the court or watch games, you see how other players react and what decisions they make. You will find out if you can achieve the same results once you get on the court. I'm a firm believer in watching the game and listening to coaches or successful players. Building knowledge is gathering information. If a play is stopped, consider your other options for keeping the play successful. You should be able to read situations on the floor and make split-second adjustments. This could be on the offensive or defensive end. An important aspect of basketball is avoiding the tendency to predetermine what you are going to do. Stick to your game plan if you see that it can work, but realize that you must have flexibility. Sure, you might know what offense you need to run against a 2-3 zone defense. But maybe the inside has been taken away and the outside shot on the weak side is available. Use it if it's there. Your skills play a vital part in this combination. You may want to make a certain move or pass. Now you need to have the proper fundamental skills to make it work. The worst feeling is to see a potential situation and not be able to complete it because of a weakness in your game.

To become proficient at basketball, you need to learn many skills: footwork, jump stops, defensive stance. The list goes on. This may sound a little tedious, but there's no getting around learning these skills. This may also sound as if learning the skills takes the fun out of the game. That may be somewhat true, but before you can scrimmage—and definitely before you're ready for a game—you have to know these skills. The minute details are what separate you from your teammates and opponents. Good coaches will recognize these details, and you will have the advantage.

Learning the Basics

Is it any wonder that the 2010 UConn women's basketball team might be the best ever in our game? Yes, Geno Auriemma is a great hall of fame and Olympic coach, and sure, his team has stars. But his players have also mastered the simple fundamentals: the extra pass, boxing out, setting and using screens properly, on-the-ball defense, and rotations. I could go on and on. These are the basics, and the UConn players use them over and over again to improve and win!

Auriemma's story is an amazing model of consistency. He has been able to share his belief system and mind-set with the players who continually come into his program, and he has made women's basketball the talk of sports. UConn's amazing 90-game winning streak is now legendary.

When you are working out by yourself or with a friend, you can continue to make workouts fun and competitive while still using each of your skills correctly. As your skills improve, you will begin to see how these skills combine as major aspects of the game. For example, you may be a great shooter, but if you have problems shaking the defense or have poor footwork, you may never get a chance to perform the skill in which you excel.

You need to learn the skills and their uses. In addition, you must know the "why" behind basketball skills and strategies. For example, you need to know the purpose for using a bounce pass in a certain situation or the purpose of boxing out rather than crashing the boards for a rebound.

Communication between players and a coach is key. If you completely understand how to do something, you will have the ability to do it. If you're not sure, that's where guessing starts. Guessing does not contribute to your game.

With so much information available, you can easily gain insight about basketball skills and strategies. You can attend clinics, read books, call coaches, network with other players and experts, watch videos, and watch high school, college, and professional basketball on television. The resources are unlimited. How does a player get better? Get some references. Look to the experts. Find the people who know. When I wanted to learn more about shooting, I watched my former teammate and current SMU head coach Rhonda Rompola. She had perfect form, follow-through, and results. I also read the writings of the "Shot Doctor," Ace Hoffstein, who wrote the book *(Hoops) I Missed!* Ace is one of the best at teaching shooting, and I respect his advice.

I probably own every book and video on the market. I began building my basketball library long ago, and I am always adding something to it. I want to keep up with the latest changes. Young players may need to rely on their parents and coaches to help them find the latest information on basketball. A good place to start is your local library. I'm sure your coaches subscribe to coaching magazines. Ask them to let you read their copies.

Here's some advice:

- ***Watch the game:*** Watch it in person or on television. Watch good high school or college teams play. Mental imagery is important. You can see others who use mental imagery. They won't be difficult to spot. They will be the players who make good decisions on the floor and have low turnover ratios.

- ***Tape the game:*** Have your own library of tapes to watch. A tremendous number of women's college games are shown on cable and more recently on network television. At your leisure, you can watch a particular game or player. You can use slow motion (if available) to watch specific moves or plays.

- ***Read about the game:*** Read any basketball material you can find. These could be instructional books or magazines, or even autobiographies. You'll get a sense of how others play or coach the game, and you'll learn about situations and games that others have been in.

• ***Talk the game:*** Find teammates or other basketball players who want to talk about the game. This is very informational. The more you talk, the more your focus is mental. I love to find basketball junkies. Talking basketball is the purest form of staying in tune to the game. It's fun to hash out the game you're going to play or an opponent you will be guarding.

• ***Read scouting reports:*** Read reports not only about your opponent's tendencies, but also about your own. This enables you to see what others think about your game or your team.

Never Stop Learning

Because I've played through the '70s, '80s, '90s, and '00s—even coming back at the tender age of 50 in 2008 to play for the WNBA's Detroit Shock against the Houston Comets—I've seen drills, skills, and strategies change. I still find that learning is the staple to improving a player's game. Women's basketball is a more athletic, up-tempo game today than it was 30 years ago. It certainly is crowd pleasing. I have found a way to stay current with all the new offenses and defenses by talking to other coaches and players. I am always learning. Even when I became the first female head coach in the NBA developmental league (I was the coach for the Dallas Mavericks' team in this league), NBA coaches were very gracious to offer any help I needed. Larry Brown (of the Bobcats), Alvin Gentry (of the Suns), Rick Carlisle (of the Mavericks), Del Harris, Bob Hill, and many others were fantastic in sharing their knowledge of the game.

Incorporating Knowledge and Skills Into Your Game

Players have various ways of incorporating knowledge of the game and knowledge of what skill to use and when to use it. See what works for you. Basic decisions must be made on offense and defense. Depending on your coach's style, you should have options to use. It always helps to find out what works or doesn't work in practice. Some of the drills your coach might put you through can be competitive-type drills that highlight a combination of thinking or reacting, then using the proper skill to complete the drill. Remember to keep your mind sharp so you don't get sloppy on the court. Be competitive in all drills, but have fun doing them.

Start the process by evaluating what kind of player you are. Start with the basics. Are you a post player or a guard? Are you an inside or outside player? Are you a scorer or a rebounder? Are you a team leader or a role player? Now, define your strengths and weaknesses. Through this process, you'll begin to understand the skills you need to develop in order to accentuate your strengths and correct your weaknesses. You can target these skills and work on them in practice.

The Future Is Now!

In 1974, a friend and teammate read in the *Long Island Press* newspaper that tryouts were being held for a U.S. team that was playing exhibition games against a Russian team. We went to Queens College on a Saturday morning. I couldn't believe it—250 girls were there. Tryouts lasted all day. Finally, after many cuts, my number was still around. The committee selected 10 players out of 250. As a 15-year-old high school sophomore, I was one of them. Three other tryouts like this had taken place, and 10 players were selected at each one. We all went to a precamp tryout in New Mexico. Forty women went at it for three days. Ten were selected to move on to the tryout camp with all the veteran players. I was one of them. After three days, I injured my ribs—the diagnosis was that they were broken. A member of the selection committee and the head coach drove me to the airport so I could go home. Alberta Cox, the coach, looked at me and said with a warm smile, "Nancy, you work hard so you can make the 1980 Olympic team." I was startled. I looked at her and said, "Coach, that's six years away. I'm going to make the 1976 team." She thought I had potential for the future. I wanted to reach that potential right away. Don't let people tell you what you can't be; show them what you can be. I had no greater joy than calling that coach after we won the silver medal in 1976 and thanking her. She gave me the incentive to prove her wrong!

Want to be a better shooter? Incorporate all the necessary skills—concentration, coordination, rhythm, mechanics, balance, follow-through—into improving your shooting. Even if you are not going to be a post or power forward, you should work on rebounding. Learn how to box out. My responsibilities as a point guard included shooting, bringing the ball down the court, passing off to teammates, and directing the offense. With my experience, it was easy for me to define my style and evaluate my skills. As a teenager, it's not so easy. My advice is to experiment. Find out where your strengths lie through the process of elimination, and eventually you'll be able to define your game.

If your coach tells you that you have potential, ask him or her what you can do to realize that potential. Make your coach be specific. All potential means is that at some point—maybe next year, maybe in 20 years—you may excel at the game of basketball.

Try not to be stuck with the "potential" label. Keep working and don't be satisfied. Use potential as motivation. Enjoy the challenge of being better or working harder than your teammates and friends. Only you can make it happen. Set goals for yourself. Motivation and goals go hand in hand. When your skills and mental game come together, you will see tremendous improvement in your overall game.

Using the skills and strategies you've been taught means making the most of your time. Be positive. Always walk away with something positive. There will be times when it's not easy. There may be times when you get down and think it doesn't matter. It does! If you are getting to the next level, you're encountering better players. If you are a sub, push the starters to be better. This will help you and the team. Be competitive with them. Respect them, but don't back down. If your coach puts you in a game during garbage time, be the "garbage queen." Get the most you can from the time you get to play. Don't allow any situation to pull you down.

Playing My Best

In 1975, I played for the U.S. squad in the world championships in South America. I wasn't playing much, so I sat at the end of the bench and pouted. Mind you I was only 16 and a star of my high school team. In international basketball, it's more difficult to substitute because there are fewer breaks in the action. But I didn't realize this; I only knew that the coach wasn't letting me play. I remember telling Pat Head (Pat Summitt, as you know her), my teammate, who now coaches at the University of Tennessee, that even if the coach put me in, I wouldn't go. Pat set me straight. She told me that even if I only played 10 seconds, I was going to give it my best. She told me that I had to make the most of my playing time—long or short—because game experience is where you test all the skills and knowledge you've learned. That lesson is still with me.

Think of your basketball skills as the foundation of your game. Above all, you want to be solid in the fundamentals. Think of it this way: Before you can work calculus problems in school, you have to know algebra. And before you can handle algebra equations, you have to be able to add, subtract, multiply, and divide. Your basketball skills are the addition, subtraction, multiplication, and division. You put those skills together and you're ready to learn basketball strategies. Finally, you're ready for competition. Start early so you won't have to play catch-up.

Using Creativity

Many women enjoy watching basketball. When you're not playing, you should be watching—high school, collegiate, and professional basketball. One reason to watch is because you can learn something every time. Another reason is that you can enjoy watching. Basketball is entertaining; it's fun. It's also amazing what some players can do.

Basketball players today are stronger and better athletes than their counterparts from decades past. That means they can do much more on the court. Basketball is in an era of marketability. Athletes must, in a sense, sell themselves on the court. They must promote their talents. If basketball isn't interesting, people won't come to watch. You always see a crowd whenever UConn and Tennessee, Texas and Oklahoma, or other top rivals meet in women's basketball. These teams are enjoyable to watch because they play a fast-paced brand of basketball. They also have players who know how to entertain crowds.

Being creative on the basketball court is an important part of your game—but remember, it's only one part. Being creative in the right situations can make you a more valuable part of your team, make you a better player, and get your teammates and the crowd fired up.

Building Creativity

Basketball is supposed to be fun. You often hear professional basketball players say that they'll keep on competing as long as the game is fun. They've got the right attitude. Sure, it's a business for them. But basketball is a game too, and people who play it are supposed to enjoy themselves—even the professionals. Making basketball fun takes a little creativity on your part. Play mind games with yourself. I'm sure you have done this before—shooting the game-winning basket just before the imaginary buzzer sounds. That's what basketball is all about. Funny thing, as you get better you expect to make more and more of those game-winning shots. Don't be surprised when you start making them in real games.

Creativity comes through practice. There's no other way to learn it. Creativity gives you options. You perfect those options in practice. You have the ball above the key. What are your options? You can go forward, double clutch, and try to draw your opponent into committing herself. You can go right, go left, or step back and pop a jumper. Doing those things doesn't just happen. They are acquired skills. And as you've heard several times already, you acquire those skills through practice.

The truly great women's basketball players come from different backgrounds and environments. But there's a common thread—the blacktop, school yards, and parks. Call them what you want. That's where freedom and creativity are nurtured—playing one-on-one, two-on-two, or three-on-three games. When you get it, you can't lose it. These are great places to learn the sights and sounds—learning basketball and the game's lingo. You develop shots and moves that you never knew you had. Maybe it's a drive, a spin, and a finger roll to finish the play. This is part of experiencing what your limits are and can be.

Not a Surprise

At Old Dominion and when I played for the Phoenix Mercury, my teammates and I would often practice taking half-court shots (after practice, of course). Many of us routinely knocked down a few. We were relaxed and confident.

During my senior year at Old Dominion, I happened to make half-court shots in two straight games. Of course, I just looked at my teammates like "What did you expect?"

I remember asking Harlem Globetrotter legend Meadowlark Lemon how he made those incredible hook shots all the time. The crowds were always shocked when he did, but Meadowlark wasn't surprised when the shots went in. He said, "Nancy, I've been practicing those shots for years. I expect to make them."

Get DirecTV and TiVo some women's college games. Get your remote and slow down the action. Watch some of the sweet moves that are made and how they develop. In 1992, the University of Virginia had one of the best backcourts in the history of women's basketball. With three-time All-American and two-time Player of the Year Dawn Staley and her teammate Tammi Reiss, Virginia was exciting. The two were great for the game; they were well worth the price of admission. Not only did they have style, but they were also true winners. Dawn could do it all—slice through the defense with incredible ballhandling skills or make a no-look pass to the Burge sisters on the inside. If the defense went with Dawn, there was Tammi Reiss to knock down the perimeter jumper. Inside or out, both players had the ability to break down the defense and get the ball to an open teammate. Today, Oklahoma State point guard Andrea Riley can dazzle you with her moves, defense, and intensity. UConn's Maya Moore is a four-time All-American and a monster to defend, and she continues to improve each year!

If you work at a skill or shot long enough, you'll be able to tell if you feel comfortable and if you're improving. The important thing is to use your creativity when practicing on your own. Use it in free time and in pickup games. Work it until you're ready to show it in team practice and competition.

Incorporating Creativity Into Your Game

Adding creativity to your game is an extension of building your creative skills. It involves developing your options. If you can pass with your left and right hands, shoot with your left and right hands, take the ball to the hoop, and hit from the outside, you're going to be difficult to guard. The more options you have, the more opportunities you have to be creative.

People think being creative is driving to the basket, spinning 360 degrees, and laying the ball in the basket. They're right. Being creative, however, is also reading defenses well. Stanford's Jennifer Azzi wasn't flashy. But she was the best at getting the Stanford offense in high gear. She could spot weaknesses in an opponent's defense and take advantage of those weaknesses. Watch the players in the WNBA and today's college stars. Angel McCoughtry, a young superstar for the WNBA's Atlanta Dream, is described as steady and hardworking. She led her collegiate team (Louisville) to the NCAA finals and showed the country why she was one of the elite players today. The former number one pick in the 2009 WNBA draft, McCoughtry is a perennial all-star and MVP candidate, and she has continued to expand her game on both the offensive and defensive sides of the ball. Sheryl Swoopes also wasn't flashy—just amazing. She was one of the most difficult players to guard. She was dangerous in so many ways that opponents didn't know how to stop her. Whether it was handling the ball, moving without it, or rebounding on the offensive end, she found ways to score and hurt Texas Tech's opponents.

I remember a play that Swoopes, Krista Kirkland, and their Texas Tech teammates worked to perfection. No matter how many times they ran it, their opponents couldn't counter the attack. Swoopes would post low on one side of the basket with another Tech teammate. Two teammates would post low on the other side and then clear out to the corner. Swoopes would cut hard to the high post, looking as if she would receive a pass from Kirkland. Swoopes' defenders began to overplay her. They'd cheat to try to deny the pass. Then, Swoopes and Kirkland knew that if Swoopes faked high, she'd be all alone if she cut back toward the basket. The result was an easy backdoor layup.

Some people aren't going to be as creative as others. Don't force it. Stay with your strengths and do what you can to incorporate them into your game.

My former coach at Old Dominion, Marianne Stanley, saw that our team was talented and creative. She let us make our own decisions. She gave us parameters. She didn't force us to run a set offense with no variations. She gave me the green light to make decisions. Sure, we could beat our opponents playing a half-court game because we had outside shooters and we had strength inside. But we wanted to beat them downcourt. Coach Stanley let us improvise; she let us be stars. In many ways, her coaching style in the late 1970s and into the '80s was ahead of its time.

Coaches such as Geno Auriemma of UConn, Gail Goestenkors of Texas, Nell Fortner of Auburn, Tara VanDerveer of Stanford, Pat Summitt of Tennessee, and Bill Fennelly of Iowa State are changing the game of basketball with the way they run their offenses. Their plan is to look for the three-pointer first. These coaches and many others begin by recruiting the top outside shooters in the country. Then, they encourage them to look for the three-point shot. If they don't beat their opponents downcourt for a layup, the players look for an open three in transition. If it's not there, they run their half-court offense, still looking for an open three-point shot. The players aren't afraid to shoot from the outside. They don't have to worry about being taken out of the game if they miss several shots early. They know that if they miss four times, they'll have a chance to make the next four. Remember that you can't do something if you don't try it. Many of these coaches have enough confidence in their players' outside shooting to let them try.

Remember, when it comes to creativity, don't get impatient. Just because you can't match your friend's moves doesn't mean it has to stay that way. You can catch up if you practice. Another important thing to remember is that creativity doesn't always mean flashy passes and flashy moves. Some of the most creative players in the history of basketball weren't the ones who had 40-inch vertical jumps or could dunk in a dozen ways. Being creative on the court means using all your options and making the best decision for the moment.

KEYS TO SUCCESS

A winning attitude means better conditioning and better preparation. It means having the confidence to know that in easy or tough situations, you'll make the right decision for you and for your teammates. It's also that aura about you—regardless of whether you are outspoken or shy. It's your look, the way you walk, and how you perform. The mind-set of a winner is a great asset to have working for you.

You must develop this part of your game, and you must feel comfortable about your efforts. Many of the top players have an extraordinary mentality. Through hard work and extra effort, they have become superstars.

Desire

Success on the basketball court begins with desire. No one said success was going to be easy. Hard work and discipline are the elements for success! There's no room for shortcuts if you want to be great.

To achieve greatness, you must have a desire to be better than the others around you. Having that desire enables you to work out longer, stay focused on your goals, and do the things that enhance your game. That could be finding better players to practice and play with, or it could be seeking out camps, summer leagues, or other places to get extra court time.

Desire is hurdling obstacles to reach your goals. It doesn't matter if it's too hot, too cold, or too windy. Desire is eliminating excuses for why you can't practice. Desire is your effort to find opportunities to work on your game. You can do this if you really want to.

Building Desire

When you watch others achieve a high level of success on the court, this helps you build desire. See how they have achieved it, and dedicate yourself mentally and physically to wanting to be that good. You build desire from the ground up. It's the little things you do that give you the love and dedication needed. Focus your time around the game; make sacrifices in your daily schedule so you have proper time to work on your game or watch others play. Desire means you must allow yourself to dream of greatness—to know and see that it can be done. Competitiveness will also fuel your desire for success; each level you achieve in your game will make you want to reach the next. If you dream about making the all-star team or the state finals, you should never expect anything less than what your goals are.

Incorporating Desire Into Your Game

Incorporating desire means challenging yourself. Get out there and get better. Self-improvement is in your hands. Do the basic drills with intensity. I always recommend playing against players who are better than you. This makes you strive for another level. You have to be focused and concentrate harder. Desire to improve comes from your love for the game—that's right, the game. Go out and practice it, play it, compete. You can do this at the school yard, at the YMCA, in the gym, or in tournaments such as Hoop It Up, the national three-on-three tournament. These tournaments are everywhere. Find one and challenge yourself to be better.

Discipline

Discipline and desire work together. It takes discipline to stay 15 minutes after practice and shoot another 40 or 50 free throws. It also takes desire to want to stay after practice when your teammates are on their way home.

Discipline doesn't just dictate when and how much you practice. It also dictates what you practice. We all have parts of our game that are better than other parts. Some people are better at being defensive stoppers, while others excel at perimeter shooting. So why not practice only those things that you do best? The biggest reason is that you won't be your best if you work only on your strengths. Instead, you have to focus your time and energy on your weaknesses. Pick the parts of your game that are the weakest and spend your time changing those weaknesses into strengths. Repetition is key. If you have trouble going to your left, spend more time using your left hand. Use your imagination to create gamelike situations when you might need to rely on that particular skill and how you would respond.

Discipline also means putting your team first. The better you are individually, the more valuable you will be to your team. That means practice and sacrifice. You need discipline and good decision-making skills to know when to pass up the 15-footer and find your open teammate for the layup. Your coaches can help you become a more disciplined player. You will come across many knowledgeable coaches. Soak up their wisdom, styles, and philosophies. Apply the ones you like and tuck the other information away for another time.

I Thought I Had to Score to Be Noticed

I started my freshman year at ODU in 1976 as a heralded Olympian with a silver medal. I thought I had to score 20 points or more a game to live up to what was expected of me. I also thought that's how I would get noticed for individual honors. Although ODU was on its way to its best season, I became my own focus. My mind-set was "me first, and my teammates second." As my sophomore season approached, Coach Marianne Stanley asked me to pass more and make my teammates more valuable and better players. At first, I couldn't understand what she meant. What, me give up scoring? But she was saying, "Nancy, we will be better as a team if you become more of a team player. Score less, and we will win more often." She was right. In each of my next three seasons, my scoring average dipped sharply. But our winning increased greatly: 30-4, NWIT champions; 37-1, national champions; and 34-1, national champions.

The real question is, do you focus on yourself, or do you focus on the team? If you make others around you better, you will win more consistently. As I became a better team player and we won as a team, I still achieved my personal goals (and was two-time National Player of the Year) and so did many of my teammates. Yes, you can have it all!

Discipline means being an individual, but this can still be applied to putting your team first. Yes, you must want to be good, very good. But you can achieve that in many ways. Can you make your teammates better? Can your ability, attitude, and leadership help others on your team get better? Absolutely. In a team sport such as basketball, the more weapons you have on the court, the better chance you have to win. That's why team play usually wins out over individual success. Discipline can also mean sacrifice. You may want to take a certain shot, but maybe a teammate has the better percentage shot underneath the basket. Sure, you've hit that shot before with someone hanging on you, but now's the time to make the right decision. Give it up. You may score fewer points, but you will help your team more when you hit the open teammate instead of taking your shot. This type of play can go a long way toward winning. It shows your teammates that you trust and believe in them and that they can be counted on. It builds a solid respect and communication among the players. Believe me, when the game is on the line, you'll have your chance to win it or lose it. Coaches respect team players. Being this type of player shows your willingness to do what's best for the team.

Building Discipline

Discipline is mental. Before you do something or say something, you think it. Repetition is the key to building discipline. You must build discipline first. Then you can apply discipline in what you expect your work habits to be. How do you treat and talk to teammates and opponents? Do you apply discipline when listening to your coaches? You should. You build these traits by being focused, having a basic plan of attack, and carrying out that plan without deviation.

Incorporating Discipline Into Your Game

Applying discipline means being in control. Don't force a situation on the court if it's not there. If you are a great 15-foot jump shooter, don't allow the defense to push you out to 20 feet for your shot. Be disciplined and mentally tough enough to know what you want—and to get what you want! You can work for the shot you want to take. Don't be satisfied or settle. You can also incorporate discipline into your game by being on time to practices, games, and meetings. How do you handle yourself on the court with teammates, opponents, coaches, and officials? Are you courteous? Do you lose your cool? This is all part of discipline. You're in control of your actions.

Donovan and Nissen

In my senior year (1979 to 1980), Old Dominion University had a problem—a very good one. We were the defending national champs, and Anne Donovan—the heavily recruited 6-foot-8 player who was the National High School Player of the Year—was coming to Old Dominion. At any other school, starting would have been a lock for Anne. At Old Dominion, we had 6-foot-5 All-American senior Inge Nissen. I waited eagerly to see those giants battle for supremacy in the paint. It became quite clear that the veteran wasn't giving her spot to the rookie and that the slender rookie wasn't afraid to go right at the vet. Each worked diligently on her favorite moves and tried to develop new ones to use against the other. Anne developed the Jabbar hook shot, and Inge worked on increased mobility and her outside shot. The time and discipline that each "twin tower" used to expand her game and help the other improve were big reasons why Old Dominion went on to win its second straight national championship. It took a lot of discipline for Inge to realize that Anne could and would block her shots underneath. It took discipline for Anne to realize that she'd better play defense with her feet moving because Inge was so quick off the dribble from the high post.

You can put discipline into or out of your game. It's up to you. Are you in control on the court? Or are you out of control?

Persistence

Persistence is your attitude. It's your frame of mind. It's not being satisfied. If you are persistent in basketball or in life, you can be successful. That quality will help you with skills and strategies. Eventually, you will figure out why you are successful on the court. Desire and hard work are a function of persistence. It's the only way to achieve success. Persistence has a domino effect. Everyone benefits except maybe your opponents. You've got the desire to play your best, and if your opponents can't match that desire, watch out.

Building Persistence

You build persistence when you are willing to settle only for the best. There will be times in practice when hard work, repetition, and persistence pay off. Continue working when you think you can be better at a skill, a drill, or learning the game. Don't be afraid to ask questions of coaches, mentors, and players. Get it right in your mind. That's how you can build persistence into your game. Persistence is always doing, asking, and making sure it's correct. No matter how much or how hard you work at something, you must apply those habits all the time. You'll be amazed at how being persistent can change a coach's or teammate's opinion of you. If you play hard for 2 hours in practice, your persistence should show your coaches that you can give the same effort in a game. Take that focus and desire and use it every time you practice or play.

Incorporating Persistence Into Your Game

You can incorporate persistence by being repetitive in drills and games, watching tapes, and reading about whatever area you are trying to improve. Don't let anyone talk you out of wanting to do more. Your game, as we have talked about, has strengths and weaknesses. Everyone has some of both. When you are working to improve, don't get discouraged. Continue to be persistent with your goals and desire to improve. Look at the positive changes you are accomplishing. Persistence is as much mental as it is physical. It's a battle you must keep winning. Don't ever fear success. Success is in all of us!

A Little Persistence Pays Off

In 1987, I was playing in the USBL for the Long Island Knights. Our team was loaded with talent, including Michael Ray Richardson, a three-time NBA all-star, and Geoff Huston, a former NBA regular. Both had played with the New York Knicks. Remember, I was the only woman playing in this league.

We were playing the Rhode Island Gulls, and talk in the locker room before the game turned to the Gulls' 5-foot-3 Tyrone "Muggsy" Bogues. Richardson, the former NBA all-star at 6-foot-3, was telling anyone who wanted to listen how he was going to post low against Bogues and knock him across the head with a forearm if Bogues got too close to him.

The first time Richardson had the ball, he obviously was thinking of how he was going to put his plan into action. Bogues, however, had other ideas. He stripped the ball from Richardson and raced down the court for an easy basket. The next time Richardson got the ball, it was the same story: a steal and two points. The third time, Richardson pump-faked, and Bogues stole the ball. Here's a player going against a three-time NBA all-star and getting the best of him. Three possessions, three steals. Richardson told our coach, Dean Meminger, that he wanted out of the game—right now. I had been on the bench telling Dean that I could guard Bogues. "I know I can; let me try," I told Coach. Dean kept saying no. I kept up my persistence. I wanted a chance.

After Richardson took himself out of the game, Coach looked down the bench and asked who wanted to guard Bogues. No one volunteered, so I did again. My persistence and desire to play paid off.

Shortly after I entered the game, Huston and I were working to trap Bogues as he worked his way downcourt. Bogues started to spin when he saw Huston close in. I took advantage of Bogues' momentary distraction and stole the ball. As I raced downcourt, I knew that Muggsy was close behind. Although I am a half foot taller than Bogues, I didn't forget that he had a 40-inch vertical jump. Instead of risking getting my shot blocked by my much shorter opponent, I drove to the basket and passed off behind my back to Huston, who was trailing on the play. Two points.

By telling this story, I don't mean to sound as if I'm bragging. I merely want to show how players who may not be as tall or as strong as their opponents can compete as long as they have desire and are persistent. Bogues didn't let his size stop him, and I didn't let being the only woman in a men's league slow me down.

COMMUNICATION

Communication is a major asset to winning. You need to have an understanding of what your coaches and teammates think and feel. That eliminates the unknown. If you completely understand, it becomes easier for you to be properly prepared to play the game.

You can be a good leader through communication. This can be done by talking, patting a teammate on the back, using a wink or a smile, or pointing to a teammate after she makes a good pass. Some players don't have the same ability as you. You can bring their level up with how you communicate with them. You can help a teammate by giving her a subtle word of encouragement or pointing out a better way of using her skill. How you say it can hurt or embarrass a teammate. Remember, once you say something to someone, you can never take it back. Take time to understand how and what others are thinking and feeling. Spend time with each of your teammates. This could help you understand how each will respond in different situations. Some are more tolerant or sensitive than others. You don't have to always hang out with all your teammates, but you can get valuable information from spending some time with them. This information can help you and the team on the court. Spending time with your teammates can let you know how they feel about winning and losing. Do they like the system? Are they confident? Do they like hard passes or bounce passes? Besides, communication skills will remain with you long after your playing days are over.

Teammate to Teammate: Can We Talk?

Criticizing a teammate should be the job of a coach, but a positive compliment can go a long way. You can suggest to your teammate an option that she didn't think of, but you should do so in a positive manner. If it's done in a negative way, you run the risk of being tuned out. We all know when we make a mistake. Try not to compound it. There is definitely room on the floor to use communication for success. Here's an example: "Jackie, great pass to Nikki in the corner. If the defense reads it next time, look under the bucket. Yolanda is wide open on the switch." Give your teammates positive options if you sense that those options are available. If you are not sure of a situation, don't give an answer. Go to your coach for help. Talking with your coach can also help the coach know what you are seeing on the floor.

Keep It Positive

I wish players' self-esteem was not tied to the actual minutes they play on the basketball court. I think that hurts them sometimes. Everybody has a role on a team, and I know this better than anybody. I've been the best player in the world, I've been a role player, and I've sat on the bench. I've played 3 minutes, I've played 15 minutes, and I've played 40 minutes. In men's leagues, I was happy just to get on the court. Regardless of your playing time, you have to be ready for your moment. You have to be basketball alert. You have to stay mentally focused, and you can't let people pull you down.

Winning is about the team. Think of Steve Kerr, a role player who won five NBA championship rings with the Bulls. With time ticking down in Game 6 of the 1997 NBA Finals, Michael Jordan told Kerr to be ready because Michael was going to be double-teamed. And it played out exactly that way. Kerr hit the shot, and the Bulls won another championship. Just because you're not the star doesn't mean you can't contribute; you have to be ready for your moment, no matter what or when it is.

Coaches Coach—Players Play

Your job as a good teammate is to try to raise not only your level of play, but also your teammates'. Be a positive force on the floor. It's the coach's job to teach and instruct. The players' responsibility is to carry out the plan. Encourage your teammates to stick with what the coach is teaching. Be a supporter, not the teacher.

On the Court Sometimes, the court is the most difficult place to communicate with each other and your coach. The pace is frantic, and emotions are high. Crowds can be loud at times. Many games have been won or lost with a team's momentum. Whether you are up or down, pull your teammates together in dead-ball situations—after a foul and definitely after a shooting foul. Get your strategy in order.

Be Yourself Being yourself sounds easy, and it can be. As you watch many of the great stars of collegiate or Olympic basketball, you may think, *I wish I was her.* I hear that quite often—players want to be like Olympians Katie Smith, Sue Bird, or Candace Parker. It's OK to want to be the best. But you need to be yourself. Develop your own style, moves, and on-court attitude. Borrow the good qualities of these players to use for your own. But don't lose yourself in order to be them. Women's basketball needs lots of new stars. There will be plenty of time for you to figure out how big, how fast, and what position you will play. Continue to work at your overall game no matter what. Who knows how far you can go? Remember, you should always want to "be your own hero."

Officials—They've Got a Tough Job No matter what you believe, the officials truly try their best. Yes, they will miss calls. In many cases, however, the calls will even out. Be respectful of the men and women with whistles and stripes. The worst thing you can do is get a bad rep as a complainer or whiner. This will only draw attention to you. Let the coach deal with the officials. Be a good sport when faced with calls that you believe are incorrect. Remember, the officials are human and are using their best judgment. They will never please everyone.

BEING A TEAM PLAYER

If you are the star of your team, you need to project leadership on and off the court. You may want to take a teammate to the side and compliment her on a great effort, or even verbally praise her in front of the others. This can build an individual's and a team's confidence and pride. It can bond teammates.

If you're not sure of your coach's preferred system or type of play for you, go directly to your coach and ask. This way, you'll know exactly what is expected of you as a player. Let's face it, you are not always in control of your reputation, but you own your character. Your character should shine through all the time.

If there is a word to describe winning, it's *teamwork*—everyone blending together, sacrificing areas of their game to make the coach's philosophy and system successful. That means believing in each other and not always being concerned with individual achievement. The greatest feeling in improving as a team is achieving it together. If you believe that playing together is the most important aspect, your thinking is correct. You win as a team and lose as a team. That's where trust and relying on each other come in.

The Team Is Always First

I'm always amazed at how University of Tennessee Coach Pat Summitt's teams continue to be true champions. It's not only the eight NCAA titles; it's the fact that very few players on her teams have extraordinary scoring averages. Yes, Tennessee has its All-Americans, but the objective for each of these outstanding players is to win the national championship. If they achieve individual success, it's a bonus.

In 1984, the U.S. Olympic team finally won its first gold medal in women's basketball. In 1988, the team went to Korea to defend that medal. It was one of the most talented U.S. teams ever: Teresa Edwards, Katrina McClain, Andrea Lloyd, Cynthia Cooper. I could go on and on. As a group, each player respected her teammates' talents. Each player's goal was to work together—no matter who played the most minutes. The mind-set was gold medal first, individual recognition second. This philosophy worked, and the U.S. team earned a second consecutive gold, which proved that a team working together will, in most cases, beat an opponent featuring a great player. It was a beautiful sight to see the greatest women basketball players in the world team up for the overall success of their country.

Filling a Role

Doing your part takes no ego and lots of confidence and pride. There's nothing better than for your coach to clearly explain what your role on the team is—what you can do to contribute to the overall success of the team. Look at this role definition in a positive way. Basketball is a team sport; each player is very important. You are simply a piece of the puzzle. And remember, role players are looked on as elite figures on a team. So set that ego aside and do whatever is asked of you by your coach. You might be asked to score, set monster screens, play tough defense, or maybe perform a combination of these tasks. You are capable of giving your coach and team the advantage they need. You must be able to explain what your role will be to help your team win.

Filling My Role

During my first year in the women's professional league with the Dallas Diamonds, my coach, Greg Williams, came up to me after a game in New Orleans. I was down. We had lost. I played terribly that night and hadn't quite adjusted to what my place on the team was. I wanted to be a team player by passing, but I was forcing my passes too much. Coach Williams said, "Lady Magic, we know you want to make your teammates better, like you did in college. But this is the pros, and we are paying you to score. I'm running plays for you, and you keep passing up easy shots." At that moment, I realized that my value to the team was more in scoring than in passing. This defined my role and answered many of the uncertainties I was feeling. With that, the Diamonds went on to play in the championship series against the Nebraska Wranglers. I was scoring points because that was my best contribution to the team's success.

Sometimes, it's easier to be a role player or a substitute. Less can be better. Less responsibility can mean more results. Coming off the bench is not a negative. If you are a sub, you should watch the game. Read the tempo and flow. What does your team need? Is it rebounding? Are your teammates up or flat? Subs need to uplift a team. You're the spirit if the starters are tired or struggling. If the starters are hot, it's your job to keep the fire going. Give your best—for 1 minute or 30 minutes. Effort is what counts.

Enthusiasm for Your Teammates' Accomplishments

There's no greater feeling than when you are sincerely excited about your teammates' achievements. Showing your enthusiasm lets the teammates know that you respect their hard work and accomplishments. They appreciate your support and how you respond to them. I've seen players who fail to show support when their teammates play well. Not wanting a teammate to do well is selfish. Keep the team goal in sight. There will be a point when you'll need and want your teammates' support, as you have given them yours. Be real!

Just Plain Happy for Her

When people do something that's kind of cool, tell them. Over time, when you get older, you start reflecting a bit more. When I signed on to be the head coach of the Dallas Mavericks' team in the NBA developmental league, I received phone calls from Martina Navratilova, Deion Sanders, Terrell Owens, Dara Torres, Jackie Jackson, and many of my friends at ESPN, including Stuart Scott and Jay Harris. Dwight Howard's family congratulated me, Cappie Pondexter texted me from Russia, and WNBA president Donna Orender and NBA commissioner David Stern contacted me. The list goes on and on. It was great to know that people cared.

I love to text or call my friends when they have had a great night or when something special has happened for them. I may send a text to Tamika Catchings with the message "You were absolutely off the chain the other night." Or I may text this note to Diana Taurasi: "Congrats on the MVP, girl! Way to uphold the integrity of the game."

Be happy for people. Compliment and congratulate them. There's nothing wrong with it, and your support can mean the world to them. Don't be negative because someone's in a place you want to be. Support the player and get better. This is important both in sports and in life.

SUMMARY

Perhaps what you need is the mental edge. Regardless of your level of talent, playing smart and staying focused can be exactly what you need to win. Here are some things to remember:

- You need to develop a strong mental attitude.
- Hard work and repetition lead to developing desire, discipline, self-confidence, and persistence.
- You should learn your basketball skills early. You can then incorporate strategies into your game.
- Team players have winning written all over them. It takes sacrifice, learning your role, communication, and teamwork.
- As a student of the game, your focus doesn't waver.
- Motivation keeps you focused on continued achievement.

chapter

3

Training for the Game

As we've seen, attending to your mental game is a necessary step in making your basketball efforts pay off. Another important step involves improving your physical condition. Here are 10 points to think about as you begin your road to achieving top physical condition:

1. Accept every challenge.
2. Have a good mental and physical approach.
3. Set your goals high.
4. Don't be afraid to succeed.
5. Play to win.
6. Have heart and desire.
7. Help people get better.
8. Have a sense of humor.
9. Don't worry about things you can't control.
10. Accept the challenge to play against people who are better than you.

CONDITIONING FOR BASKETBALL

My favorite subject is conditioning—training for the game. I've been doing it my whole life, and amazingly, I have been able to continue playing hoops and other sports at a high level even into my 50s because of how I train and take care of my body. Lucky me! You are in control of your training. They can say you're too young. They can say you're too old. They can say you're not this or you're not that. But they cannot say you're not in great shape if you've done your work. And if you don't have to worry about your conditioning, then you have more time to concentrate on the actual skills and drills that you need to work on in order to improve your game.

On the other hand, you can't be good at what you do if you're not in shape. Conditioning is your responsibility, and it determines whether you'll be successful. If you're in great shape, you'll have a chance to be great. If

Wearing Them Down

Conditioning was one of the strengths of our team at Old Dominion in the 1978 to 1979 season, which was the season that we won our first AIAW national championship. In the championship game, we trailed Louisiana Tech by about a dozen points at halftime, but we weren't discouraged. We knew we could wear teams down with our size and conditioning. For us, the game turned into a mental and physical battle that we knew we could win. And we did, by 10 points. I attribute the 20-point swing to conditioning, depth, and execution.

you're in good shape, you can be good. But if you don't think that training is important, then you will struggle no matter what your goal is. And the last thing you want to do is injure yourself or wear down because you're not in shape. Your body will determine much of your health and success. Look at Orlando Magic center Dwight Howard. He was a skinny little kid in high school. He got pushed around a lot, but then he finally said he had enough of it. Now, he has the best physique in the NBA, in my opinion.

On TV, I was once asked when Diana Taurasi would be the MVP of the WNBA. I said, "When she gets her body in shape." And that's what she did. In 2009, Diana Taurasi's body finally caught up to her game when she lost 20 pounds. That year, she became the MVP of the WNBA!

The four main aspects of physical training are enhancing your flexibility, building your strength, improving your endurance, and being aware of other training issues (including diet) that can make a difference in your athletic career. In this chapter, we talk briefly about each of these areas and point out some other important training considerations. Then we look at a training program and some conditioning exercises that you can use to achieve a new level of physical conditioning.

Your training program should concentrate on the following areas of fitness:

- Flexibility
- Strength
- Endurance
- Nutrition

Your training program should also consider the following:

- Speed and agility
- Balance
- Core strength
- Plyometrics or jumping ability
- Rest and recovery

Prehab Conditioning

You've heard of rehabilitation and rehabilitative training. I'm a big supporter of *prehab* training. If you're a one-sport athlete, you might think that as soon as the season's over you don't have to worry about physical training until next season. With today's high level of competition, athletics are full time, even though you may take a break from your specific sport and focus on another. Cross-training is the key. You'll reach your potential if you continue to train. The off-season is the time to hone in on your weaknesses and turn them into strengths. If you're a multisport athlete, you have an advantage. You have the luxury of keeping in shape while you play other sports. Your disadvantage is not being able to personalize your training to improve your basketball game. It's OK to use other sports to supplement training, but be sure to leave time to work on your main sport.

Prehab, simply put, is taking preventive steps to keep you as healthy as possible. Prehab training means that you never fall out of shape. You'll always have a foundation for your physical training, and you'll be doing all you can to prevent injury. Too many great athletes have lost their jobs to someone else because of injury. Many athletes get hurt because their bodies are not ready to handle the strain of intense off-season or preseason conditioning. Your chances of injury will be reduced if you stay in prehab condition.

When you do get injured, the trainers and doctors take over. They will put you through many tests to diagnose the injury and decide how to best get you on the road to recovery. Trainers and doctors can be an injured player's best friends.

Staying in prehab condition means working out and training hard. An off-season spent on the couch watching television and eating junk food will erode your foundation of physical conditioning. When it's time to get ready for the coming basketball season, you don't want to have to start from scratch. You can increase your exercise program as the season draws near. When it's time to step on the court for the first day of practice, your teammates and coaches will notice.

Training Periods

The basketball year includes three main seasons: off-season, preseason, and in-season. The off-season lasts roughly from late spring to August. You should be training to train during the off-season. This means getting in shape and building your fitness foundation in preparation for the coming season. You should work to increase your flexibility, strength, and endurance while improving your basic basketball skills. You should also correct any poor nutrition habits you may have.

The preseason usually includes September and October, starting 6 to 8 weeks before your first official practice. Now you are strong mentally and physically. You are training to compete and raising your level of performance in all areas. You should maintain your flexibility and continue to increase your strength and endurance; at the same time, you will continue to refine your basketball skills.

The in-season period stretches from November to March. You are ready for competition. You've trained hard and worked on your skills. You are now ready to show your teammates, coaches, and competitors that you have put in your time. You are ready for every challenge. Continue to maintain flexibility and strength, while increasing endurance, between actual practices.

Many coaches provide their players with specific workouts for all three training periods.

ENHANCING YOUR FLEXIBILITY

The off-season is the time when most of your progress in strength, endurance, speed, and quickness will be achieved. (That's right, you really don't have an off-season if you want to improve your game; training is year-round for most of us!) You don't have to hold back on anything during the off-season because you have time to work on your overall conditioning, flexibility, and basketball skills.

When the season ends, you should take 7 to 10 days to have fun and let your mind and body recover before you get back to work. As your training progresses, you will be making changes in your conditioning as the season approaches.

This is a terrific time to work on flexibility, which will help you reduce the chance of injuries. Flexibility is the ability of the joints to move through a full range of motion. Range of motion refers to the degree to which movement occurs around a joint. To have pain-free mobility of the muscles and bones, you must maintain a full range of motion at all joints. Flexibility will give you an appearance of ease, smoothness of movement, graceful coordination, self-control, and total freedom. It will help you perform more skillful movements with greater self-assurance and amplitude. Flexibility can mean the difference between an average performance and an outstanding one.

Flexibility is especially important in basketball because of all the movement you must make on the court: stopping, starting, leaping for a rebound, making a move to the basket, playing defense, and so on. The more flexible your body is, the quicker it can react to the move you are asking it to perform. If you are tight and stiff, your reaction time is greatly reduced. Think of your body as a rubber band. The more flexible it is, the more it can stretch and do whatever you need it to do. If it's tight, it will stretch only so far without breaking. Basically, without flexibility, your physical ability to perform is limited. My advice is to stretch, stretch, and stretch some more. Adding yoga to your training, especially hot yoga for stretching and reducing injuries, can help. One torn muscle can put you on the sidelines for months. No matter how talented you are on the court, if you are injured and on the bench, you have hurt yourself and your team.

Make sure that your muscles are warm before you start to stretch; one way of doing this is through aerobic exercise, as suggested on page 57. Proper breathing while stretching can allow you to relax and stretch farther than you think you can. By taking deep breaths and blowing out while in the stretch position, you are relaxing your body. Remember to always breathe while stretching.

Improving and maintaining your flexibility can be accomplished through simple stretching and calisthenic exercises. These can be incorporated into your weight training regimen and endurance exercise workout—topics we'll address later in this chapter. Take a few minutes before each workout to make sure your muscles are loose and ready for work.

Warming Up

The warm-up is essential in preparing muscles to work and stretch without being injured. The warm-up raises your body temperature and increases your heart rate, breathing, and blood flow.

You should warm up your body for about 5 minutes *before* beginning any stretches in order to avoid damaging cold muscles. To begin your warm-up, walk or jog around the court three times. This will get your blood flowing. Some players also like to get their blood flowing by taking shots. The increased blood flow will reduce stiffness and send oxygen to all areas of your body. Now your muscles are warm even before you stretch.

Stretching

After the short warm-up, it is time to move into your stretching routine. As with most things, there is a right and wrong way to stretch. A relaxed, slow approach is the most useful. Players will often bounce while stretching, and that can cause injury. If you bounce throughout your stretch, your muscles will tighten, not relax. Remember, your body needs time to loosen up each of the muscle groups before it can perform to its maximum. The old adage "No pain, no gain" should not apply to stretching. The last thing you want to do is injure yourself while stretching.

Stretch Lightly Hold your stretch for 10 to 20 seconds. Remember, no bouncing. Go easy and breathe out as you extend your stretch. As you start to feel tension, hold your position and keep breathing. The muscle will continue to loosen as you hold the stretch. Then, relax after about 20 seconds.

Use Repetition Do each stretch two or three times. Each time you should try to extend the stretch farther. Again, hold it at the point of tension. Don't force your stretch. Ease back if you are uncomfortable. It could take some time for you to recondition and loosen various muscle groups.

Breathe and Count This combination is so important. The breathing allows you to relax and exhale all the tension as you are stretching. When people feel pain or tension, they often hold their breath. Doing so will only make you more tense. Breathe normally and count slowly. Don't rush through the 10 or 20 seconds of stretching time.

You need to know the correct techniques for stretching. Keep the following points in mind:

1. Stretching reduces muscle tension.
2. With proper breathing, you can learn how to relax while stretching.
3. If you stretch properly, your coordination will improve on the court. Your movements will be freer and easier.
4. Stretching also allows you to have a sense of awareness of your body—what hurts and where you are tight.
5. Prehab training may help reduce the number of injuries you will have.

I've picked five simple stretches that you should incorporate into your stretching routine. These stretches will help you get loose and prevent nagging injuries.

Achilles Tendon Stretch

Stand upright 4 or 5 feet (122 or 152 cm) from a wall. Bend one leg forward and keep your opposite leg straight. Lean against the wall while keeping your body in a straight line and keeping your rear foot flat and parallel to your hips. Exhale, bend your arms, move your chest to the wall, and shift your weight forward. Hold and relax for 10-15 seconds. Repeat on the opposite leg.

Hip Flexor Stretch

Stand upright with your legs straddled 2 feet (61 cm) apart. Flex your right knee and roll your left foot under so the knee and toes rest on the floor. Place your hands on the floor. Exhale and slowly lean or push your left hip toward the floor. Hold and relax for 20 seconds. Repeat on the opposite leg.

Lower Leg Stretch

Sit upright on the floor with one leg straight and the other positioned so that its heel touches the opposite thigh. Exhale, bend forward at the waist, and grasp your ankle or foot. Exhale and slowly turn your ankle inward. Hold and relax for 10 seconds. Repeat on the opposite leg.

Triceps Stretch

Flex one arm, raise it overhead next to your ear, and rest the hand on your shoulder blade. Grasp the elbow with your opposite hand. Exhale and pull your elbow behind your head. Hold and relax for 10 seconds. Repeat with the opposite arm.

Back Stretch

While standing with your legs shoulder-width apart, gently interlock your fingers behind your back, keeping your arms straight. Bend at the waist, keeping arms straight to stretch your back. Hold and relax for 10 seconds.

Cooling Down

Cooling down after working out helps your breathing and heart rate return to normal. It also prevents blood from pooling in your extremities (the blood that has been pumping to your working muscles during the workout). After you have finished your workout and while you are still warm and stretched, you should cool your body for 5 minutes by simply decreasing the intensity of your activity—for example, by walking or jogging a few laps. Then, continue to cool down with some light stretching exercises before you are finished.

BUILDING YOUR STRENGTH

Being strong is exciting. You'll see it in the way you look, and you'll feel it in the way you play. Opposing players, much to their dismay, will see it and feel it, too. Strength gives you confidence to go out and match up with any player—big or small.

Strength is an acquired edge, and improving your strength starts in the weight room. Weight training, or external resistance (ER), exercises include leg and jump squats, leg presses, lunges, walking lunges, step-ups, high step-ups, pull-downs, pullovers, combo curls, presses (including bench presses), and so on. Such exercises emphasize power in the muscles. They tone and redefine your body, giving you added strength in the large and small muscle groups. You'll discover muscles you didn't even know you had. Weight training can also help increase your flexibility. But you have to learn to train properly. Correct techniques include breathing naturally, lifting through the proper range of motion, and not lifting too much or too fast. By lifting weights using proper technique and by committing yourself to a regular training program, you'll get a tremendous return on your investment. You will begin seeing and feeling positive results in a relatively short time.

Experts have many different theories about weight training. Therefore, you have several choices. For example, you may use resistance bands, free weights (barbells and dumbbells), or weight machines. Each option has its good training points. Your preference and your individual needs will determine which program is best for you. Before you begin lifting weights, consult your coach for information about strength training. Your coach can help you find literature about strength training and can direct you to someone with additional expertise on strength training, such as a fitness instructor at a weight training facility. Do not begin lifting without proper instruction! This could lead to injury or failure to meet your strength potential.

Different Programs for Different Players

Athletes often say, "Give me a workout program." Sounds easy, but it's not. As we said before, there are many theories about how a person should perform strength training. And players may have different goals that they want to achieve from their strength training programs. We'll briefly examine the basics of strength training, giving you the main points. Use these points to get started. Be sure to consult with your coach or another expert on strength training who can help you identify your goals and preferences. This person can also help you design the program that's best for you.

Determining Sets, Repetitions, and Weight

The first step in designing your workout is to determine how much weight to lift (the load or amount of resistance) and how many times to repeat the movement (repetitions and sets). A set involves performing a particular number of repetitions before stopping. We'll look at two ways to structure your repetitions, sets, and weight—the multiple- and single-set approaches.

The multiple-set approach to strength training suggests that you complete three sets of 5 to 8 repetitions for developing strength, and that you complete three sets of 10 to 20 repetitions for developing endurance. For example, when selecting your load for developing strength, you need to select a weight that allows you to perform all sets at a point somewhere between 5 and 8 repetitions. If you can perform more than 8 repetitions, then your weight is too light. Likewise, if you can't reach 5, you're lifting too much weight.

Another popular approach to strength training is the single-set approach, or high-intensity training (HIT). In this approach, you should lift an amount of weight that will permit you to perform one set of at least 8, but not more than 12, repetitions during an upper-body exercise. For a lower-body exercise, the weight should allow you to perform at least 10, but not more than 15, repetitions. You then increase the amount you lift when you are able to perform 12 repetitions of an upper-body exercise and 15 of a lower-body exercise.

We recommend that you lift for strength during the off-season, lifting more weight for fewer repetitions. Most strength training experts agree that this is when you'll make the greatest strides in your strength development. During the season, you should lift less weight and perform more repetitions for more of a maintenance routine—this enables you to stay toned and not lose strength. Heavy workouts during the in-season period can lead to burnout or fatigue while playing. Always keep stretching during your lifting. You never want to lose your flexibility.

Allowing Time Between Exercises

Limit your workout to 12 to 14 exercises. Select a core group of about 10 exercises that will develop the five major muscle groups in your body (lower back and buttocks, legs, torso, arms, and abdominal muscles). Then choose 2 to 4 additional exercises to specifically meet your particular needs or interests.

Time spent in the weight room should be short, 45 minutes or so, especially during the season. In the off-season, you can design a longer workout to add more strength. Limit the time between each exercise to less than 1 minute. Allowing time between workouts is also important. You might want to use a split routine for your workouts, exercising the upper-body muscles one day and the lower-body muscles the next. (Exercise the abdominal muscles each day.) This gives you a full day between workouts. If you want to exercise all of your muscles in one workout, an alternate-day regimen (Monday-Wednesday-Friday or Tuesday-Thursday-Saturday) might be best for you.

Weight Training Tips

The following suggestions will help you get the most out of your strength training workout:

- Before you begin any workout, be sure to warm up properly. Use the mirrors in the weight room. Take a good look at your body. Identify the areas where you want to make gains.
- Get a buddy—someone who competes as hard as you do or who is even more competitive. Compete with each other using the proper technique for each exercise.
- Use the weight you can handle with proper technique. Throwing around heavy weights isn't the answer.
- Check out some of the books or tapes on weight training and be sure to include your coach in your efforts. The more you understand, the better you'll be at it.
- Always drink fluids when you work out. Fluids cool your system and allow you to keep working hard without dehydrating. Water or sports drinks are equally effective.
- Always use weight training gloves if you can. Gloves will help prevent sore hands or calluses that keep you from lifting or playing. Use a weight belt to protect your back from injuries due to having weight or stress on your lower back during various exercises. For example, squatting and dumbbell exercises that require bending at the waist place stress on your lower back.
- Record all weight, pool, and track workouts.

IMPROVING YOUR ENDURANCE

Endurance comes from many sources—including running, weightlifting, and playing basketball. After working on these three areas, you'll probably notice improvement in your speed and endurance on the court. The stronger you become, the better your muscles function. Increased speed and endurance are natural results. Some players are solid for 5, 10, or even 20 minutes. But if you want to become the best player you can be, you must work to become solid for the entire game and beyond. The more endurance you have, the more mental discipline you will have. Decisions that you face on the court will come easier because you won't be distracted by fatigue.

Basically, endurance is how many times you can repeat a certain function without getting tired. Exercise that improves endurance is commonly referred to as aerobic fitness or cardiovascular endurance training. Aerobic activity—such as biking, cross-country skiing, dancing, hiking, yoga, rowing, running, skating, and swimming—stimulates your body's ability to sustain an activity for an extended period of time. This involves the ability of the heart, lungs, and circulatory system to supply oxygen to the muscles during exercise.

Running on the road or at the track is a tremendous way to gain cardiovascular endurance and to challenge yourself mentally and physically in the process. Running provides a mental battle with the conditions—wind, weather, and the feeling of being uncomfortable. It's all there; it's something to attack and conquer.

I suggest you look at the big picture: You have 4 months of off-season running, weightlifting, and basketball. Make sure you don't go from having no base training to doing everything at once. Learning to build your conditioning in stages gives you the right steps to overall success. If you have worked out for a few weeks and you are tired, don't feel guilty about taking a day off here and there. This will allow your body to rest and recover.

I firmly believe in having a plan. You should chart each day of running, weight training, and basketball playing. This will allow you to see progress, how you felt, and what improvement you made. Be detailed in recording each day's workouts. How far did you run? How did you feel? Was it easy or difficult? What were the weather conditions? You should strive to make each workout more productive than the previous one, even if it's only one-half second better, or you did another repetition while lifting. Your chart lets you see your progress and pushes you to consistency.

ADDITIONAL TRAINING METHODS

To improve your athleticism, your total program should also include extensive core work and plyometrics.

Plyometrics

Plyometric training is a specific type of workout designed to improve jumping power. This is accomplished by training the stretching and shortening actions of muscle contraction. During the stretching phase, a greater amount of elastic energy is stored in muscle. This elastic energy is then reused in the muscle's ensuing shortening action to make it stronger. The key is to shorten the time it takes for the muscle to switch from the lengthening (yielding) phase to the shortening (overcoming work) phase. If not properly used, however, plyometrics can add a high risk of injury. The risk of injury occurs when the volume and frequency of the program are excessive. Proper technique is essential.

Consistency, intensity, and safety are key when doing plyometrics. A complete plyometric workout is beyond the scope of this book. You may want to consult other books, such as *Jumping Into Plyometrics, 2nd Edition* (1998, Human Kinetics) by Donald A. Chu or *High-Powered Plyometrics* (1999, Human Kinetics) by James C. Radcliffe and Robert C. Farentinos, for more information.

Core Training

Core work consists of exercises such as an abdominal circuit (e.g., medicine ball throws, medicine ball rotations), twist and movement drills, and speed and agility movement drills. Core exercises work many muscles simultaneously, improving stability, enhancing power, and reducing the risk of injury. This, my friend, is why it is so important to build core strength.

A complete core training workout is also beyond the scope of this book. For more information on core training, you may want to consult other resources such as *Core Assessment and Training* (2010, Human Kinetics).

BUILDING YOUR FOUNDATION

As you begin, think of training as a pyramid. The bottom of the pyramid is your base. This will be a 3- to 4-month process during the off-season of building strength and endurance through longer running and heavier weight training. Table 3.1 shows a sample 2-month chart to use as a guide. Your training should have you running 1 to 4 miles at the start. It's OK if your time is slow the first few times. Try to improve your time, even if just by 1 second. Keep improving. As your conditioning improves, vary your running routine to include the track. Add speed training to your endurance training. Your routine might include 3 days of running on the track and 2 days of long-distance running (2.5 to 3 miles); Saturday might be a day for a long, leisurely run of approximately 4 miles. When you're finished running, do your weight workout. This will add strength and endurance. Finally, finish the day out by playing basketball.

During the first several weeks of your training regimen, you're going to be tired and sore. Remember, when you are sore, ice is your best friend! Stay mentally tough. After a few weeks, you'll start feeling stronger. Your recovery time, aches, and pains will decrease. You will start to see progress. Push yourself mentally and physically to finish each training session. Soon, you'll reach the point where running, lifting, and playing basketball several hours each day will feel great. You're now hitting the middle of the pyramid program.

You should run 1 to 4 miles during your 3-day-per-week program. You have to determine where you are with your conditioning. You might want to start at 1 mile and push yourself to increase your time and distance until you begin to see that 4 miles is a distance that you can achieve.

Table 3.1 Sample Weekly Training Chart

Week	Sunday	Monday	Tuesday	Wednesday	Thursday	Friday	Saturday
1		1-mile run Strength training Basketball		1-mile run Strength training Basketball		1-mile run Strength training Basketball	
2		2.5-mile run Strength training Basketball		2.5-mile run Strength training Basketball		2.5-mile run Strength training Basketball	
3		3-mile run Strength training Basketball		3-mile run Strength training Basketball		3-mile run Strength training Basketball	
4		4-mile run Strength training Basketball		4-mile run Strength training Basketball		4-mile run Strength training Basketball	
5		2-mile run Strength training Basketball		3-mile run Strength training Basketball		4-mile run Strength training Basketball	
6	**Select the days on which you want to play ball. Choose three days.**						
7		1-mile run for time		3-mile run Strength training Basketball		3-mile run Strength training Basketball	Leisurely 4-mile run Basketball
8		2-mile run for time Strength training Basketball		2-mile run for time Strength training Basketball		3-mile run Strength training Basketball	Leisurely 4-mile run Basketball

After you have run hard, lifted hard, and played ball 3 days per week for approximately 5 weeks, you should take 1 week off to relax, to play ball, and to let your body recover and refuel.

On the first Monday after your days off, run 1 mile for time. Give it your all. Record your time. On Wednesday, run and continue lifting weights and playing basketball. Do the same on Friday. On Saturday, run 4 miles at a leisurely pace.

For the next week, run 2 miles on Monday, Wednesday, and Friday. You should have a solid base of endurance, strength, and stamina after 8 weeks of training. You should be playing basketball as much as you want—a minimum of 3 days per week. The next step will be to add speed and quickness (through plyometric training, for example).

As you may have guessed, it doesn't matter to your heart and lungs whether they are working hard because you are running, swimming, biking, or climbing stairs. You can take advantage of this to incorporate variety into your cardiovascular training and to minimize the potential for overuse injuries. If you have to run in your sport, then the majority of your cardiovascular training should come from running. You may be able to get into great shape by swimming or by using a stair-climber, stationary bike, elliptical machine, rowing machine, or upper-body ergometer. But the only way to develop the skill of running is by running. You can use other cardiovascular tools to minimize the stress that running can place on your joints, but you still must run if you are going to be effective.

SEASON SCHEDULE

In this section, you'll find suggestions for how you should schedule your off-season, preseason, and in-season training regimen. The focus is on training, but to be a good basketball player, you must play basketball all the time.

Off-Season

The off-season is where your strength training starts. In the off-season, you have the time to build muscle and add strength. Your training regimen should include 1 day per week of strength exercise, 3 to 4 days per week of external resistance, 3 days of plyometrics, 4 days of distance running, and 4 days of core work.

As you progress from off-season to preseason, your training regimen should change slightly. You will move from building your foundation to increasing your speed and quickness.

Here are some tips:

- Use three different workouts per week.
- Focus on all body parts during each workout.
- Use 1 to 3 exercises per body part.
- Use 12 to 14 exercises per workout.
- Do 10 to 15 repetitions for lower-body exercises; do 8 to 12 repetitions for upper-body exercises.
- Keep the order of each exercise consistent.
- Work out for 30 to 45 minutes.

Preseason

In the preseason, you will continue to do strength training as part of your overall workout. Your training regimen should include 1 day of body work, only 3 days of external resistance, and 2 days of plyometrics. You should add sprinting on 3 days and reduce distance running to 1 day. You are now trying to add more speed and quickness to your training mix. You should still do your 4 days of core work. You can always work on that area. Use two different workouts per week and follow the other off-season rules.

In-Season

During the season, your strength training is geared more toward maintenance rather than building strength. Your training regimen should include 1 day of body work and 2 days of external resistance. You can see how your training regimen has been reduced from the off-season to the preseason and now to the in-season period. Your in-season training should also include 1 day of plyometrics, 1 day of distance running (a long, leisurely run), and 2 or 3 days of core work. Use two different workouts each week; each workout should include 7 to 10 exercises. Work out for 20 to 30 minutes.

Strength training overloads your muscles in order to achieve muscle growth. You must overload the muscle no matter what workout program you do, especially during the off-season and preseason. During the in-season period, you should focus on more reps and lighter weights. This is a maintenance workout. For off-season and preseason workouts, you will use more weight to build strength and muscle. If you can complete more sets with proper technique, you should increase the weight. When you can rest for shorter amounts of time, this means you are getting stronger. Try to cut down your recovery time, but never eliminate it altogether. If you are willing to work out, make it worth your time and effort. Concentrate and don't get sloppy with technique.

Keep these tips in mind:

- The slower the movement, the greater the tension.
- The greater the tension, the harder the muscle works.
- The harder the muscle works, the stronger it becomes.
- The stronger the muscle, the stronger the joint.
- The greater the speed of movement, the less force production from the muscle.
- Preventing injuries means increased playing time.

Lady Magic Tips

- Always have proper supervision.
- Never try to do one-rep max.
- Do basic exercises.
- Always use extreme caution.
- Stretch as you work out.

OTHER TRAINING ISSUES

You need to consider some other training issues in addition to flexibility, strength, and endurance. Good nutrition is very important to sound physical fitness. Some people eat for taste, and some eat for fuel. I eat for fuel. It's not always sexy or fun. But I make sure I know what's going into my body. A related issue involves making the right choices regarding alcohol and drugs. In this section, we also discuss the mental aspects of being in good physical shape.

Good Nutrition

Dr. Robert Haas, author of the best seller *Eat to Win,* changed my eating habits forever. He taught me that people can recondition their body, as well as their tastes. When you improve your eating habits, you are helping your body, which will enable you to enhance your performance on the court. You will be able to play at a higher level for a longer time because of the excess energy you have. When it comes to diet, everyone has a different answer. You have to find out what works for you. That being said, keep in mind the following information.

In 2011, the U.S. Department of Agriculture (USDA) replaced the food pyramid with the food plate. On this plate, the five major food categories consist of grains, vegetables, fruits, dairy products, and proteins (see table 3.2). Oils are not considered a food group, but you do need some for good health. For more information, visit www.choosemyplate.gov.

If you consistently include these food groups in your diet, you will maintain energy storage, maintain the muscle tissue you have built up during your training, and reduce your body fat. Your body has only so much energy. Don't waste it by consuming saturated and trans fats, cholesterol, sodium (salt), and added sugars. Those ingredients take away from your strength and energy levels.

The way you treat your body is determined by how much respect you have for it. Athletes train hard to achieve results, but sometimes they overlook the importance of nutrition. You have to eat right.

Table 3.2 The Five Major Food Categories

Grains	Vegetables	Fruits	Milk	Meat and beans
Make half your grains whole • Eat at least 3 ounces of whole-grain cereals, breads, crackers, rice, or pasta every day • 1 ounce is about 1 slice of bread, about 1 cup of breakfast cereal, or 1/2 cup of cooked rice, cereal, or pasta	Vary your veggies • Eat more dark-green veggies like broccoli, spinach, and other dark leafy greens • Eat more orange vegetables like carrots and sweet potatoes • Eat more dry beans and peas like pinto beans, kidney beans, and lentils	Focus on fruits • Eat a variety of fruit • Choose fresh, frozen, canned, or dried fruit • Go easy on fruit juices	Get your calcium-rich foods • Go low-fat or fat-free when you choose milk, yogurt, and other milk products • If you don't or can't consume milk, choose lactose-free products or other calcium sources such as fortified foods and beverages	Go lean with protein • Choose low-fat or lean meats and poultry • Bake it, broil it, or grill it • Vary your protein routine—chose more fish, beans, peas, nuts, and seeds
For a 2,000-calorie diet, you need the amounts below from each food group. To find the amounts that are right for you, go to ChooseMyPlate.gov.				
Eat 6 ounces every day	Eat 2 1/2 cups every day	Eat 2 cups every day	Get 3 cups every day (for kids aged 2 to 8, it's 2 cups)	Eat 5 1/2 ounces every day

Adapted from www.choosemyplate.gov/downloads/MiniPoster.pdf.

Here are some suggestions:

- **Eat pasta rather than steak.** Carbohydrates are easier to break down and digest. Your body exerts energy to break down food.
- **Remember that vitamins and supplements can give your body what it is missing nutritionally.** For example, I dislike milk, so I obtain the calcium I need from vitamins.
- **Drink as much water as you can.** Water prevents cramping and dehydration. The water you drink on the day of competition can never replenish what you have sweated out. Store up on water by drinking it the day before competition.
- **Give yourself adequate time to eat your pregame meal.** I recommend eating 3 to 4 hours before game time to properly digest your food. You don't want to play feeling heavy, nor do you want to be thinking that you're hungry.

Drugs, Alcohol, and Tobacco

I'm sure you remember times when people told you, "Don't do this," "That's bad for you," or "You can ruin your life or die." Man, those are harsh words. But you wouldn't be at this level if you made bad choices. You're smart, and there's enough information about drugs, alcohol, and tobacco for you to understand how these substances can affect what you want out of your career and life. Be selfish—don't let anyone pull you down or away from achieving your dreams. It's tough today. You face peer pressure and temptation. But I just don't understand how an athlete can work so hard to train, and then go party, causing the opposite effect on her body. While some are choosing this route, others are working in the gym, taking care of their bodies, and getting the rest they need to be the best.

That's why I love basketball. It keeps you focused and limits your exposure to these temptations. When faced with a choice about these substances, your decisions are easy. Ask yourself, "Is this good for my career?" You're trying to make all-state and win the championship. Will this make it easier? I'm sure you'll agree. No! Stay strong.

One Fatal Mistake

In 1986, Len Bias, a college great from the University of Maryland, was headed for the big time: money and fame. He was the number one draft choice of the Boston Celtics. Bias was being compared to Michael Jordan. He was a clean-cut guy who didn't party. After his return from Boston, he celebrated at school by trying cocaine. He used enough coke that by early morning, the country was shocked to hear of his death. Bias died of an overdose of cocaine. It's sad. He had it all—talent, skill, money, and a great family. Bias' death taught me and millions of players one thing: One mistake is too many.

Mental Aspects of Conditioning

Whenever you play basketball, you should also be playing a mind game. Think about how you might gain a small edge over your opponent. There will be times during games when you'll be drained. Although you are just about to run out of energy, you should *never* let your opponents know that you're tired. If you need to catch your breath during a break in the action, turn your back to your opponents. Don't let them see that you're tired.

At the same time, if you see an opponent put her hands on her knees while trying to catch her breath, you know that you can take advantage of her weakness. Go at her the first opportunity you get. It's all part of the mental game we play on the basketball court.

Sending a Message

Your physical conditioning can send a message to your opponents that you mean business. Two months before the Olympic tryouts for the 1992 women's basketball squad, I turned up my training routine a notch. I was already in shape because of my prehab conditioning, but it was time to really get serious. Each morning at 7:00 a.m., I worked out at Creighton University with Mike Thibault, coach of the 1993 CBA champion Omaha Racers (he is now the head coach of the Connecticut Sun and is one of the top coaches in the WNBA). He put me through drill after drill. Mike has coached with the Los Angeles Lakers and Chicago Bulls, and he knows that basketball drills are not exactly exciting. I trained 6 days a week—lifting weights, running, playing pickup games, and working on my skills. I was "drilled" out after 2 months, but my basketball game was at its best.

When I reported for the tryouts, I sent a message to members of the selection committee by walking onto the court confident—mentally and physically. I wanted them to know that I was taking these tryouts seriously. I wasn't going to be left off the team because I was out of shape.

I didn't make the 1992 Olympic squad, which was disappointing. In a way, however, I accomplished my goal. I sent a message to the stars and future stars in women's basketball that being 30 doesn't mean your basketball career is over. If just one person, after seeing me play at age 33, said to herself, "I hope I can play like her when I'm 33," then I accomplished something.

And remarkably, I accomplished something else. I continued to train hard, and in the inaugural year of the WNBA in 1997, I became the oldest player in the league at the age of 39.

PUTTING IT ALL TOGETHER

Use the summer months to play a lot of basketball and to get into the weight room for a properly supervised workout. Add your track conditioning and be mindful of your diet. You will begin to see a change in yourself. As you start to see muscle definition, you will develop more confidence and self-esteem. If you see the changes, others will too.

When you walk into the gym on the first day of organized practice, it will be immediately clear to everyone that you went the extra distance. They might not know how you did it, but make no mistake, people will notice. This will speak volumes about your dedication and work ethic. Every coach wants a leader. Every teammate needs a role model. Be one.

The Buddy System

I'm a strong believer in using the buddy system during physical training. There's a reason why people hire trainers, and there's a reason why we have coaches. It's just a lot easier for somebody else to push you to the places you really don't want to go. And you can be more successful with your training if you have somebody to hold you to a high level of accountability and responsibility. When I was training with Martina Navratilova, we relied on the buddy system on the days that one of us didn't want to train. If she was feeling unmotivated, it was my responsibility to help her get there mentally and have a goal and purpose at that practice. This really helped. The buddy system is essential.

Improving Your Skills

This is where your coach comes in. After the season, if your coach hasn't yet called you in for a face-to-face meeting, you should take the initiative and schedule one. Ask how you can improve. Ask your coach for drills that you can use to work on the areas that need improvement.

Your coach should know your weak areas. Once you get the information you need, it's up to you to achieve the results. Playing in the off-season is important, but knowing what you should be working on will give you direction and focus. Then you can use your basketball workouts properly.

You can make great strides by doing the following:

- Know what areas need work.
- Know which drills to use.
- Be efficient by being organized and focused.

Whether you are playing basketball, running, cycling, or lifting weights, your workout habits will determine if you are successful.

10 Ways to Work

1. Have a plan.
2. Always think about improvement.
3. Use the correct form.
4. Be mentally prepared.
5. Be physically prepared.
6. Have the right equipment.
7. Always stretch first.
8. Have a good attitude.
9. Always challenge yourself.
10. Never rest until you are the best.

For me, the off-season was great. You should view the off-season as a great opportunity. By being dedicated to your mission of overall improvement, you will begin to see areas of weakness turn into strengths. This should give you the attitude of wanting more and should motivate you to work hard. It won't happen overnight, but you will see gradual improvement. And a lot of gradual improvement will mean major steps in becoming a better overall player.

OFF-SEASON RECOMMENDATIONS

The off-season is one of the few times when you won't always have coaches around giving you instruction. Enjoy the freedom of having your game in your own hands. I recommend the following:

- Work on the fundamentals through drills; the fundamentals are vital at the next level, especially in college and above.
- Play in as many pickup games as possible.
- Play a lot of half-court games (one-on-one, two-on-two, and three-on-three games).
- Find some friends who have the same dreams as you and work out together.
- If you have the resources, consider private lessons. One-on-one attention can go a long way.
- Be willing to make sacrifices if you want to be the best. It's a small price to pay.

If you want to drill on the court, here are a few of my favorites:

- Beat the All-American (see page 117).
- Two-player shooting to 50—shoot, rebound, pass. Run at the shooter with your hands up.
- Foul-Shot Golf (see page 112).
- Horse. Play by the traditional rules or make up your own.
- One-on-one.

Pushing Myself

At the 2007 WNBA All-Star game in Washington, DC, I did a demonstration of a skills challenge for the players. After seeing me do the demonstration, Bill Laimbeer, coach of the Detroit Shock through 2009, asked me if I still played. Bill asked, "Would you like to make history next season?" I told him yes, and we talked about the possibility of the Shock signing me to a seven-day contract. He then asked, "When do you turn 50?" I said, "July 1st, 2008." So we had a date with history.

Bill's part was giving me the opportunity. My part was getting my body into elite-athlete shape again! For 3 months, I trained 5 days a week with my trainer, Brian Darden, in Dallas—lifting, running, core strength, explosive movements, jump rope, lateral slides, sprints, and more. Then, I did on-court work—one-on-one, full-court games with the guys, and so on.

All of this for one game. Why? Because I got it; I knew that it would influence generations of kids and would help adults focus on being better and accepting the challenge placed in front of them! It worked. I received over 20,000 letters and texts from fans and friends from all over the world, telling me that I had inspired them. Many of them asked me, "How did you get your body into that kind of shape?" My answer? Hard work!

Keep in mind that training should be fun and competitive. Treat your body right. Get plenty of rest so your body can recover from training. Your diet can be your edge; be selective in how you eat. Stretching properly can prevent injury and give you a better chance to succeed. It's easy to train when you feel good. Complete the program each time. Ask yourself, "Am I feeling soreness or pain?" Soreness will go away, but if you feel pain, see a doctor or trainer. Stay focused. Improvement will come—sometimes quickly, sometimes slowly. Be patient, but be persistent. As your conditioning improves, find new challenges on the track, in the weight room, and on the court. Continue to strive for excellence. The opportunity is there for you to succeed; now you must take advantage of it.

SUMMARY

Conditioning programs are designed to build your strength, stamina, and endurance from the ground up. If you have worked through the off-season, you need to continue that pace throughout your preseason. Be mentally and physically strong. Your self-discipline will allow you to continue your journey to excellence.

Here are some things to remember:

- Commitment to mind and body starts with playing basketball, lifting weights, running, and following a proper diet.
- Flexibility reduces the risk of injury.
- Building strength starts with weight training.
- Preseason conditioning builds speed and quickness.
- In-season conditioning is basketball specific.
- You are what you eat.
- The serious athlete must say no to drugs, alcohol, and tobacco.

chapter

4

Becoming an Offensive Threat

To be a good offensive player, you must be balanced, and you must understand angles. You should be playing lower than the level of the defender's shoulders, especially when you're in the red zone—the three-point line or in. The lower you are, the more you attack the body of your defender; you'll have more leverage, taking away a defender's recovery step. A defender needs space. If your first move is to your right, a defender can slide and cut you off at that angle. Instead, your first step should be at the foot of the defensive player (with your left arm protecting the ball), and you should lean in on the defender's hip and get up underneath her chest or shoulder area. That way, you are in control of the action because the defender has nowhere to recover to. In baseball, they always say that the most difficult ball for outfielders to catch is the one hit right at them. There's no angle, so the outfielder can't tell if the ball is going to fall in front of him or behind him. It's the same thing in basketball. The most difficult player to defend is the player coming right at you. As the offensive player, you are the action. The defense should be the reaction.

In this chapter, we emphasize improving and refining your offensive skills. You'll learn some simple moves and discover the ways to use them successfully. Basketball, in many ways, is like a chess match. You move; the defense counters. This chapter helps you explore your options. You'll learn to be mentally and physically challenging to your defenders. We show you ways to read the defense's reactions and then make your move. It's a game of cat and mouse. If you have the advantage, you'll keep the defense guessing. You know exactly where you want to go.

Jab Step and Go

The jab step can also be used to drive past a defender. With the ball in a triple-threat position, jab-step straight at your defender with your front foot while keeping your pivot foot on the floor (figure 4.3*a*). Always attack the foot that is up. This forces the defender to retreat, opening up as she drop-steps. At this point, you should explode past her hip on the dribble (figure 4.3*b*). This will take away her recovery angle to stop your drive. Make your first step explosive because it is the most important one. Stay balanced and low, and use your momentum as you move forward. Always keep your head up and look at the basket, not the floor.

Remember, if you jab-step and go to your right, you should dribble the ball with your right hand. Use your left hand to protect the ball. If you jab and go left, switch the ball on the move to your left hand. Lefties should remember that their left foot should be slightly ahead. Their pivot foot is their right one.

Figure 4.3 Jab step and go.

Jab Step and Crossover

This move is good to use when the defense is close. With the ball in your hands, jab-step to the side of the defense (figure 4.4*a*). Then, step across and by the defense with your front foot (figure 4.4*b*). If you are right-handed, jab with the right foot. If you are left-handed, use the left foot. The defense will react and try to take away your strong-side drive. Now, you can cross over in the opposite direction. You must protect the ball, taking it from the outside hand farthest from the defender. For example, if you cross over with the ball in your right hand, do not leave the ball open between you and the defense. Quickly switch the ball low from right to left using your right arm and body to protect the ball. The dribble begins before you pick up your pivot foot. Instead of going to the side that the defense will open up toward, make your defenders use a drop step. It takes longer to drop than to slide. Attack the defense's weaknesses. Stay close to your defender's body so she cannot get an angle and catch up with you.

Figure 4.4 Jab step and crossover.

Rocker and Swing Move

Stay in your triple-threat position, but expand it. For example, keep your left foot on the ground as your pivot foot, and jab at the defense with the right. Rock back and forth and stutter-step from side to side, even putting your right foot behind you or crossing it in front of the left (figure 4.5*a*). This will draw the defender to you and force her to move back and forth or side to side. If you catch the defender leaning or off balance, you should make your move (figure 4.5*b*).

Figure 4.5 Rocker and swing move.

Jump Stop

When a player lands on both feet at the same time, she is using a jump stop. When you perform this move, your legs should be shoulder-width apart for proper balance, and your knees should be bent slightly. Your head should be over your knees.

The two-step jump stop is used when a player lands on one foot and then the other. The second foot should land slightly ahead of the first so that you can be in a triple-threat position (figure 4.6). From that stance, you can shoot, pass, or dribble. With your feet in a staggered stance, you can use either foot as your pivot foot. Jump stops are most effective when you are driving the defense back. As you jump-stop, your defenders are still moving backward. Jump stops will create space for you and will release defensive pressure.

Figure 4.6 Jump stop in triple-threat position.

Hop Drive

This move is being performed more and more often. The player drives hard to the basket, and as the defense closes off the drive, the player hops with both feet past the defender or past two defenders (figure 4.7). Not only does the hop drive help the player split two defenders, but it also allows her to stay in balance for her shot or pass.

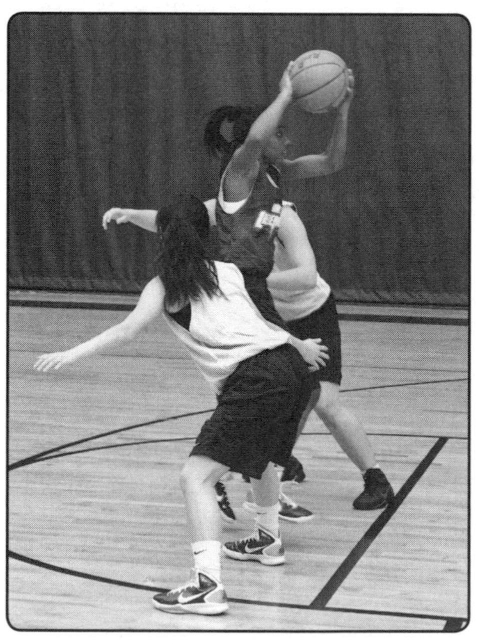

Figure 4.7 Hop drive.

Pivot

The pivot is the most important aspect of footwork; it is a valuable tool for changing direction. The pivot allows you to gain leverage, remain in balance, and create space between you and a defender. It also allows you to break double teams. The pivot is a must for success.

You can pivot both forward (called a front turn, or forward pivot) and backward (called a reverse turn, or drop step). The pivot foot is the foot that you turn (or pivot) on. In the front turn, you should keep your pivot foot planted while stepping forward with the nonpivot foot (figure 4.8*a*). In the reverse turn, make sure your pivot foot stays planted while dropping back with your nonpivot foot (figure 4.8*b*). Don't be shy about establishing your space and position. Be physical, but not illegal.

Figure 4.8 Pivot: (*a*) front turn; (*b*) reverse turn.

For drills specific to the triple-threat position, see page 79.

Checkpoints

- ☑ Keep your head up. If you are looking down, the defense knows you are not a threat to score. See the whole floor and the basket.
- ☑ Go somewhere with the dribble. To get by your defender, you should always go ball first, feet second. Push the ball past the hips of the defense, not next to your feet.

- ☑ Protect the ball on your fake. Keep the ball close to your body on all ball fakes.
- ☑ Plant your lead foot—the one that starts the drive—as close to the defender's foot as you can. This takes away her angle to recover.
- ☑ Remember that you will find success attacking the front foot of the defense. Make the defender drop and open.
- ☑ Protect the ball on the drive. Follow this simple rule: you, ball, defense. To get to the ball, the defense must go through your body, arms, and knees.
- ☑ Stay low. The lower you are, the more speed and quickness you have.
- ☑ Sell your fake. If your fake is believable, you'll have your defender constantly coming out of her stance.
- ☑ Play a lot of one-on-one with a one- or two-dribble limit. This will make you work on using your jab fakes in a game situation. You have to be quick and read defenses to make your move.

FOOTWORK

If your footwork is great, you're going to be great. Look at LeBron James, Lauren Jackson, and Candace Parker, to name a few. They use their pivot foot. They know how to attack the defender. They have great positioning. Watch Kobe Bryant from the waist down sometime—his footwork is amazing!

The proper position for good balance is to keep your head over your knees while leaning forward. This positioning also gives you more speed. Stay on the balls of your feet and try to be as light on your feet as possible. Relax but keep your feet moving. You'll notice that your center of gravity is lowered, thus allowing you to move more effectively and making it easier to change direction. If you are flat-footed or off balance, it will take longer and more energy for you to get going.

Good footwork is not an inherent trait. You can improve your footwork if you work on it. Jumping rope, running short sprints, and practicing changes in direction are just a few ways that you can improve in this area.

For drills specifically designed to improve footwork, see page 82.

A Good First Step

Becky Hammon, a guard for the San Antonio Stars, has one of the best first steps I've ever seen. At about 5-foot-6, Becky always keeps her feet moving when attacking the defense. She has a tremendous understanding of change of pace and change of direction, which keeps players off balance when they are trying to guard her. She consistently takes her opponents off the dribble and uses simple head, ball, and jab fakes. Boom! Her moves freeze her opponents, and she is gone.

Checkpoints

- ☑ Jumping rope increases speed, quickness, and endurance. It keeps you light on your feet.
- ☑ Sliding drills improve lateral quickness and strength.
- ☑ Short sprints increase leg muscle strength and explosiveness.
- ☑ Line jumps (front and side) increase speed and quickness going in different directions.
- ☑ Transition sprints (with change of direction) improve explosiveness and help decrease the time it takes to change direction.
- ☑ Knee highs focus on hip flexor muscles and help you respond more quickly when sprinting.

TRIPLE-THREAT DRILLS

Practicing the following drills will help you become better at executing your offensive options during the game. Once you are comfortable with each drill, create goals for self-improvement, even if it's only performing the drill one more time through. Challenge yourself with the clock. Remember, you must always practice proper form. Don't sacrifice form for more repetitions or faster performance. A good way to rest is to take five foul shots between each drill. You'll improve your free-throw shooting as well.

One-on-One Jab Drill

PURPOSE

To work on your jab step and taking opponents off the bounce.

PROCEDURE

1. Place basketballs in at least five spots around the perimeter of the court. Come from behind the ball in a low, balanced stance.
2. Pick up the first ball, get in a triple-threat position, and jab at an imaginary defender. You should be about 20 feet from the basket.
3. Make a move—jab and drive, jab and cross over, or jab and shoot. You have the option of the shot. Make a quick decision. If it's a jab and shoot, make your ball fake violent and rise up for the jumper.
4. After completing that move, run to the next ball. Come at it in a balanced stance. Bend your knees, not your back. Pick up the ball, do a jab fake, and perform a crossover dribble. Take the drive or shoot.
5. Use the same continuation after your fake and crossover. Next time, use a different move. Always take the shot or layup to complete the drill.
6. Finish performing jab fakes from all five spots. Take five foul shots while you're tired.
7. Repeat this drill two times.

(continued)

One-on-One Jab Drill *(continued)*

VARIATION

Instead of a jab step, use a ball fake, head fake, shoulder fake, or crossover dribble from any spot on the court.

LADY MAGIC TIPS

- Make believable jab steps and ball fakes even without a defender. Each jab step should be 6 to 8 inches (15 to 20 cm). That way, if you back the defender up, you can rise up to take your shot without moving your foot back. Be efficient.
- Jab directly at the defense. This drill can be used with two players. Use the second player as a defender at each ball. After completing the moves at five spots, shoot five foul shots and switch positions.
- Remember that solid technique means consistency when practicing.

Jab Step Drill

PURPOSE

To work on making a believable jab step while attacking the defense. You will also practice going somewhere on your dribble after the jab step (dribble with a purpose). The drill will help you strengthen your strong and weak hands.

PROCEDURE

1. Get in a triple-threat position. Place the ball on the floor. While balanced, pick the ball up and jab at the defense.
2. The first time through the drill, jab and take one quick dribble right, going somewhere off your dribble.
3. Get back in your triple-threat position, jab at the defense, and take one quick crossover dribble left.
4. Repeat each jab step and dribble three times in each direction.
5. Do the same drill, adding two dribbles off the jab step. Take two dribbles to your right, then two dribbles left off the crossover. Repeat this three times each way.

LADY MAGIC TIPS

- You need to jab at the defense. Attack your defender; don't avoid her. Usually a 6- to 8-inch jab step will keep her off balance.
- Right-handed offensive players should jab with their right foot; left-handed players should jab with their left foot. This forces the defense to take away the strong-side drive.

X-Out One-on-One Drill

PURPOSE

To work on one-on-one moves off a triple-threat position. This drill will improve your quickness, your reaction, and your ability to make split-second decisions while recognizing what the defense has given you.

PROCEDURE

1. Player 1, the offensive player, starts on the block at the foul-lane line with the ball. Player 2 is the defender. The defender is on the opposite side of the basket on the foul-lane line on that block.
2. Player 1 rolls the ball to the middle of the foul line or beyond, near the key area, and sprints to pick it up. Player 2 sprints up the lane line, then slides across at the foul-line elbow to defend against player 1.
3. Player 1 picks up the ball in a low, balanced position and pivots to face player 2.
4. Using assorted jab and ball fakes, player 1 makes player 2 react.
5. Player 1 and player 2 compete one on one until player 1 scores.
6. The players each shoot five foul shots when finished.
7. The two players reverse positions and repeat the drill. Each player is the defender twice and the offensive player twice.

LADY MAGIC TIPS

- Player 1 must roll the ball to the foul area, not bounce it.
- The offensive player should keep her head up and use a good, believable jab step at her defender.
- The offensive player should read how the defender is guarding her.

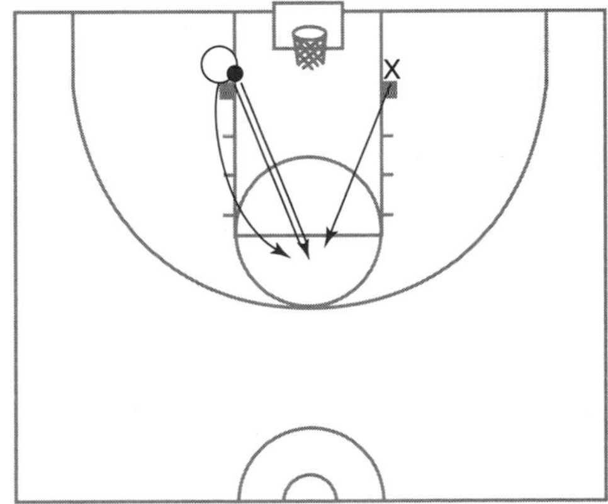

FOOTWORK DRILLS

Practicing the following drills will help you improve your movement and speed on the court. Once you are comfortable with each drill, create goals for self-improvement. For example, you can challenge yourself with the clock. Remember, don't sacrifice form for more repetitions or faster performance. To rest between drills, take five foul shots after each drill.

Knee High Drill

PURPOSE

To increase the power and explosiveness in your running. By drawing your knees high, you create power. The more you do these drills, the better endurance and strength you will have in straight running and in transition.

PROCEDURE

1. Start by standing in one place. Jump upward. Bring your knees up as high as you can.
2. Place your arms by your sides for balance. Use them for momentum and power as you drive your knees up.
3. Jump for 30 seconds. Rest for 30 seconds. Complete four sets of 30 seconds each.

Change Drill

PURPOSE

To work on changing speeds and direction. This drill also enables you to work on conditioning and helps you focus on your change of direction.

PROCEDURE

1. Start on the baseline under the basket. Sprint straight down the court as hard as you can. Change direction instinctively. Stay low, planting your lead foot and pushing in the opposite direction.
2. Start with 30-, 60-, and 90-second change drills. Rest between drills when necessary.
3. You should be creative in structuring this drill. For example, you might want to sprint up and down the court several times without stopping, followed by several quick turns. Keep your running off balance. Try not to get into a rhythm.
4. Complete three change drills. You can determine how long each one lasts (30, 60, or 90 seconds).

LADY MAGIC TIPS

- Use your imagination and focus to keep changing your direction as if you were in a real game.
- Have a watch in your hand so you can monitor your time during this drill.

Lane Slide Drill

PURPOSE

To increase your lateral speed, quickness, reaction time, and ability to change direction.

PROCEDURE

1. Start on one side of the foul lane. Get in a good, balanced stance with your head up, knees bent, feet apart, and arms out in the passing lanes.
2. Slide from one side to the other and back (up and back is one repetition). Stay low in your stance.
3. Touch the lane line with your inside hand, then slide back in the opposite direction. Once again, touch the lane line with your inside hand.
4. Do not cross your feet or bring them together, because this will cause you to be off balance and slow. Use a crablike slide.
5. Do this drill as fast as you can for 1 minute. Rest for 1 minute. Complete three sets of 1 minute each.

Backboard or Net Touch

PURPOSE

To strengthen your lower legs for quickness and explosive repetitive jumping. This drill is great for rebounding, too.

PROCEDURE

1. Stand under the net or backboard.
2. Jump 10 times off both feet and touch the net or backboard with your right hand. Then jump 10 times using your left hand to touch the net or backboard.
3. A total of 20 touches equals one set. You can also use a one-step takeoff.
4. Rest for 60 seconds. Repeat three times.

LADY MAGIC TIPS

- Be explosive to the spot you are trying to touch.
- Use your arms, as well as your legs, to generate power.
- Come down and quickly go back up.

One-Foot Running Jumps

PURPOSE

To combine sprinting, maintaining balance, pivoting, sprinting again, and jumping. All the transition moves you might have to make during a game are included in this drill.

PROCEDURE

1. Start at the baseline under the basket, sprint to the foul line, and touch it with either hand.
2. Lower your center of gravity as you approach, or you'll be off balance.
3. Pivot and sprint back to the basket, jumping as high as you can off one foot. Touch the net or backboard.
4. Repeat this exercise 5 times on each side for a total of 10 times—5 on the left side using your left hand for the touch; 5 on the right side using your right hand for the touch.
5. Rest for 60 seconds after each repetition (perform a total of three sets).

LADY MAGIC TIPS

- Have a goal of touching a specific point (net or board), or jump as high as you can.
- Be quick on sprints.
- Be a high jumper (jumping up), not a long jumper (jumping out).

Reaching New Heights

When I was 11 and growing up in New York, my favorite place to play was PS 10. The park had five courts, but one had an 8-foot rim. This became our dunk court. Our goal was to be the first to touch the rim and the first to dunk. I used an unusual method to increase my vertical jump—one that my mom didn't appreciate. Every time I left a room in our house, I'd jump and touch the top of the door. As I got bigger and stronger, my dirty little fingers went higher and higher until I could reach the ceiling. Finally, I could touch my whole palm on the ceiling. But success meant punishment. My mom didn't appreciate my progress. All the jumping and repetition really helped me dunk on that 8-foot goal. Later, as a 5-foot-8 high school senior, I could dunk on a regular rim. People didn't expect to see that from a girl.

Jump Rope With Two Legs

PURPOSE

To increase endurance and foot speed. This exercise is a great conditioner when done at a solid pace.

PROCEDURE

1. Warm up slowly for 3 minutes.
2. Rope sprint for 25 consecutive jumps. Rest for 25 seconds. Five sequences of 25 jumps (reps) equals one set. After completing one set, rest for 1 minute.
3. Cool down slowly for 3 minutes.

LADY MAGIC TIPS

- Keep your body fairly straight for proper balance.
- Keep your knees flexed and eyes straight ahead.
- Stay on the balls of your feet.
- Have a good, solid pace and rhythm.
- Push yourself on the sprints; complete the number of jumps as quickly as possible.
- Use your forearms and wrists, not your arms, to create speed.
- To add variety to your workout, complete the drill using just one leg. Then complete the drill using the other.

Jumping Line Drill

PURPOSE

To gain rapid improvement in jumping skills by practicing and executing jumping in all directions with maximum intensity.

PROCEDURE

1. Stand sideways to any line on the court. Place your feet together. Stand on the balls of your feet and jump from side to side using your arms for proper balance.
2. Don't drag your feet on the slide. Jump over the line and clear it. You are working on movement as well as speed.
3. Do three sets of line jumps, side to side. Each set lasts 30 seconds. Rest for 60 seconds. Repeat three times with 1 minute of rest in between.
4. Do three sets of line jumps, front to back. Each set lasts 30 seconds. Rest for 60 seconds. Repeat three times.

(continued)

Jumping Line Drill *(continued)*

LADY MAGIC TIPS

- Stay balanced. Use your arms for speed and momentum in each direction.
- Keep in mind that intensity is the key.
- Keep your knees and feet together.
- Keep your knees slightly bent; do not lock your knees.

SUMMARY

Becoming an offensive threat can be challenging and fun. By dedicating yourself to being more of a threat offensively, you will work on areas that can lead to overall improvement. You must work on the following:

- Triple-threat positioning—passing, shooting, dribbling
- Triple-threat options to enhance your offensive game
- Drills that improve your footwork

chapter

5

Shooting the Lights Out

Most players love to shoot. Fans, coaches, media, and teammates love to watch a player who can score almost at will. But it's never as easy as it looks. For a player to be proficient in any part of the game—especially shooting—technique, concentration, and repetition are vital.

Few players have ever been proficient in sports without mastering the fundamentals. The truly great shooters have been unbelievable: Sheryl Swoopes, Jennifer Azzi, Becky Hammon, and, maybe the purest shooter I ever saw or played against, Montclair State's Carol Blazejowski. All of these players had confidence and worked hard.

In this chapter, we take you through the necessary fundamentals, concentrating exclusively on shooting, offensive moves, and a variety of drills to make your game better. Shooting isn't just doing it; shooting also involves thinking and visualizing yourself taking and making the shot.

SHOOTING FORM AND TECHNIQUE

Preparation is one of the keys to becoming a great shooter. Being ready means your hands are up waiting for the pass. Your knees are flexed so that when you do catch the ball, you can go right into your shot. Your feet are balanced and squared to the basket, ready to explode up into your shot. Your eyes are focused on the court. You see all your options before you shoot the ball.

The Hands

Always be prepared to catch the ball even if you're not open. Keep your hands up in front of your face or in front of your body. It takes time to move your hands up from your sides to catch the ball. If you already have your palms to the passer, she knows that you are ready if she passes to you. Spread your fingers apart and keep them slightly flexed; this gives you "soft hands" and enables you to catch the ball more easily (figure 5.1). Have your shooting hand open and ready to catch the ball. Your off hand is positioned to be on the side of the ball. This allows you to have a quick release once you have received the pass.

Figure 5.1 Hand position for catching the ball.

Once you receive the pass, your grip becomes the single most important feature of good shooting. Start the process by spreading the fingers of your shooting hand wide apart. Next, when you place your fingers behind the ball, use the pads of your fingers. Don't use your palm. Apply pressure on the ball by grabbing it with your thumb and little finger. Then, place the middle three fingers on the ball in a gentle but firm manner. To achieve the greatest accuracy, point your middle finger at the valve on the ball and aim that finger at the rim. Place the ball in your hand with the seams across your hand. If you shoot the ball with the seams across, you can see if you have proper rotation on your shot. When the pros are catching the ball, they rotate the seam up so that the ball has beautiful rotation after release.

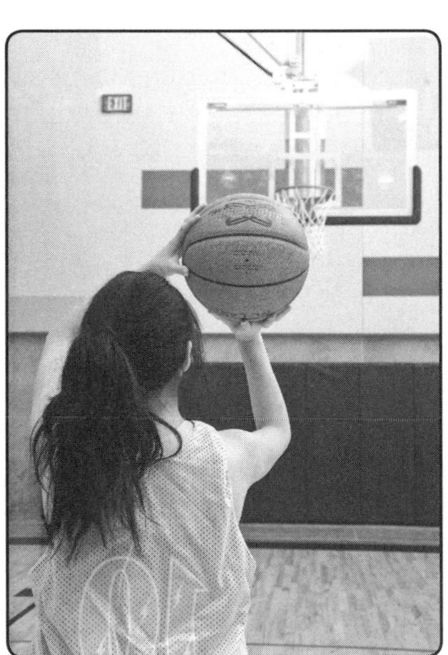

Figure 5.2 Proper shooting form.

Your nonshooting hand will help guide the ball straight at the target. Place your nonshooting hand on the side of the ball, with your fingers pointing to the ceiling and with your thumb toward your ear (figure 5.2). Apply gentle pressure. The real secret is for you to think of pushing your shooting hand (with the ball) through your guide hand (with your fingers pointing upward) and to finish with your guide hand staying in the same spot. Your shooting hand is extended into a limp release by extending your wrist and elbow forward and outward; your hand ends "down in the basket."

Footwork

As you learned in chapter 4, footwork is the key to balance and speed. Footwork is also important to your shooting game. Proper footwork enables you to be where you want and to be ready to shoot. Every great shooter has excellent balance before taking her shot. A shooter's foundation comes from good footwork and legwork before the shot.

When you are preparing to shoot, your feet should be pointed to the basket, straight ahead, and at the middle of the rim (figure 5.3). For good balance, your weight should be on the front foot to help keep you in a flexed and ready position. Your knees should be slightly flexed to allow for a deeper flexing movement of the legs, which will help generate an easy fluid upward motion. The quality of your footwork will determine the quality of your shot!

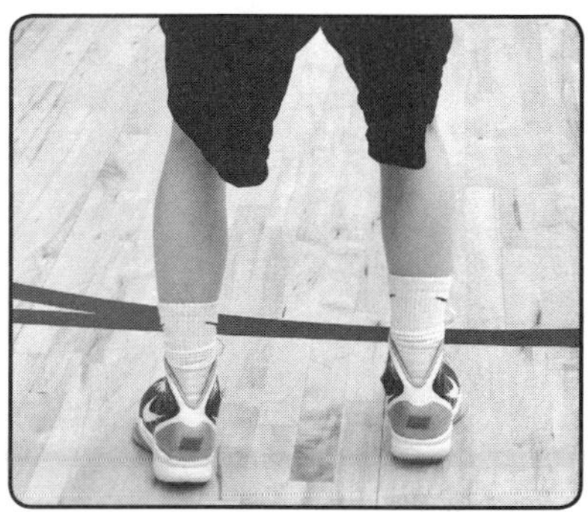

Figure 5.3 A right-handed shooter keeping the feet straight and the knees bent. If the shooter is right-handed, the right foot should be slightly ahead of the left.

Figure 5.4 Low shooting position while body is up.

Body Position

The best way to be ready to explode into your jumper is to catch the ball while you are already low in your shooting position (figure 5.4). This way you can go straight up with the shot. Many players catch the ball while their body is straight up. Then they have to go down to gain strength to make the jumper. Starting in a lower position permits a more efficient motion. (Remember, too, that a low center of gravity is better for speed and balance if you choose to drive instead of shoot from the triple-threat position.) Start low; this way you only have to go in one direction—up.

As you prepare to shoot, square your hips and shoulders to the basket and keep your head slightly forward. Your head is the heaviest part of your body.

If it is leaning back, it will pull your shoulders back. Subsequently, your shot will be short. You want to be leaning into your shot—toward the basket and your defender—not away.

Figure 5.5 Forming an L with your shooting arm.

Arm Position

Make an L shape with your shooting arm; the underside of your arm should be parallel to the floor (figure 5.5). Do not use a V-shape arm formation with your elbow pointed toward the ground. Pretend you are a waitress—your hand is the tray, and the basketball is the food. Once you have achieved this "tray" position, you want your long shooting finger and your shooting elbow pointed right at the middle of the rim. The fingers of your shooting hand are generally pointing to the ceiling.

When you are ready to launch the shot from your favorite "groove" or "pocket," the area where you like to catch the ball, you now know the spot where you'll hit from with consistency. You must learn and know where your "shot spot" is. To maintain a good pocket routine, in other words being consistent with catching and shooting from where you like to catch the ball, keep your shooting elbow out over your front, or shooting, foot. Make sure your elbow is not outside of you. This will help your alignment and lead to an easy, effortless release of the shot.

Sighting

To prepare for your shot, you must learn how to sight or aim. Take aim by staring and concentrating on the front of the rim. Don't follow the flight of the ball—if you do, more often than not you'll watch as you miss the shot. Always have your head up, whether you are shooting or not. If your head is up and you are seeing the floor, the defense doesn't know if you are going to take the shot, pass, or dribble. Keeping your head up also allows you to quickly shoot the ball because you can see the rim.

The Finish

To check your finish, exaggerate pointing your shooting finger and shooting elbow. Move your wrist and elbow in an outward and forward motion toward the rim (figure 5.6). Release your shot so that you cannot see the back of your hand, and try to put your hand "into the basket." Check the rotation of your shot by placing a piece of tape on the ball and counting the rotations of the ball.

Exaggerate your follow-through. Shoot up, high above the rim, not forward. You need air under your shot—shooting up will make sure your shot is not flat. If you can't get the ball over the 10-foot rim, your shot won't go in. With more arc, your shot will have a better chance to hit the rim or backboard and fall through the hoop.

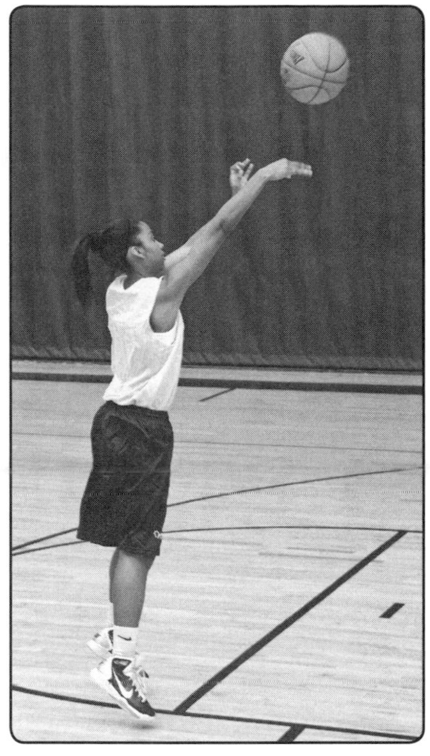

Figure 5.6 Proper hand and arm position for the finish.

Reading Your Shot

If you hold and shoot the basketball with correct form, you will be able to "read" your shot. If you are shooting correctly and your shot is short, you need to add more arc and power. If your shot is too hard, you may need to use less leg strength. To figure this out, think about how you are shooting. If your form is correct and your shot is still too hard, you should let up with your legs. If you are getting good leg strength into your shot, check your form. Alternatively, you might be pushing the ball. Has your L become a V? If your elbow is facing the ground, you might be pushing the ball toward the rim instead of shooting high above the rim. If your shot rebounds to the right, chances are your hand went to the right on your follow-through. By shooting the ball correctly and holding the ball with the seams, you can read the rotation of the ball and the direction the ball is moving. Once you are able to find the problem, you can make the proper adjustment in your shot.

Keep Trying

We all have games when we shoot well and games when we don't. To be a complete player, you must be able to control the bad shooting days. Believe me, I've had games when the basket looked like a coffee cup and others when it looked like the ocean. Even though I may have been shooting poorly, I tried to read my shot and make the proper adjustment. In my college days, many times I was 5 for 20 but was able to come back at the end and hit the last three or four shots. Don't ever give up.

Perfecting Your Technique

The more you work on your shooting technique, the better your chance for success. Good technique means less chance of mechanical breakdown in your shot. Less breakdown means successful shooting. This all goes back to repetition and practice. The more you practice with the correct form, the more likely it is that you will accomplish your goal of proper shooting technique. Here are some common errors and checkpoints for self-correction of your shots.

Short shooting (front rim or air ball): Caused by leaping up for the shot and releasing the ball on the way down.

Correction: Shoot the shot during your upward jumping motion by releasing the ball as you are going up or at the peak of your jump. You must maintain a good L position and keep your guide hand in place. Finish with your hand "in the basket."

Shooting side to side (right or left): Caused by poor hand position.

Correction: Recheck your hand position on the ball and keep your shooting hand in the middle of the ball. Point your elbow at the basket and finish your shot so that you can't see the back of your shooting hand. Keep your guide hand firmly in place and push the shooting hand through the guide hand. To practice getting the feel of the proper hand and arm position before the shot, you can make an L with your shooting arm against a wall.

Long shooting (back rim or backboard): Caused by going forward instead of straight up on the jumper or by hurrying the shot.

Correction: Release your shot with a higher arc, with your shooting arm fully extended, and with your hand in the hard finish position. Keep your eyes strictly on the basket, not on the flight of the ball.

Checkpoints

- ☑ Square up to the basket. Keep your feet parallel, with one foot slightly ahead of the other. If you are right-handed, your right foot is forward. If you're a lefty, your left foot is forward.
- ☑ Remember that your toes, knees, hips, elbow, shoulders, wrist, and follow-through should be facing the basket.
- ☑ Make sure that your shooting elbow is directly above your knee on the same side. This indicates that you have proper form. If your elbow is outside your knee, the elbow is not in close enough—your form is incorrect, and the angle will cause you to push the ball.
- ☑ Lean into your shot. Be balanced.
- ☑ Follow through high above the rim.
- ☑ Make sure that the seams are across your palms.

SHOT SELECTION

Shot selection is pure discipline. You must learn to recognize what is a good shot and what isn't. Why settle for a 22-footer when an 18-footer is better? You can control shot selection. Good shot selection means using your dribble to square up to the basket or using your footwork to get into the right position. You must change your mentality—don't shoot a shot, *make* a shot.

Shot Fake

The shot fake is one of the most underrated aspects of basketball. First, you must make the fake believable. This can be done in a variety of ways. Use whatever it takes—fake with your head, eyes, shoulders, body, arms, and feet. If you fake with the ball, be quick and keep your elbows close to your body. If the ball is extended too far out, the defense has a greater chance of slapping it away. When you shot-fake, the ball goes up, but you should stay down in an attack position (figure 5.7).

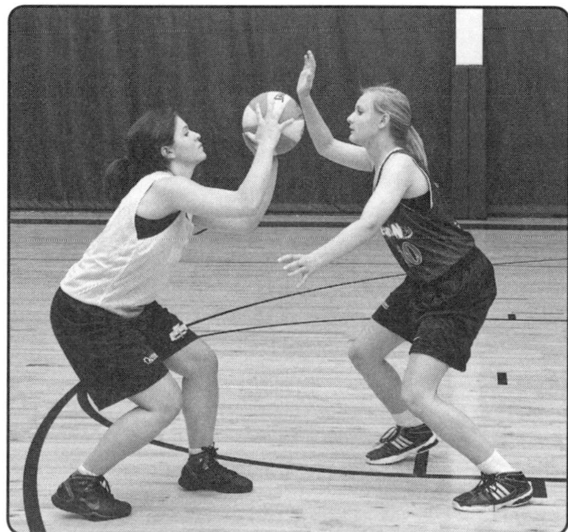

Figure 5.7 Shot fake.

A properly executed shot fake can create an easy shot or an open drive to the basket. When an offensive player fakes a shot to the basket, she must react to the defense. If the defender does not come out and defend the shot, the offensive player should take the shot. If the defender closes in on the offensive player and comes out of her defensive stance, the offensive player should step to either side and go by the defender.

Pump or Double-Pump Fake

Pump faking is a great way to get to the free-throw line. It is an essential part of the game, especially when competing against opponents who regularly try to block your shot. In a pump fake, the player fakes a shot to draw the defender up before taking her real shot. The goal is to avoid a block or to draw a foul. The double-pump fake (two pump fakes before an actual shot) requires you to be strong and creative; you must be able to adjust your body while taking a variety of shots. Only exceptional athletes can go up for a shot, be covered by the defense, and then change shots in midair—all while concentrating on the follow-through to the basket.

Pump-fake the ball to get the defense to jump or react. For example, as you leave the ground to shoot, you draw the defense to you. When your defender comes close, you should double-pump. Once your defender is in the air, you can draw contact and get to the free-throw line. Remember, you must make the pump fake believable, as if you are really going up with the shot.

SHOT VARIETY

The most important aspect of shooting is putting the ball in the basket. Because your shot opportunities may be available anywhere on the court, you need to have variety and creativity in your game. The great thing about the game of basketball is that you never really know what your defenders will give you. You may want to take a jumper, but it might not be available. You might have to penetrate and shoot a layup or a bank shot. The more shots you have in your arsenal, the better equipped you will be to score in any situation. Let's look at various types of shots that you might have to take in a game or in practice.

Layup

You make layups with your eyes. Keep your eyes fixed on the box on the backboard; use this as your guide. The layup should be the first shot you master; it's a high-percentage shot. When shooting a layup, make sure you leap at a 45-degree angle to the basket. If you are starting from the left side, plant your right foot, then dip your right leg. This allows you to generate momentum going from a forward motion to an upward motion as you move the ball up in unison with your shooting knee (in this case, the right knee) on the drive to the basket (figure 5.8). Keep your head up and your eyes focused on the square above the basket. Your back and waist should be straight. Push off your right leg and use your left knee to explode up to the basket. Shoot the ball straight up. Follow through by extending your elbow, wrist, and fingers. Always keep two hands on the ball until you release it. Use your off hand to protect the ball. Don't worry about getting fouled. Finish the shot. Remember to jump up, not out. I always stress getting up as high as you can, even to the point of touching the backboard or dunking. If you long jump, you float out of bounds and out of the play! If you cannot go hard for layups on both sides, you do not have a complete game.

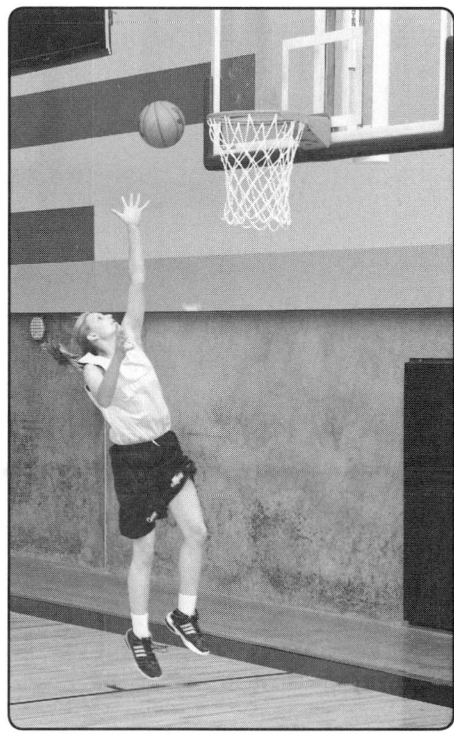

Figure 5.8 Shooting a layup.

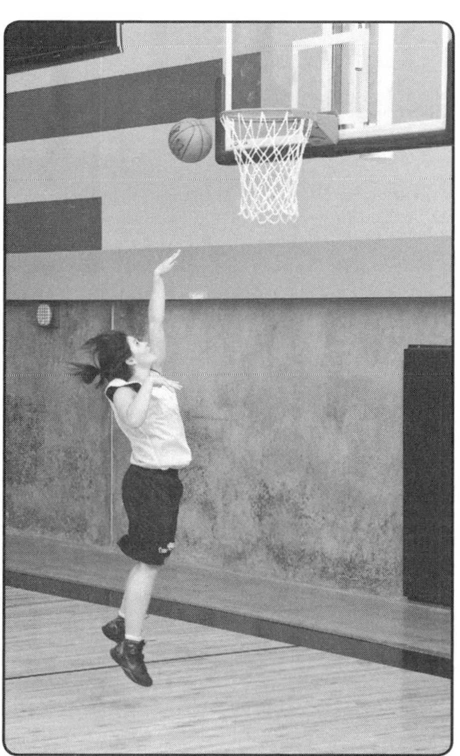

Figure 5.9 Shooting a power layup.

Power Layup

The power layup is slightly different from the regular layup. For this shot, you use both feet simultaneously—performing a jump stop—and explode toward the basket (figure 5.9). Release the ball as you are airborne. A power layup keeps you in good rebounding position and allows you to maintain proper balance. Keep your eyes focused on the basket. This is a good move to use for drawing fouls as you jump into the defense in order to create contact under the basket. Be sure to use your inside arm to protect the ball from your defenders.

Reverse Layup

This layup is great when going baseline or using the proper 45-degree angle while making your move to the basket. The reverse layup puts the basket between you and the defense. Start on the opposite side of the basket. Concentrate on the backboard as you float past it during the shot. As you go up with your shot, you need a little spin on the ball—but not a lot, because too much will make the ball spin off the glass. The shot requires a soft turn and flick of the wrist (figure 5.10). As always, remember to work on performing the reverse layup with either hand.

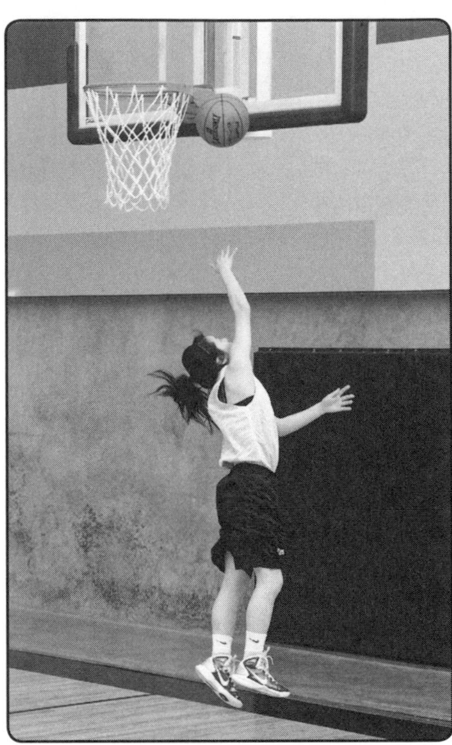

Figure 5.10 Shooting a reverse layup.

Jump Shot

The one-hand jump shot is the most efficient and most used outside shot. Like any shot, the ball is controlled with your fingertips; the seams are parallel to the floor. You should always have the proper L position when shooting. Your head should go toward your target. Your knees are slightly flexed, ready to explode into your jump shot. When you are in the ready position to shoot, spring up off your toes and jump as high as you can. Release the ball near or at the top of your jump (figure 5.11). Focus on the basket as you release your shot. Your follow-through hand and index finger should be pointed just above the rim. Remember to "finish hard" with your wrist. The lower you are when you catch the ball, the quicker you can jump up for the shot.

Figure 5.11 Positioning for the one-hand jump shot.

Add another dimension to your jump shot by mastering the fallaway jumper. The shot is exactly the same as a regular jumper except the jumping movement is different. In a game situation, you might lean in slightly and then pivot away from the defense and the goal. Instead of jumping into your shot, you jump and fade backward. This is a tough shot for the defense to block because your backward momentum creates space between you and the defense.

Stationary Shot

The stationary shot is usually taken from long range when a player has plenty of time to set and shoot. This shot is still very effective for many players, especially against a zone. The one-hand set shot is the preferred shooting style today. It is similar to the jump shot with the exception of the actual jump. The ball is shot more with the arms than with the legs. This shot can be tried whether you are in one place or moving. A shooter must find the open shot on the outside and be ready to shoot the uncontested set shot.

Bank Shot

The glass and square above the rim give you good sight lines, making the bank shot a high-percentage shot. You can bank layups, short jumpers, or even outside shots. The ball should hit within the square. Avoid using too much spin on your shot. Ideally, your bank shot should hit and drop through, barely touching the front of the rim.

Even on the fast break, you should use the glass. Using the glass will soften your shot even when you are out of control. The key to the bank shot is knowing angles and where you are on the floor. A 45-degree angle is the best place from which to shoot the bank shot—whether it's a layup or a three-pointer. Tim Duncan has brought the art of using the glass back to the game. Using it can increase your shooting percentage.

Free Throw

How many games have been won or lost at the line? It happens at all levels—the pros, college, high school, and rec league. Developing a consistent, reliable foul shot can change your success and your team's success. With all the bumping and grinding you deal with during a game while trying to shoot over a defender, the free throw is a blessing. When you are at the line, no one is in your face playing defense. You have worked hard to get to the line. Now take a deep breath, relax, and concentrate. Here are some things to remember:

- Take deep breaths; relax your muscles. Take a moment to catch your breath. You rarely go to the line rested.
- Line up properly. Most indoor courts have a nail placed in the middle of the foul line. Line up your foot with that nail. Line up with your

right foot if you are right-handed, or with your left foot if you are left-handed.

- Remember that repetition is important. Take a few dribbles before shooting to find a rhythm. Do the same routine before each foul shot.
- Use a consistent technique; each shot must be the same motion. Foul shooting is rhythm, routine, and mechanics. Stay balanced. Keep your elbow in; lean into your shot. Fix your eyes on the target and follow through.
- Think positively; you must believe in yourself and have confidence that you will make the shot. Confidence comes from success. Success comes from practicing your free-throw shooting every day.

Checkpoints

☑ ***Pole ready***—The proper foul-shooting position evolves from what is called the pole ready technique. Use a pole that is 6 to 7 feet (183 to 213 cm) in length. You and your teammates, one at a time, should assume your normal shooting position. Take the pole and place it vertically on the floor at the middle of your shooting foot. Have your hand in front of the pole and your buttocks behind it. Your knees should be slightly flexed so you will be in a ready position before your shot. Any time you miss a shot short (front rim or air ball), you should lean farther forward. You will seldom miss the second shot as a result of the lean. If you miss a shot long (back rim), adjust your shot by using a higher arc. Again, you will seldom miss the second try.

☑ ***Elbow***—Whenever you shoot free throws, maintain a good L position with your shooting arm and, more important, look down at your shooting foot and make sure your shooting elbow is over it. This is an excellent alignment test and prevents your elbow from going out of the shooting line.

☑ ***Guide hand***—The wall can help you maintain a consistent straight shot. Go to a wall and, if you are a right-handed shooter, put your left shoulder against the wall and place your shooting hand across your body. Hold the ball up against the wall. Get a teammate to stand about 10 feet (3 m) away, facing you. Push the ball along the wall toward your teammate by using your shooting hand. You will find that the ball hugs the wall when your shot is pushed. Develop this slogan: "If the wall is straight, the ball is straight." Now you should be ready to make your guide hand become your "wall," with your fingers pointing to the ceiling. Keep your guide hand (wall) in place, and push your shooting hand through the wall, which you have pointed toward the basket. Finish your shot by putting your hand "in the basket" so you can't see the back of your shooting hand.

Specialty Shots

Having a few specialty shots in your arsenal can give you a tremendous edge over your opponents. We'll discuss three shots—hook shots, tip-ins, and dunks—that require skill and a lot of practice. These shots won't be appropriate for all players; physical limitations might prevent you from performing them successfully.

Hook Shot

The hook shot has been very successful for a few great players, including George Mikan, Kareem Abdul-Jabbar, my former Old Dominion teammate Anne Donovan (who is 6-foot-8), and most recently, Becky Hammon. It is a great close-up shot. Even Magic Johnson, a guard, mastered what he called the "baby hook." When shooting a hook shot, extend one leg and plant it in the direction you're going to hook the ball. Use your inside arm to create space and protect the ball. Hold the ball with the hand you will use to shoot it. Lift the ball to the basket with a full extension of your arm to a point by your ear—all in one fluid motion (figure 5.12). Flex your wrist and fingers. As you release the ball with a feathery touch to the basket, keep a wide base for proper balance. As you half turn (pivot), use your body to create the space needed to shoot over your defender. To be more effective, practice with both hands. Becky Hammon uses the early-release floater in the lane. She gets it up high, before the bigs can come out to try to block it.

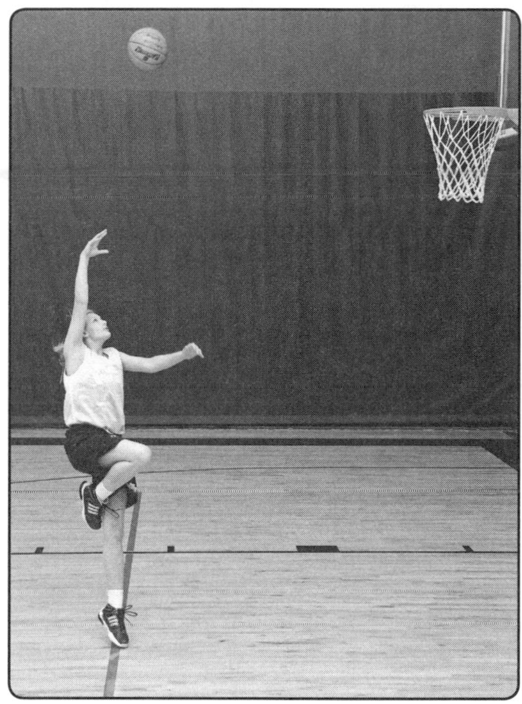

Figure 5.12 Shooting a hook shot.

Tip-In

The tip-in is the part of the game that I practiced as a young girl in the school yards. We played "21," and the only way to score was by making your foul shots or tipping the ball in off a missed attempt. Only two tips were allowed on each missed free throw. Although many girls and women don't yet play above

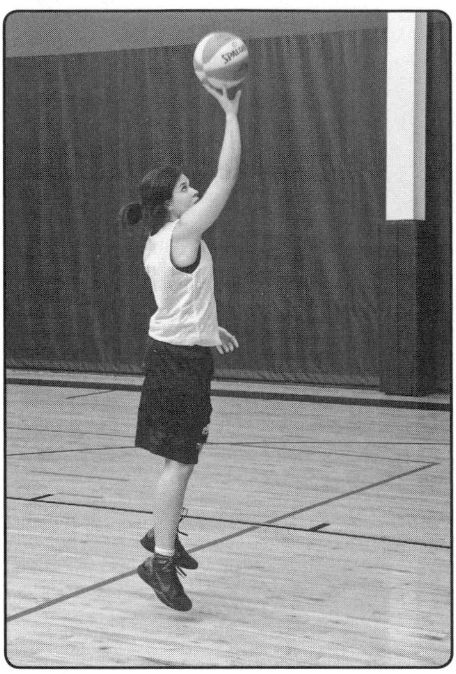

Figure 5.13 Tipping the ball into the basket.

the rim, they can still tip the ball into the basket. Practicing tip-ins helps you develop control, touch, and a mentality to always go for the ball—even if you cannot gain full control. The proper position for a tip-in is to have your body straight and knees flexed in a jumping position. Use your arms to help you accelerate up to the basket. Then, use your wrist and fingertips to guide the ball to the rim or backboard (figure 5.13). As with passing and dribbling, you should practice with both hands.

Dunk

Yes, the dunk is a part of women's basketball. It's the most electrifying shot in the game. The dunk represents power and authority. It changes momentum. And it's the highest-percentage shot in the game. So if you can dunk the ball, do so! It's a great weapon.

Players use a variety of dunk shots, from the basic one-hander to the two-hand dunk. You can dunk off one foot or two. Successful dunking requires good timing on your jump as well as the ability to palm or hold onto the ball long enough to power it home. Obviously, you need to jump as high as you can. Clear the rim with the ball, and then dunk it by using a downward wrist action.

Experience the Feeling

Although some women can't dunk on a 10-foot rim, that doesn't mean they shouldn't practice the shot. Each summer at my basketball camps, we have a slam-dunk contest for the little kids and the bigger girls. We lower the rims to 5 feet or so for the itty bitties, and to 7 feet for the others. This contest is one of the highlights of camp. Kids get a chance to express themselves. Campers choose the winners. A lot of clapping by the campers means a pretty nasty dunk. For some participants, it's the first time they've touched the rim. Their confidence gets a boost.

FORM AND TECHNIQUE DRILLS

The following drills focus on correct shooting form and technique. The drills give you checkpoints to see if you have accomplished correct form by working on ball rotation, strengthening your wrist, and being able to constantly hit your target. Repetition is important to improve form and to increase confidence when shooting.

One-Arm Shooting

PURPOSE

To develop proper shooting form and technique. (Checkpoints are used to make sure your mechanics are correct.) This drill will teach you to maintain the same shot no matter where you are on the floor. What will change is the power from your legs and hips. I call this your power base. This drill will also help your concentration, confidence, and development of a shooter's soft touch.

PROCEDURE

1. Stand directly in front of the basket. Hold the ball with your shooting hand out in front of you, palm up. Slowly turn your wrist inward. This will drop your shoulder and put your arm in the proper L position. The ball should be on your fingertips and approximately head high. Place your opposite hand behind your back. Shoot the ball high, exaggerating your form and follow-through. Your fingers should point up over the top of the rim for a high arch.
2. Make five shots in a row from the same spot. Take one step back and repeat, again trying to make five in a row. Continue to repeat the drill until you have made it to the top of the key. The farther you step back, the more difficult it is to keep your form. Use your power base to explode into your shot and lean in.
3. Move to the block on the side of the foul lane. Using a 45-degree angle, repeat the drill on each side. The only difference is that now you're working on your one-arm bank shot. Lean in and follow through.
4. Make five in a row, then take one step back each time until you hit the wing and are about 18 feet away.

LADY MAGIC TIPS

- Remember that proper form is the key. Make sure everything is lined up to the basket: feet, knees, hips, shoulders, arm, and follow-through.
- Always lean into your shot.
- Be relaxed in your ready position and when you shoot. Keep your elbow in the L position, over your knee. Release the ball with a soft touch. Focus on your target, not the ball.
- Exaggerate your follow-through until the ball drops through the net.

One-Hand Flip Shot

PURPOSE

To discover your true shooting range by performing one-arm shooting with proper form.

PROCEDURE

1. You will shoot from five areas—in the areas running from the basket to each corner where the sideline and the baseline meet, in the areas running from the basket at a 45-degree angle on either side of the foul line, and in the area running from the basket to the top of the key.
2. At each of the five areas, start shooting 5 feet from the basket and back up and away from the basket in 3-foot intervals until your last shot is from 20 feet.
3. Shoot at least 3 shots from each distance (18 in each area—a total of 90 shots for all five areas).
4. Record your attempts and shots made.

LADY MAGIC TIPS

- Always lean into your shot.
- Remember, the farther you are from the basket, the more you must use leg strength.
- Keep your shooting arm in the L position.

Chair Shooting

PURPOSE

To exaggerate lifting the ball to the basket and to help you learn to shoot the ball instead of throw it. Sitting in a chair forces you to keep your head up and stay focused on the target.

PROCEDURE

1. Place a chair about 8 feet in front of the basket. While sitting in the chair, shoot 25 shots. Rest for 1 minute. Then shoot 25 more shots. Rest.
2. Move the chair to bank shot position at a 45-degree angle 8 feet from the basket. Sitting in the chair, take 25 shots. Rest for 1 minute. Then shoot 25 more shots. Rest.
3. Move to the opposite side of the court and repeat the drill.

LADY MAGIC TIPS

- Concentrate on a point over the rim. Focus on your target.
- Work on developing fingertip, wrist, and arm strength.
- Use the correct L position.
- When you are low in a chair, follow through hard, extending your elbow while using a soft touch and backspin.

Floor Form Shooting

PURPOSE

To work on rotation and follow-through, developing a soft touch, and learning to read the spin of the ball by holding it across the seams. Lying on your back will allow you to check if your elbow is in, if your arm is in the L position, and, most of all, if the ball has backspin.

PROCEDURE

1. Lying flat on your back, relax your shooting hand as you are holding the ball over your chest.
2. Check your elbow alignment.
3. Shoot the ball directly up into the air, completely extending your elbow, wrist, and fingers. The ball should come back into your hands.
4. Shoot 25 form shots. Rest for 1 minute. Then take 25 more shots.

LADY MAGIC TIPS

- Keep your elbow in place and your shooting hand relaxed.
- Create backspin.

Wall Shooting

PURPOSE

To simulate your shot using a strong finish (follow-through) and putting good rotation on the ball. This drill will strengthen your wrist and help you with consistency.

PROCEDURE

1. Mark some spots on a wall.
2. Sit on the floor, facing the wall. Hold the ball in your shooting hand.
3. Aim above the lowest mark on the wall. Shoot the ball up high and accurately, using a nice, easy wrist and elbow extension.
4. Keep your fingers down. Repeat this action above each spot until you have shown an exaggerated finish and good form.

VARIATION

If you have a teammate, sit facing her about 4 to 5 feet (122 to 152 cm) away. Using good shooting form and rotation, shoot the ball as high as you can to your teammate. You and your teammate should take about 20 shots until you both finish your shot simulation.

LADY MAGIC TIPS

- Concentrate on proper form and follow-through on each shot.
- Keep your head up to follow the flight of the shot.

Power Layup

PURPOSE

To work on balance and power as you go strong to the hoop. A power layup is often a great way to draw a foul.

PROCEDURE

1. Place one chair at each foul-line elbow. Start outside the lane and flip the ball in front of you toward the hoop. Run and get the ball. Perform a hard ball fake and go off two feet. Explode up to the basket.
2. Get the rebound and dribble between the two chairs, going to the opposite side. After you turn the corner around the chair, again flip the ball toward the hoop. Go to the ball. Perform a ball fake and go up strong for a power layup using both hands.
3. Jump as high as you can on each shot. Make five on each side. To challenge yourself, see how many you can make in 60 seconds.

LADY MAGIC TIPS

- Toss the ball toward the basket as if you were going in for a layup.
- Run the ball down. Be balanced. Make your ball fake believable.
- Go up strong, lean in, and jump as high as you can.
- After the rebound, when you are on the left side, use a right-handed dribble to split the chairs; when you are on the right side, use a left-handed dribble. (The ball should always be in your outside hand.)

Reverse Layup

PURPOSE

To gain options around the hoop by using the backboard and rim as another form of protection from the defense. The reverse layup is a great shot to use in traffic. You should be able to shoot with either hand. Steve Nash practices this before each game.

PROCEDURE

1. Stand under the backboard with the ball, directly in line with the rim.
2. Jump as you plant your right foot (inside leg) and shoot with your left hand, using a flicking motion of your wrist. Spin the ball with your wrist inward, using the square above the rim as the target you would want to hit.
3. Concentrate on each shot. Use your off arm to protect the ball. You are always shooting while facing the entire court.
4. Make 10 reverse layups on each side.
5. Shoot 10 foul shots. Repeat the drill three times.

LADY MAGIC TIPS

- Always keep your head up and jump as high as you can on the shot. As the ball comes down through the net, catch it, and this time plant your left foot (inside leg) and shoot a reverse layup with your right hand.
- Start under the backboard so you have to use your wrist to spin the ball off the glass.
- Push yourself to game speed when comfortable.
- Follow through on all shots.

JUMP SHOT DRILLS

Learning to shoot on the move will improve your chances of making shots on the move in games. With practice, your shots off a fake or dribble will become one fluid motion.

X-Out J

PURPOSE

To work on shooting a jump shot. In this drill, as in a game, you will be shooting while active rather than stationary. The faster and more accurately you can position yourself for the shot, the better your success rate will be as a shooter.

PROCEDURE

1. Start with your outside foot on the block and with your back to the baseline.
2. Roll the ball past the foul line.
3. Pick the ball up after it crosses the foul line. Then pivot and face the basket.
4. Shoot the jumper and follow your shot. (The ball shouldn't touch the floor after it goes through the net.)
5. Repeat until you make 10 shots.

X-Out Shot Fake J

PURPOSE

To work on shooting a jump shot off a fake. In games, defenders will run out to guard you as you receive the ball. Working on a fake in practice helps prepare you for using one in a game, and you'll be more likely to knock down the shot when it counts.

(continued)

X-Out Shot Fake J *(continued)*

PROCEDURE

1. Start with your outside foot on the block and with your back to the baseline.
2. Roll the ball past the foul line.
3. Pick the ball up after it crosses the foul line, but add a shot fake when you turn and face the basket.
4. Take a dribble before you shoot the jumper.
5. Repeat until you make 10 shots.

X-Out Combo From Wing

PURPOSE

To improve your ability to create space between you and a defender for an open shot. This drill also helps you practice proper shooting form off the dribble.

PROCEDURE

1. Start with your outside foot on the block and with your back to the baseline.
2. Roll the ball past the three-point line.
3. Pick the ball up after it crosses the three-point line. Then pivot and face the basket.
4. Perform a shot fake and then dribble to the elbow or baseline for your jumper. Follow your shot.
5. Repeat until you make 10 shots.

Fallaway Jump Shot

PURPOSE

To work on executing a fallaway jump shot. When you use the proper shooting form, this shot allows you to create space between you and the defender. This drill also develops your ability to be balanced and to stay low before your shot.

PROCEDURE

1. Start at the foul line extended (the T). You should be in a triple-threat position.
2. Make a hard drive to the basket and quickly plant your outside foot. Make sure your weight is on this pivot foot before pushing off it.
3. As you go up for your shot, push back, leaning away instead of leaning in. Your release should be higher with more arch and a soft touch.

4. After your shot, rebound and dribble back to the extended foul line and continue the drill.
5. Make 10 fallaway jumpers on the left side and 10 fallaway jumpers on the right side. Take 10 foul shots. Repeat three times.

LADY MAGIC TIPS

- Use the proper shooting form. The only change is that you're falling away instead of leaning in.
- Plant hard with your outside foot to drive the defense back.
- As the defenders retreat, fade back on your shot. This is where the space is created.
- Use a high arch, and follow through using a soft feathery touch.

Baseline Jumper Off the Glass

PURPOSE

To help you see and feel where the defense is behind you. You will shoot on balance while turning baseline for a jumper off the glass. The drill will improve your ability to catch the ball off the jump stop and turn (pivot) baseline to face the defense in a ready position.

PROCEDURE

1. Starting under the basket in front of the rim, toss the ball above the low block outside the lane. Catch the ball. Then, using your jump stop, check for the defense on either side by looking over your shoulder.
2. Pivot with your inside foot and turn baseline, squaring up to the defense. You should be in a low triple-threat position, driving the defense back.
3. You can go straight up with the baseline jumper or use a few ball fakes. When you shoot, aim for the near corner of the square above the rim. Use proper shooting technique.
4. Rebound after your shot.

LADY MAGIC TIPS

- Catch the ball and use a balanced jump shot.
- Use ball fakes to make the defense commit.
- Shoot high and use the glass.

BANK SHOT DRILLS

Bank shots can improve your shooting because they help your sight lines. The square on the glass gives you a target to focus on. All layups and angled jumpers should come off the glass.

Toss and Shoot

PURPOSE

To work on getting in the correct and balanced shooting position. This drill will help you focus on catching the ball in a low position as you turn to attack the defense. You should catch and shoot the ball in one quick motion.

PROCEDURE

1. Use a 45-degree angle from both sides. Start under the basket and toss the ball out at a 45-degree angle to a spot that you think is within your shooting range on the wing.
2. As you approach the ball, perform a jump stop, grab the ball, and turn with your body square to the basket. Stay balanced with your elbow in the L position and your shooting foot slightly forward.
3. After the shot, rebound and return under the basket to start again.
4. Shoot for 1 minute. Record the number of shots made. Take 10 foul shots. Repeat this drill three times on each side.

LADY MAGIC TIPS

- Stay behind the ball in a ready position.
- Pivot around and square up to the basket in one motion.
- Make sure your hands are ready to shoot.
- When you shoot the bank shot or your jumper, aim for the square above the rim. Jump up and in slightly. Follow through hard, pointing toward the target.
- Look for the offensive rebound.

Bank Shot Off Dribble

PURPOSE

To work on your speed dribble with either hand and to practice exploding into your shot.

PROCEDURE

1. Start near the sideline, at the foul line extended. Toss the ball out in front, go get it, and jump-stop in a balanced position.

2. In one motion, speed-dribble to an area at a 45-degree angle. Stay within your shooting range.
3. Stay low and be ready to rise up and shoot the bank shot. Concentrate on the top near corner of the box above the rim. Always follow through hard; exaggerate your follow-through.
4. Follow your shot and change sides. On the left side, speed-dribble with your left hand. On the right side, speed-dribble with your right hand.

LADY MAGIC TIPS

- Jump-stop and receive the ball in one motion. Make your move for the speed dribble.
- Plant your inside foot and jump as high as you can.
- Stay focused on the box above the rim.

Bank Shot Off Spin Dribble

PURPOSE

To work on getting your bank shot off after shaking the defense with a spin dribble (see page 146 in chapter 7). The spin dribble is another way to create a shot. You should work on ballhandling, focusing on executing the spin dribble with each hand in the proper position. Stay balanced. The drill will also condition you to go for the offensive rebound.

PROCEDURE

1. Start slightly back of the key area. Using your left hand, speed-dribble to the foul-line elbow on the right side. As you approach the elbow, stay low and balanced. If you are too high and out of control, you will be off balance when you move into your shot.
2. With your head up, begin your spin to the outside.
3. Switch the ball to your right hand (outside hand), using your left to protect the ball. Find your shooting range and pull up for a bank shot (45-degree angle).
4. Jump slightly in and follow through to the square above the rim.
5. Always follow your shot to work on offensive rebounding. After grabbing the rebound, dribble back to the starting point.
6. Make 10 bank shots off your spin dribble on each side. Take 10 foul shots. Repeat this drill three times.

LADY MAGIC TIPS

- Don't leave the ball behind you on the spin. Pull it around, then switch hands.
- Spin with your head up so you can see the defense and the floor.
- Square up in a balanced position for your bank shot.

FREE-THROW DRILLS

These drills are solely for repetition and concentration. The more free throws you shoot, the more confident you'll be at the line.

Nail It

PURPOSE

To develop good work habits, confidence, and concentration. Relax and get into a good rhythm and routine. You can use this time to work on your mechanics.

PROCEDURE

1. Step up to the free-throw line. As you approach it, look for the nail on the floor. On most wooden floors, the nail is in the middle of the foul lane. If it is not, try to center yourself in the middle of the free-throw line, directly at the front of the rim.
2. Shoot until you make 20 straight. (If you're still improving at the line, you can lower the number. Always look to improve.)
3. Shoot 10 one-and-ones.
4. Shoot until you make 20 straight.
5. Shoot 5 one-and-ones.
6. Shoot until you make 20 straight.
7. Shoot 5 one-and-ones.

LADY MAGIC TIPS

- Remember that you should be shooting at least 100 foul shots a day. Break them into sets—25 at one basket, then 25 at another. You can also shoot 20 one-and-ones. If you make the first shot, you shoot the second.
- Step back from the foul line after two shots in a row. You'll never shoot more than two unless you are fouled while shooting a three-pointer, or if a technical foul is added to a foul.
- Use proper shooting form.

Foul-Shot Golf

PURPOSE

To work on your foul shooting through repetition and concentration. This drill is a fun way to play alone or with others.

PROCEDURE

1. Start at the foul line. You play 18 holes in this drill. You earn a "birdie" by hitting nothing but net. (If the ball hits any part of the rim, it does not count as a birdie.) You earn a "par" by just making the foul shot. You earn a "bogey" by missing your foul shot.

2. You get three shots. For example, if you make your first shot but it hits the rim, you earn par. If you make the next shot and it hits only net, you earn a birdie. Now your score is 1 under. If you also hit net on your third shot, you earn another birdie. Now your score is 2 under. You have completed one round.
3. You can start your next round, or if you are playing with others, it's their turn to shoot.
4. When you have completed six rounds (18 holes), the game is over. The player with the lowest score wins. If you are playing by yourself, challenge yourself by improving your score each time.

LADY MAGIC TIPS

- Follow through with a high arch, and finish hard with your wrist straight to the basket.
- Concentrate on your target.
- Don't forget your score!

SPECIALTY SHOT DRILLS

The shots practiced in these drills give you options. You never know when a hook shot might come in handy or when you might need to tip a shot to keep the ball alive. Work on all these shots when you have time.

Mikan Drill

PURPOSE

To work on planting your inside foot and using a semihook off the glass. The drill will help you learn proper form and concentration. You will also work on pivoting with each foot, shooting with each hand, keeping the ball up at all times once you get it out of the net, following the flight of the ball, and developing speed and quickness.

PROCEDURE

1. Start directly in front of the rim. Plant your left foot to the right as if you are beginning a layup. Go up and attempt your semihook (layup) using your off hand to protect the ball.
2. As the ball goes through the net, grab it and plant your right foot. Lean left and attempt a left-handed semihook. Keep alternating left to right. Use the glass on each shot.
3. Make 10 shots on each side. Shoot 5 foul shots. To challenge yourself, see how many you can make in 60 seconds. Then take 10 foul shots. Repeat this procedure three times.

LADY MAGIC TIPS

- Make sure your head is always up.
- Don't drop the ball below your shoulders. Keep your elbows out.
- Plant your inside foot and explode up for the shot.

Two-Hand Hook Shot

PURPOSE

To help you develop confidence and proper technique and to improve your strong- and weak-hand bank shot using a crossover step. (Though mostly used by post players, this drill can be used by others as well.)

PROCEDURE

1. Start sideways in front of the rim and hold the ball above your waist. Going left, you will be shooting with your right hand.
2. Using the crossover, step with your left (inside) foot at a 45-degree angle outward, then pivot toward the basket. Your right knee comes up as you lean in to release the ball.
3. Start with the ball close to your body near your hip. Bring the ball up near your ear and the side of your head. As you extend your elbow, flex your wrist and fingers toward the basket, using your fingertips to release a soft shot with good rotation on the ball.
4. Shoot high off the glass, aiming at the near corner of the square above the rim.
5. After the shot goes up, rebound. Repeat the same drill from the other side.
6. Continue alternating your hook shot from right to left, using the crossover step.
7. Take 10 hook shots from each side. Take 10 foul shots. Repeat this drill three times.

LADY MAGIC TIPS

- Start in the sideways position in front of the rim.
- Always use the crossover step; your inside leg is at a 45-degree angle to the basket.
- Always aim high off the glass, using a soft, relaxed touch on the ball.
- Remember, a missed shot is a pass to yourself. Follow through hard and rebound.

Hook Shot With a Drop Step

PURPOSE

To work on reading where the defense might be and to improve footwork and offensive rebounding.

PROCEDURE

1. Start slightly in front of the rim, with your body sideways to the basket.
2. Toss the ball outside the foul lane above the low block. Catch the ball with your back to the basket, using a jump stop for balance.
3. Check over each shoulder to see the imaginary defense. Then drop-step baseline using your hook shot at a 45-degree angle to the basket.

4. Repeat the drill until you have completed 5 baseline hook shots. Alternate sides of the court after you complete 10 shots. Take 10 foul shots and repeat this drill four times.

LADY MAGIC TIPS

- Start sideways in front of the basket.
- Drop-step at a 45-degree angle to the basket.
- On the right side of the court, drop-step baseline with your left foot, and hook with your right hand. On the left side of the court, drop-step baseline with your right foot, and hook with your left hand.
- On the baseline hook, don't get caught too far under the backboard. Get a good angle (45 degrees to the basket).
- Rebound after each shot.

Tipping

PURPOSE

To improve strength and endurance for rebounding. When fighting for rebounds, it's not always how high you jump—it's how quickly and how well you are positioned. This drill will also improve the strength in your hands and wrists.

PROCEDURE

1. Stand on the left side of the backboard. Place the ball in your left hand. Keep your elbow in and your wrist back. The ball should be shoulder high. Use only your left hand.
2. Shoot the ball high and controlled on the left side of the backboard. Keep tipping the ball up against the glass five times. On the fifth time, tip the ball in the basket (try not to catch the ball). You should be in a balanced position (legs shoulder-width apart, knees flexed) and should be ready to jump up to meet the ball in flight.
3. Switch to the right side of the backboard and repeat the drill using your right hand.
4. Then, alternate hands. This is difficult and takes balance and coordination. Start on one side (left) and use your left hand to tip the ball over the rim to the right side of the backboard. You must slide over to the right side quickly to be in position to tip the ball with your right hand to the left side. Keep alternating sides for six tips—three on each side. The last tip goes in the basket.

VARIATION

Tipping is an advanced drill. Use a wall instead of the backboard if that is more helpful.

LADY MAGIC TIPS

- Keep the ball above your head when tipping. If it gets too low, you lose control.
- Keep your fingers spread apart, flexed, and relaxed.
- When alternating the tip, slide from side to side, quickly and in balance.

Dunking

PURPOSE

To try something you might not have tried before and to work on your timing and jumping.

PROCEDURE

1. Find an adjustable rim. Lower it to a height at which you can comfortably dunk.
2. As you begin to feel more relaxed and confident, raise the level.
3. Try a one-hand dunk, a two-hand dunk, and a reverse dunk. Do whatever you think you can do.
4. Have fun!

LADY MAGIC TIPS

- Be careful not to hit your head on the rim.
- Jump as high as you can.
- If you have small hands, use Stickum (an adhesive) for a better grip or use two hands.

Duck-In Move Drill

PURPOSE

To work on getting the pass to the post player in the paint. This drill will help you learn to position the post properly in the paint, create a passing lane, and thereby decrease the degree of difficulty for the pass. Players will learn to catch the ball under pressure and learn three offensive moves once they've received the pass. (The *duck-in* is another term for posting up.)

PROCEDURE

1. Player 1 has the ball and stands at the top of the key on the left side. Player 2, the offensive post, stands to the right of the lane. Player 3, the defensive player, stands in the lane.
2. Player 2 brings her defender (player 3) into the lane. She must break the broken circle to do this. If possible, she should line herself up so that she is in front of the rim.
3. Player 3 stays with player 2 and contests the passing lane.
4. When player 2 reaches the broken circle, she ducks in and steps over the leg of the defender, creating a lane for the pass. Player 2 now shows her free hand and calls for the ball, which she should receive in the paint near the broken circle.

5. Player 2 can now execute one of three offensive moves depending on how her defender reacts. If the defender is slow to react, player 2 executes a drop step, dribbles, and squares up for the layup. If the defender reacts and recovers, player 2 takes one dribble toward the box and executes a baby hook on the left side. If the defender recovers and positions herself between player 2 and the basket, player 2 drop-steps, performs a power dribble, squares up, and uses a head-and-shoulders pump fake before going up for a short bank shot.

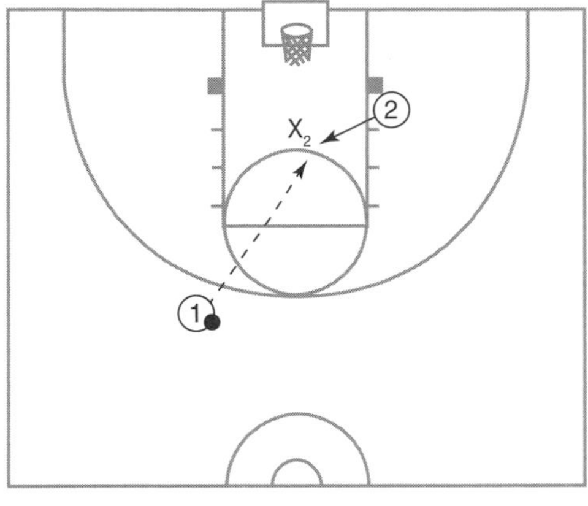

LADY MAGIC TIP

If player 2 uses a head-and-shoulders pump fake, she should not fake the ball up; instead, she should fake it from her chest to elevate the defender.

Beat the All-American

PURPOSE

To build confidence and concentration on each shot and to learn to be more selective on shots. Being selective is important because a bad shot will cost you. In this drill, you'll work on your offensive moves in a gamelike situation. Remember, it's you against the imaginary All-American—have fun.

PROCEDURE

1. Start out by shooting a foul shot. If you make it, you earn 1 point. If you miss, the All-American receives 2 points.
2. After the foul shot, you can shoot from any spot on the court (layups aren't allowed). You must keep moving, and you cannot shoot the same shot twice in a row from the same spot.
3. Ten points wins. Make sure you are in your range. Be positive and relaxed. This drill depends on great concentration for each shot.

VARIATION

You can also play Beat the All-American from three-point range. This time, you shoot only from three-point range. If you make a shot, it's 2 points for you. If you miss, the pro gets 3 points. Play to 21 points.

LADY MAGIC TIPS

- Shoot on the move—work on your concentration, shot selection, and form.
- Use all your moves and shots. Make it gamelike.
- Play to win.

Rabbit Shooting Drill

PURPOSE

This drill consists of 12 steps that will make you a better shooter. The workout is brief and must be done with intensity.

PROCEDURE

1. Toss the ball to the three-point line. Get the ball and square up to the basket. Shoot and follow your shot.

Time: 2 minutes.

Goal: 20 to 25 shots.

2. Shoot 10 foul shots. Record your score. Do not rest. Keep the shooting gamelike.
3. Toss the ball to the three-point line. Get the ball and take one strong dribble. Square up to the basket. Shoot and follow your shot.

Time: 2 minutes.

Goal: 18 to 20 shots.

4. Shoot 10 foul shots. Record your score. Do not rest.
5. Toss the ball to the three-point line. Get the ball and take two strong dribbles. Square up to the basket. Shoot and follow your shot.

Time: 2 minutes.

Goal: 17 to 20 shots.

6. Shoot 10 foul shots. Record your score. Do not rest.
7. Toss the ball to the three-point line. Get the ball and square up to the basket. Shoot and follow your shot.

Time: 2 minutes.

Goal: 20 to 25 shots.

8. Shoot 10 foul shots. Record your score. Do not rest.
9. Toss the ball to the three-point line. Get the ball and take one strong dribble. Square up to the basket. Shoot and follow your shot.

Time: 2 minutes.

Goal: 18 to 20 shots.

10. Shoot 10 foul shots. Record your score. Do not rest.
11. Toss the ball to the three-point line. Get the ball and take two strong dribbles. Square up to the basket. Shoot and follow your shot.

Time: 2 minutes.

Goal: 17 to 20 shots.

12. Shoot 10 foul shots. Record your score. Do not rest.

MULTIPLE-PLAYER DRILLS

Doing drills with a partner can be fun, whether it's one-on-one or shooting drills. Play hard and concentrate.

Full-Court One-on-One

PURPOSE

To work on various aspects of the game, including shooting, in a gamelike situation. This is also a great conditioning drill.

PROCEDURE

1. In the first game, pick up your player at half-court. Work hard, box out, and run the floor. First player to score 10 points wins.
2. After a 10-minute rest, play a second game. For this game, pick up your player at three-quarters of the court. First player to score 10 points wins.
3. After another 10-minute rest period, play a third game. Pick up your player full court.

Two-on-Two

Everyone should learn how to become a better team player. It starts with being efficient at one-on-one, then two-on-two. Two-on-two games allow a small group of players to work on specific techniques within a team concept. As a team player, you must be able to make your teammates better. Technique and precision are important in a team concept. Much like three-on-three, you learn timing and how to set picks. Most important, you must remember good teamwork.

Three-on-Three

Three-on-three continues to be a popular playground game. Three-on-three tournaments have sprung up all over the country for players at every level of ability. In a half-court situation, three-on-three gives you the opportunity to be creative, because the action doesn't get cluttered up in a limited area. This concept combines one-on-one and two-on-two. In this format, you have the chance to use your total game: passing, screening, cutting, defense, rebounding, and, of course, scoring. With three-on-three, a lot of action takes place off the ball. Timing is essential for creating scoring opportunities. The close confines of the three-on-three competition create a physical atmosphere. You must use all the fundamentals, including boxing out and setting good, solid screens.

Two-Player Shooting Drill

PURPOSE

To simulate game shooting, moving, offensive rebounding, and passing.

PROCEDURE

1. Spot up and get ready to shoot. The second player passes you the ball. You can shoot from anywhere on the court.
2. Rebound your shot and make a good pass to the other player, who has gone to a different spot on the court. Her hands are up, showing you where she wants the pass.
3. Run at that player with your hands up, defending the shooter with token defense.
4. As the shooter rebounds her shot, spot up. You become the shooter looking for a pass.
5. Continue the drill without stopping until a player scores 30 points.
6. Execute this same drill taking shots from the three-point area.

LADY MAGIC TIPS

- Concentrate on your shot.
- Make a good pass to the shooter.
- Go at game speed.

NANCY LIEBERMAN'S SHOOTING WORKOUT

Incorporate the previous drills into the following shooting workout.

Warm-Up

- 10 shots each side on the low block—pivot and score
- 10 shots each side on the low block—power move
- 20 seconds—toss and shoot, change directions

Perimeter Workout

- 2 1/2-minute shooting drill—5 spots, 10 shots
- 10 bank shots each side off a pass (half court and full speed)
- 5 free throws
- 2 1/2-minute shooting drill off penetration (use a chair—reach the spot on your first step)
- 5 free throws

- 10 bank shots each side off penetration (half court and full speed)
- 5 free throws
- 2-minute jump shot drill off a toss (turn over right and left—alternate)
- 5 free throws
- 2-minute jump shot drill off the dribble (top of key)
- 5 free throws
- Free-throw line across for 2 minutes (receive the ball from the wing—off the pass and off the dribble)
- 5 free throws
- Creative shooting drill for 2 minutes using one-on-one moves (with defense when possible)
- 5 free throws
- 2 1/2-minute shooting drill off the pass
- 5 free throws
- Transition shots off penetration (be creative) from the point
- 10 free throws
- Weak-side cut to the elbow from the wing—10 each side off a pass
- 5 free throws
- Weak-side cut to the elbow from the wing—10 each side off penetration
- 5 free throws
- Offensive boards toss—10 each side (vary your shots)
- Make 5 free throws in a row
- 2 1/2-minute shooting drill with penetration
- Make 10 free throws in a row

SUMMARY

Shooting is the thing that players do the most. So why not shoot the ball with proper technique and form? Remember the following points:

- For proper shooting form, you need to achieve proper body, hand, arm, head, and foot position.
- You should use the checkpoints to make sure you're ready for success.
- You have many types of shots to master. Doing so takes practice and proper form.
- Nancy Lieberman's shooting workouts can make you a better shooter.

chapter

6

Getting Open and Being a Threat Without the Ball

In my opinion, trying to get open is one of the most enjoyable parts of the game of basketball. It involves a lot of player-to-player moves and a great deal of deception. The player guarding you might be a great defender. To get open, you must know how to use angles and change of pace, and you must understand where you are on the court and how you're being guarded.

In this chapter, you'll learn effective ways to change your pace, use angles, and establish your position. This takes hard work, determination, patience, and intelligence. By using fakes, screens (picks), and cuts, you can free yourself to get to the position you want. This enables you not only to get open, but also to find a good shot.

SETTING SCREENS

Being able to set a good screen is essential. By setting an effective screen, you will enable your teammate to get free for a potential scoring opportunity. In many cases, you, the screener, will also get an open shot. With so much happening on the court—especially when using motion offenses, the flex, or spread offenses—setting a simple screen is no longer the only way to be effective, but it's part of executing the developing play.

To set a screen, you first need to identify the person you will screen. Once you have identified your target, begin with a jump stop, staying low and leveraged with your knees bent (figure 6.1, page 124). Maintaining this balanced position, cross your arms at chest level. You must set up in a stationary position to block the defender from the offensive player who is trying to get open. Square up to your opponent, setting the screen at chest level or under her chin.

Figure 6.1 Setting the screen.

Your screens will be much more effective if your teammates master the art of setting up the defense with a move in the opposite direction, followed by a hard cut off your screen. Here's my rule: When a teammate is screening for you, take two steps away from the screen before cutting to use it. This will allow a better screening angle for you to get open. Another effective way to set up the screen is to walk, then run. Walk your defender into the screen action, then run out of it. Conversely, running to a screen (specifically on a post pick-and-roll) can force the defense into motion and not allow them to be set.

The player with the ball must keep her dribble alive and be patient, giving her teammates time to perform screens effectively. When you screen for her, she must cut as close to you as possible (using the two-step rule mentioned previously) so the defensive player does not slip between. If the ball handler is on the outside, she'll find the open shot. If she's on the inside, she'll drive hard to the hoop. Always be alert and look for a return pass; if the ball handler drives, she may pass up the shot and make the pass to you for the score.

Reading the defense is yet another aspect of learning how to screen. If you are setting a screen on a smaller player, she will most likely fight over the screen. If all of the players involved in the screen are of similar height, the defenders may choose to switch. You might even set a brush screen, rubbing off the defender. You must try to create confusion for the two defenders as they determine whether to switch or not. This is part of the reason why an offense uses screens. Next, we'll discuss what you should do after you set a screen.

Roll to the Ball

After you set a screen, you should perform a reverse pivot as you see your teammate going off your screen. Then roll to the side that the ball handler is traveling toward. See how the defense plays the screen. If the defense switches on the screen and you have a smaller player on you (we call this "a mouse in the house"), you should automatically roll to the front of the rim. Own the paint! If you are in front of your defender after the screen, again, roll to the basket. You have the lane, and the defense is behind you. If the defense has played the screen smartly and sagged into the lane, you might stay high and look for a pass for a shot (we call this a pick-and-pop). You can't predetermine the situation. You have to read your options. If the screen is solid, the defense will be forced to switch. You could potentially have a mismatch. If the defense has jumped to the ball handler and gotten over the screen, you should keep rolling.

You might receive a quick pass as you go to the basket. Or you might be able to set a second screen if your teammate can set up her defender. Always have your hands ready to catch the pass. Try to keep the defense on your back. Use your body to shield a defender who is trying to front you. Be a big, wide target.

Screen and Roll

If the defense is not alert or is not communicating, a blind screen can be quite effective for your team and a bit painful for your opponent. The idea behind the screen-and-roll is to provide a teammate with an open shot. It is difficult for defenders to both guard their own opponent and watch for other offensive players getting in their way. This creates confusion and communication problems for the defense. Any split-second delay could create the desired shot for the offense.

To execute this option, move to either side of the defensive player who is guarding the ball handler and perform a jump stop to gain good balance. Remember, when setting the screen, you should first run to the point of the action, then remain stationary with your feet spread shoulder-width apart for proper balance. Place your arms across your chest to avoid being called for illegal use of hands.

The ball handler must then use the two-step rule to set up the screen; she then steps foot to foot with you (as close as she can get to your screen, trying not to allow the defense to squeeze between, separate the two of you, and recover) as she begins to rub the defensive player into the screen (figure 6.2*a*). The ball handler

Figure 6.2 *(a)* Set the screen, *(b)* pivot with the ball handler, and roll to the basket.

continues to dribble with her head up to watch for you as she heads toward the basket. As the ball handler goes by you, you should use a reverse pivot and roll toward the basket (figure 6.2*b*). The ball handler reads the defense to determine whether to shoot, continue driving, or pass the ball. The success of this maneuver depends on the defender's reaction to the pick-and-roll. Remember, when setting a screen, always keep your eyes on the ball handler and be prepared to catch a quick pass.

As the ball handler uses your screen and goes by you, you should notice if the defenders have switched and if you have space. If so, you can "short roll," and the player can pass the ball quickly to you. You can also "long roll" to the rim if the ball handler draws the defensive trap off the screen and pulls the defenders with her.

On either roll, use a reverse pivot and roll toward the basket. The only time you don't use the reverse pivot is when you are slipping the pick—that is, faking as if you are going to set the pick and then slipping to the basket to receive the pass. This is used before the defense can get into a trap.

Use nonverbal cues to let the ball handler know you are open. Use your hand to show her that you are open and where you want the ball thrown to you. If neither you nor the ball handler is open at this point, in many cases, you can rescreen on the other side. This takes great communication between teammates.

Step Out (Pick and Pop)

By reading the defense, you might see that the pick-and-roll isn't your best option. Let's say you have set the screen for your teammate, and her defender has gotten over the screen but is still trailing the play. Your defender might hedge out to keep the ball handler from turning the corner. Normally, you would pick and roll. But you see the defense clogging up the middle. Why go into traffic? Step away from the defense but stay within shooting range (figure 6.3). Be ready for the pass. Take the shot if you're open. If the defense takes away the pop, revert back to the screen-and-roll!

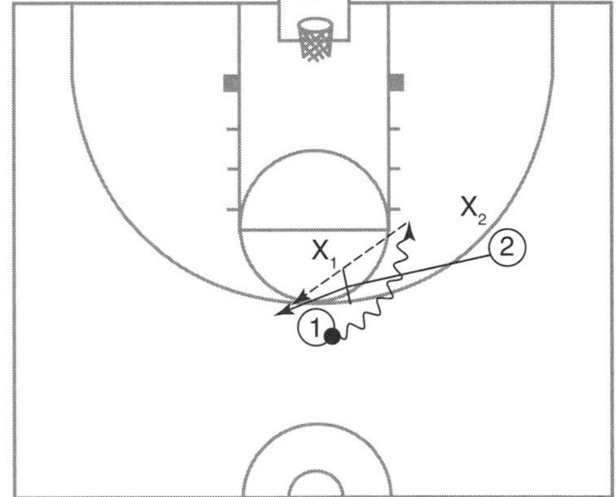

Figure 6.3 Step out (pick and pop).

CUTS AND ANGLES

Basketball is a game of angles, from how you slide to shaking the defense off a drive. The key is to use fakes and deception to get the defense leaning in the opposite direction. Change of speed, change of direction, and straight-line cuts are the best ways for the offensive player to free herself from the defense. Here are a few tips for using angles:

- Make your cuts sharp and precise. Plant hard with the foot you will be pushing off with. Explode in the other direction.
- Stay low and balanced.
- Cut as close to the defender as you can. This takes away her recovery step (the angle she needs to recover).
- Set your opponent up. When making a cut off a pick, first deceive your opponent, then make the hard cut.
- Always slide with your outside leg in the direction you are going. Do not cross your feet or bring them together.
- For speed and balance, make sure your head always leads in the direction you want to go.

Flash (Body) Cut

The flash cut is a very effective inside cut when you are coming from the perimeter to the inside and then cutting back to the perimeter. Step right at your defender. As you lean toward the defender, she will back away. Now, make a hard flash (or body) cut back to the perimeter to receive the ball (figure 6.4). Be sure to have your hands up as you make your cut.

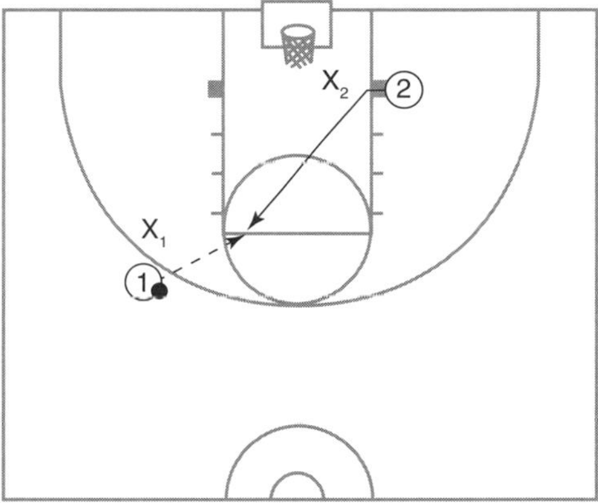

Figure 6.4 Flash (body) cut.

Pivot and Cut

The pivot-and-cut move is a great way to establish good inside position in the low-post area. Step right at your defender. Plant your foot and drive her back. You can pivot if necessary. Quickly make your cut into the lane to receive the pass (figure 6.5). Always have your hands up to receive the ball.

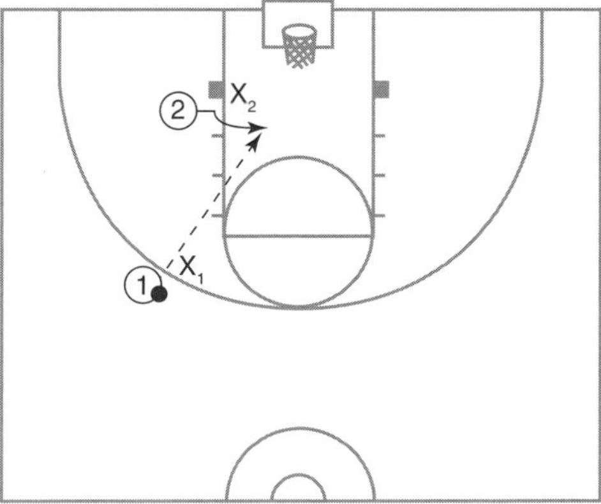

Figure 6.5 Pivot and cut.

Step and Cut

This is a great change-of-direction cut. Your first step is a decoy to pull the defense in the opposite direction. Then, you cut in the other direction away from the defense to receive the pass. Always have your hands up and ready to receive the pass. The most important thing is to plant your foot and make a believable fake or cut to lure the defense. Then, make your move to the open spot (figure 6.6).

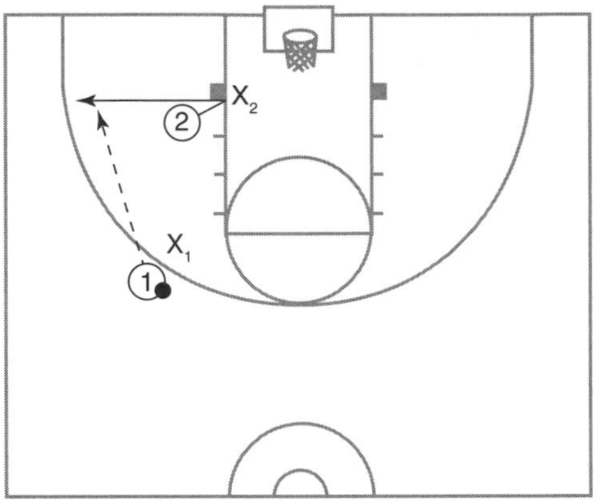

Figure 6.6 Step and cut.

V-Cut

The V-cut is the most common way for an offensive player to get open and receive the ball outside. For example, if the wing player is denied an entry pass by the defense, she makes a sharp cut toward the basket. This drives the defense back. As the defender is backpedaling, the wing player stops, pivots, and sprints back to the original spot where she wanted to receive the ball (figure 6.7).

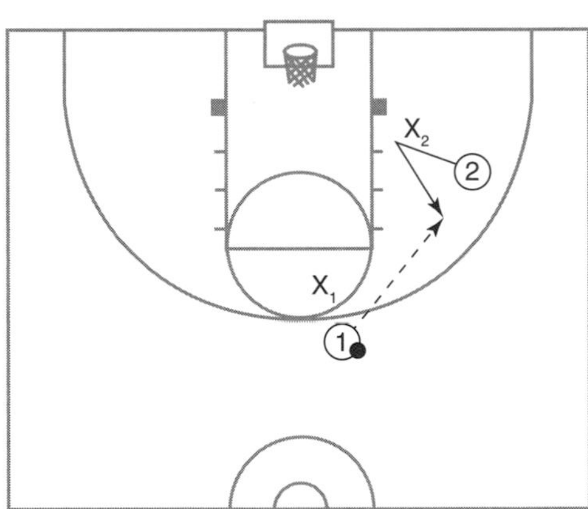

Figure 6.7 V-cut.

L-Cut

The L-cut is another option that players use to get open. You might be stacked on the block, trying to get into your offense. Come straight up the lane line and, at the foul line, plant your inside foot and explode to the outside, cutting in an L shape to create an opening to catch the pass (figure 6.8). Make sharp cuts, not ones that are rounded off. Sharp cuts take away the defense's ability to steal the ball, while rounded or banana cuts create space between you and the defender. Space equals recovery for the defense and allows them to get back into the play!

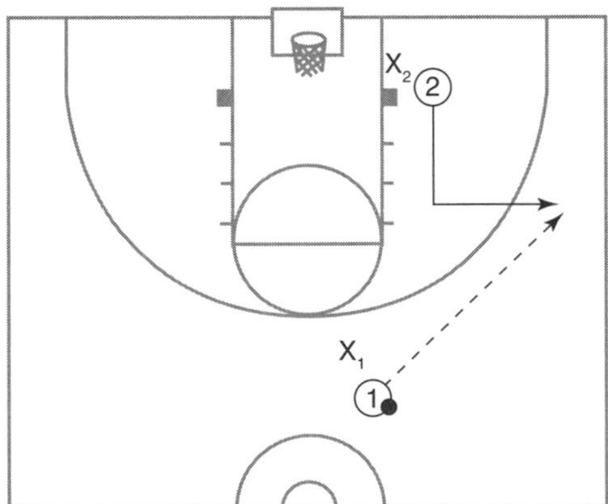

Figure 6.8 L-cut.

Backdoor Cut

Figure 6.9 Backdoor cut.

When executing a backdoor cut, start by making a short one- or two-step fake on the wing, away from the direction you plan to go next—similar to the V-cut, but at a different angle and area on the court. The defense is trying to deny the entry pass to the wing. Be aware of where you are on the court. When you reach about the three-point line, cut to the basket (figure 6.9). If you have faked the defender sharply as you execute this move, the defender will be out of position and off balance. As you sprint hard to the rim, keep your hand up, showing the passer that you are open. Expect a bounce pass, chest pass, or even a lob. Use the glass for a layup. It's best to go in at a 45-degree angle. You can use the square above the rim as a focal point for your shot. Even if you don't get the ball, finish your cut to the rim.

Give-and-Go

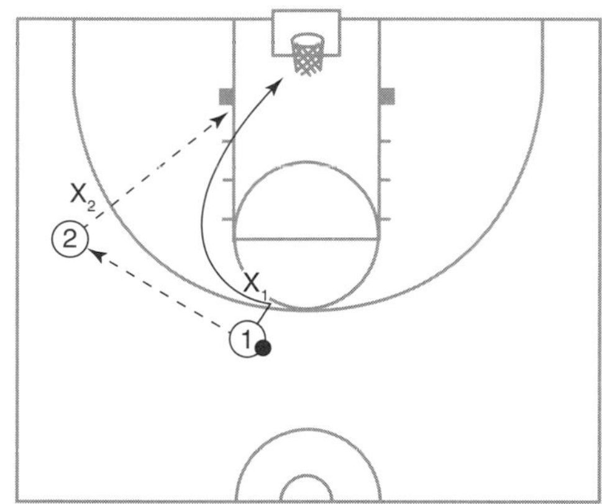

Figure 6.10 Give-and-go.

The give-and-go has been used in basketball for years. It is still one of the most effective cuts in the game, because defenders don't always adjust to the ball and force cutters to go behind them as they should. The give-and-go is a simple play where the ball handler passes to an open player and then cuts in front of the defender to the basket or an open area for a return pass (figure 6.10). This play is most successful when the defender hasn't jumped toward the ball on its flight and ends up watching the ball instead of her player, therefore getting beat to the basket. Good offensive players will exploit this type of defensive breakdown by using change of speed, change of direction, and sharp cuts.

Splitting the Post

Offenses often get bogged down because the defense is doing a great job of denying the wings. When this occurs, the point guard can call a high-post play to relieve the pressure. In a single-guard front, the point can then run off the post for a give-and-go, and the post can start the offensive play. You can run this off the opposite (weak-side) high post as well, passing and cutting off this play when the defense is overloaded on the strong side. This is called a pinch post action. In a two-guard front, the ball will often be passed to the high post to increase movement, and the guards will cut across one another to the opposite side. When this happens, the offense is trying to force the defense to make a mistake in their movement or experience a miscommunication (e.g., one defender may stay with her player while the other defender thinks it's a switch). This creates solid movement and forces the defense to be alert.

Splitting the post is one of many three-on-three concepts available in a half-court offense. The basic set is two guards and a center. The passer, usually a guard, makes the first cut off the center and rubs her defender to the outside of the court. The other guard makes the second cut off the high post to the opposite side of the court (figure 6.11). The high post needs to be alert and watch how the defense reacts. Then, the post needs to decide which cutter is open. If neither is open, the high post must look to shoot or drive to the basket. This play gives you a chance to find the best option available for scoring.

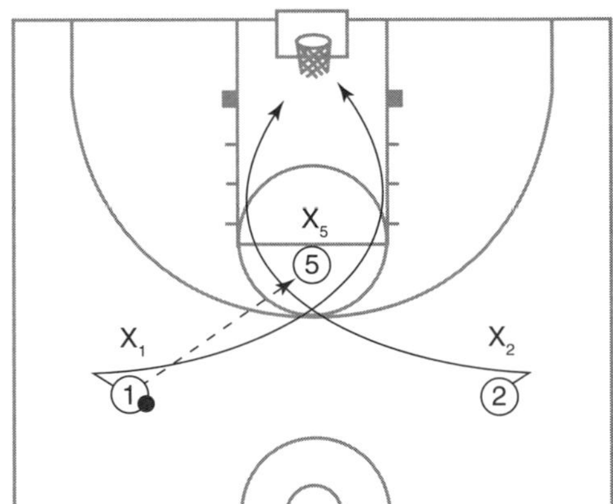

Figure 6.11 Splitting the post.

When you have a lot of cutting and movement in your offense, you must remember to keep the floor spread out and balanced. If too many players are on one side, it's easier for the defense to guard them. Spread out the defense with proper spacing.

Ouch!

Basketball is becoming more and more physical at every level. Defenses aggressively push their opponents to different areas of the floor. Offenses have to work hard to counteract this, being more deceptive in their cuts and passes and attacking the rim.

Physical players can change the game, disrupt strategies, and get into the minds of fearful players, causing doubt. As players get bigger, quicker, and stronger, you must be prepared to combat physical play rather than back away. Physical play can happen before you ever touch the ball; more and more contact is happening off the ball. So be aware and prepared for the physical part of the game. Never allow the defense to take you out of a game!

ON THE BREAK

Great athletes love this part of the game. A well-executed fast break is thrilling. To be successful, though, a fast break requires a lot of team effort. You need to be sure of the following: who rebounds, who fills the lanes, who the floor leader is, and who takes the shot. This section provides a breakdown of the responsibilities of each position and tips for getting open to score off the break. Figure 6.12 shows typical positioning for a fast break.

Figure 6.12 Executing a fast break.

In many cases, players believe that the fast break is about numbers. Do we have more players downcourt than the defense? If so, it's a fast break. If not, let's set it up. But not so fast, my friends! You can still run your break and then move right into your secondary break, running a play off this. That way, you don't allow the defense to get comfortable and set up. You are keeping them moving and keeping the pressure on.

Posts

Most of the time, the fast break starts with a defensive rebound. Running teams must remember to box out and hit the boards. After you get the rebound, keep the ball high so it's not stolen or deflected. If you're in traffic, take a quick step. If necessary, power dribble away from the defense. Always get the outlet pass out quickly.

After the outlet pass, the post player must run (sprint) the floor and trail the play. Try to beat your opponent down the floor. You must establish position for

- going to the glass and securing offensive rebounds, and
- setting picks if the break isn't there and you must move into your secondary offense.

Remember these pointers:

- ***Hit the boards.*** Your team can't have a successful fast break without first gaining possession of the ball.
- ***Outlet quickly.*** The faster your team can get the ball down the court, the better advantage you have for a successful fast break.
- ***Establish position.*** Try to beat your opponent to the other end of the court in order to establish good positioning; this way, you're available to help rebound and set up the offense if the break is unsuccessful.

Forwards or Wings

If you're a forward or wing, you must first box out. Then, it's horse-racing time. Get out on the wings and fly. Use your speed and quickness. Stay 2 or 3 feet (61 to 91 cm) inside the sideline. This will eliminate stepping out of bounds or getting too close to the ball handler, cutting down her passing angle. As you hit the opposite foul line, make that sharp 45-degree-angle cut to the hoop. Remember these pointers:

- ***Box out.*** First, try for the rebound. You don't want to allow your opponent to get a second shot.
- ***Call for the ball.*** You should get the ball from your point guard early enough to make your move. Remember to use the strategies that you've learned to get open.
- ***Cut.*** If you haven't received the ball, make your cut 45 degrees to the basket. Be ready to receive the pass.
- ***Read the defense.*** Do you have a layup or should you pull up for a short or long jumper?
- ***Draw the defense.*** If you don't have the shot, make the defense commit. Then, find your open teammate.

Point Guards

As the point guard, you are the brains behind the fast break. What do you see? Do you have the advantage (the numbers)? Should you push it or pull it back out and set up? Seeing the floor and making the correct decision are important. You must go to the ball and help your rebounder out. If you fade away, the defense will step up and steal the outlet pass. Remember these pointers:

- ***Keep your head up.*** See the floor and the defense. The defense might try to pick up a charge if your head is down.
- ***Pass the ball.*** Passing is quicker than dribbling. If a teammate who can handle the ball well is open, get the ball up the floor.
- ***Stay in the middle of the floor.*** The defense will try to force you to a side to eliminate your options. Don't help your defenders by shading that way too early.
- ***Keep track of the numbers.*** This is what the fast break is all about: advantage. Do you have a three-on-one? A three-on-two? If it's in your favor, attack. Make the defense commit. Then, find the open player. Remember, the defense is hustling back. Be quick and know who's coming from behind.
- ***Avoid forcing the numbers.*** If the numbers aren't in your favor, back the ball out and move into your team's half-court offense. Take the break only when it's there.
- ***Look off your pass.*** Use your fakes. You have the advantage; keep it! Don't telegraph which direction you are going to pass. By looking off your pass, you might fool the defense into thinking that you are passing in the other direction.
- ***Consider taking the shot.*** After passing to the wing, step in and toward the ball. Be ready to shoot if you're open on the return pass.

Shooting Guards

Quickness and the ability to make a shot are essential for shooting guards. If you are on a running team, the minute your teammate gets the rebound, it's your job to get in the outside lane and run the floor in transition. When your point guard penetrates and draws the defense, you must find the open place on the court and must be ready to shoot on the catch. You can also use your quickness to slash and penetrate to the basket. If you are a slasher, make sure you have a mid-range jumper in your arsenal. If you can knock down the three, the drive will be available to you. The mid-range shot will bring the bigs to you and open the finish at the rim. This game is pure cat and mouse; put yourself in a position to be in charge. Remember these pointers:

- ***Get open.*** Find the open spot on the floor (the spot that the defender vacated).

- ***Cut.*** Run hard, stay wide, and make your cut to the bucket at a 45-degree angle from the foul line extended.
- ***Hit your shot.*** This will open up your drive because the defense will have to play you tighter.
- ***Finish.*** When you get the ball while going to the basket, concentrate and finish the shot.
- ***Become a good passer.*** Work on that skill. A good passer makes her teammates better shooters, by virtue of where she gives them the ball. Set a shooter up for success!
- ***Rebound.*** Shooting guards can be good rebounders offensively. If you go hard to the glass and keep moving, the defense will find it more difficult to box you out because you are in motion.

SCREENING DRILLS

In all screening drills, the purpose is to get your teammate open or to enhance a scoring opportunity. When screening, you should be balanced, with your knees bent. Set the screen chest high or under the chin of your opponent. Hold the screen. If you are the screener, it's your job to get your teammate open. This is an underrated skill that is needed on every level of basketball for a team to be successful.

PURPOSE

To practice executing and using screens.

PROCEDURE

1. This drill is performed with four players, two on offense and two on defense.
2. Player 1 starts near the top of the key with the ball. Player 2 comes up from the wing at an angle to set a screen for player 1. The angle should be such that the defender can't see the screen coming.
3. Player 1 should begin 8 to 10 feet (2.4 to 3.0 m) away and should run into the screen, allowing her to turn the corner and get to the rim. This creates movement and another way for the ball handler to attack the defense.
4. At this point, player 1 has a few options. After reading the defense, she can decide to continue her drive, stop and take a jump shot, or look for player 2.

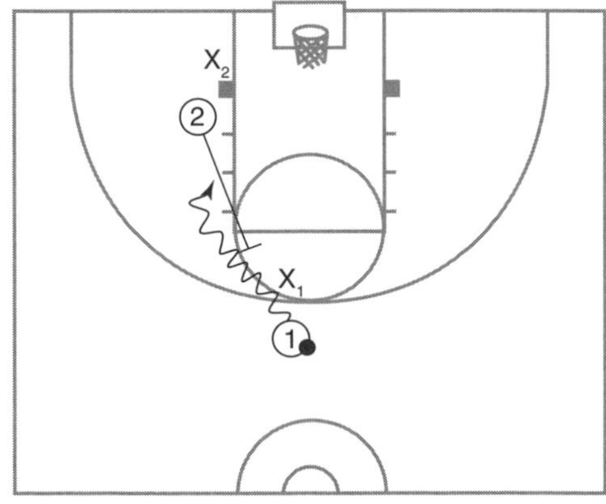

LADY MAGIC TIPS

- The ball handler must keep the dribble alive.
- The screener should focus on the angle of her screen.
- The ball handler should take one or two dribbles away from where the screen is set before using the screen.

Pick-and-Pop (With Ball)

PURPOSE

To practice screening and popping out while simultaneously trying to get the defense to overpursue the ball.

PROCEDURE

1. This drill is performed with four players, two on offense and two on defense.
2. Player 1 starts near the top of the key with the ball. Player 2 comes up from the wing or the post to set a screen for player 1.
3. Player 1 should stay as close as possible to her screener. After player 1 uses the screen, player 2 then reads the defense, popping out to an open spot on the perimeter.

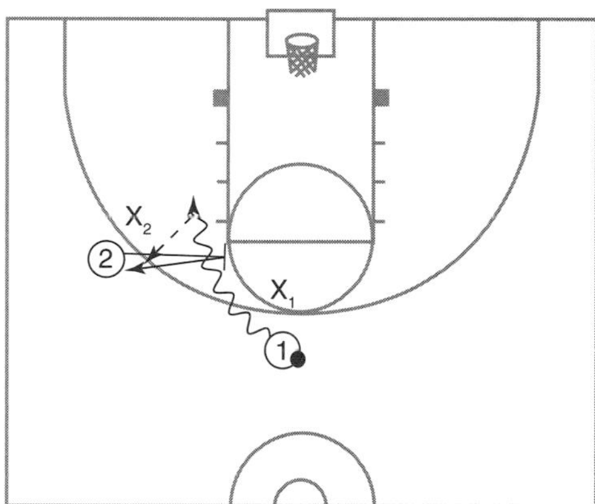

4. If player 2 is open, player 1 passes to player 2 for the shot. If player 2 is covered, player 1 can choose to stop and shoot or drive to the basket.

LADY MAGIC TIPS

- The screener must be sure to set a good screen.
- The offensive players must read their defenders. The defenders' reactions will be the offense's cue for whether the pick-and-pop is open.

Pick-and-Roll (With Ball)

PURPOSE

To practice executing and using the pick-and-roll, creating a mismatch defensively, especially with posts and guards.

PROCEDURE

1. This drill is performed with four players, two on offense and two on defense.
2. Player 1, a guard, starts near the top of the key with the ball. Player 2, a post, comes up on the block to set a screen for player 1.
3. After player 1 comes off the screen, player 2 should inside pivot and roll in the direction of the rim. Using the closest hand to the rim, player 2 should show where she wants the ball to be passed.
4. At this point, player 1 has a few options. After reading the defense, she should first look for player 2, who should be rolling to the basket. If player 2 is not open, player 1 can decide to continue her drive or stop and pop.

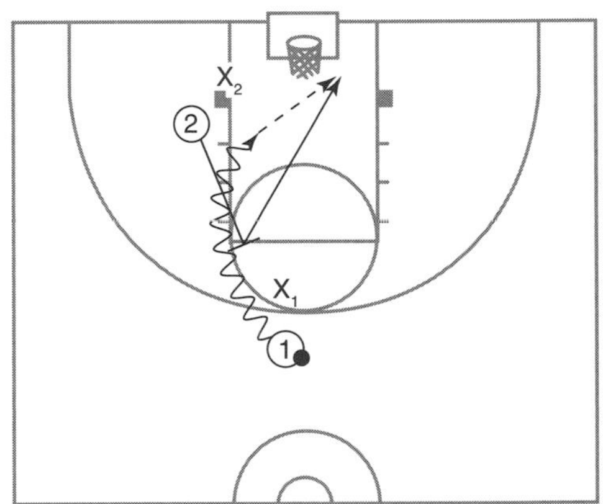

LADY MAGIC TIP

Anytime a screen is set and the defender gets caught behind the screener, the screener should pin her defender behind her, backing her down to the front of the rim. She should turn, seal the defender off, and score.

CUT AND ANGLE DRILLS

About 80 percent of basketball is learning how to move without the ball. Getting open is an art. Developing this part of your game will make you more valued and more effective on your team.

Basketball is made simple if you can master how to cut and use angles to your advantage. Space equals recovery for the defense. If you can take that away by getting into the body of the defender, you are winning that area of the game.

Flash

PURPOSE

To practice finding the open spot on the floor by using the flash cut, cutting in front or in back of your defender.

PROCEDURE

1. This drill uses four players—two on offense and two on defense.
2. Player 1 has the ball near the top of the key. Player 2 is under the basket on the weak side.
3. Player 2, who should be continuously moving, reads the defense. If she sees that her opponent has turned her head to watch the ball and has lost sight of her, she should flash in front of or behind the defender to an open spot.
4. Player 1 passes the ball to player 2 for a quick shot or layup.

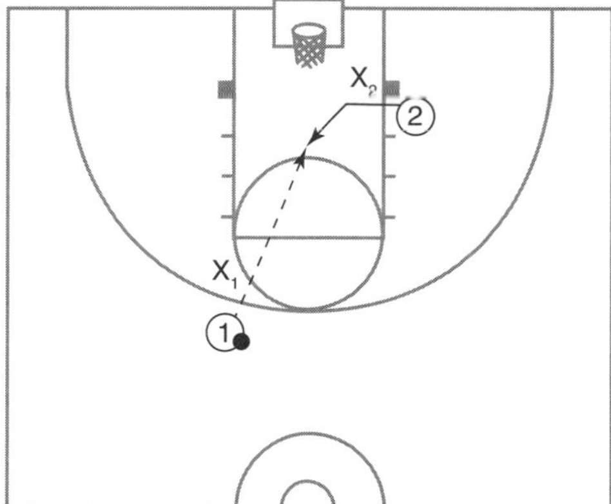

LADY MAGIC TIP

Take advantage of any defender who does not have good weak-side defensive principles.

Give-and-Go

PURPOSE

To practice the give-and-go, using teamwork and communication.

PROCEDURE

1. This drill is performed two on two.
2. Player 1 sets up with the ball at the top of the key. Player 2 fakes to get open on the wing and receives the pass.
3. After passing the ball, player 1 makes a hard fake away from the ball, then cuts into the lane.
4. Player 2 reads the defense and, if possible, passes back to player 1 for a layup.
5. If player 1's defender overplays the passing lane, player 1 can fake the cut and pop back out for the pass and outside shot. If player 2's defender cheats into the passing lane, player 2 can fake the pass and drive to the basket.

(continued)

Give-and-Go *(continued)*

LADY MAGIC TIPS

- The give-and-go is a quick, short play with explosive passes.
- If the defender is not alert and doesn't make you cut behind her, you will get layups off this move.
- When making the cut, you should not stop. Finish it all the way to the rim.

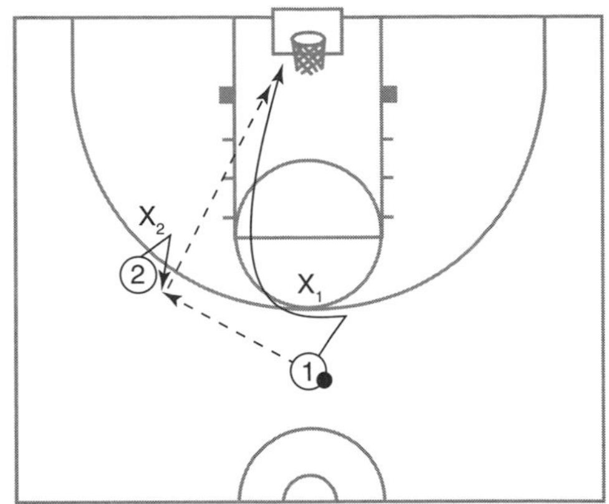

Splitting the Post

PURPOSE

To practice creating movement against the defense.

PROCEDURE

1. This drill is performed three on three; each side has two guards and one post.
2. The two guards, one with the ball, set up on both sides of the top of the key. Player 1 passes in to player 3, the post, who receives the ball at the free-throw line.
3. Once player 3 receives the ball, player 1 cuts from her position and moves down low to the opposite block; if she doesn't receive the ball, she goes through to the other side.
4. Immediately after player 1 begins her cut, player 2 follows, cutting through to the opposite block; if player 2 doesn't receive the ball, she goes through to the opposite side of player 1.
5. Player 3 can choose to hand off the ball to either player as they are passing through, or she can perform a reverse pivot and then pass to either player for a layup.
6. If neither player is open, player 3 can pass back to player 1 or 2 after those players have gone through the lane and returned to the top of the key.

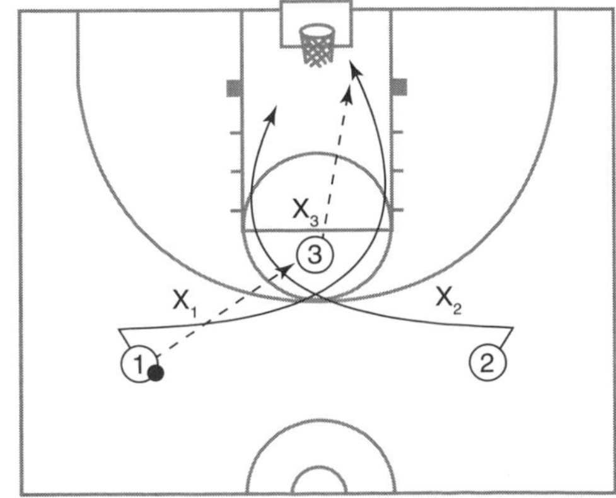

LADY MAGIC TIPS

- The first cutter is the one who has just passed the ball to the post.
- When both guards split off the post, this creates confusion for the defense about whether they should switch, stay, or ask the post's defender for help.

FAST-BREAK DRILLS

Most players love to run and have the freedom to attack opponents in the open court. The fast break should be performed with speed; players need to pass the ball quickly up the floor before the defense can recover. Forcing the tempo of a game is a great asset. Defenses are in scramble mode as players try to get back, identify their player, and help out teammates. This causes confusion and mismatches, and it can tire a team out.

Four-on-Zero Fast-Break Layup Drill

PURPOSE

To practice filling in positions on the fast break.

PROCEDURE

1. Four players participate in this drill, with no defenders. Players set up in front of the basket along the baseline; players 1 and 4 start at the blocks, and players 2 and 3 start in the corners.
2. Player 4 tosses the ball off the backboard and rebounds. Player 1 cuts to the middle for an outlet pass, while players 2 and 3 run down the outside lanes for a pass at the opposite end.
3. Whoever receives the ball from player 1 takes the ball to the basket for a layup; player 4 sprints down the court for a rebound.
4. Whether the shot is made or missed, player 4 grabs the ball and makes an outlet pass once again to player 1, and the fast break is executed on the other end.

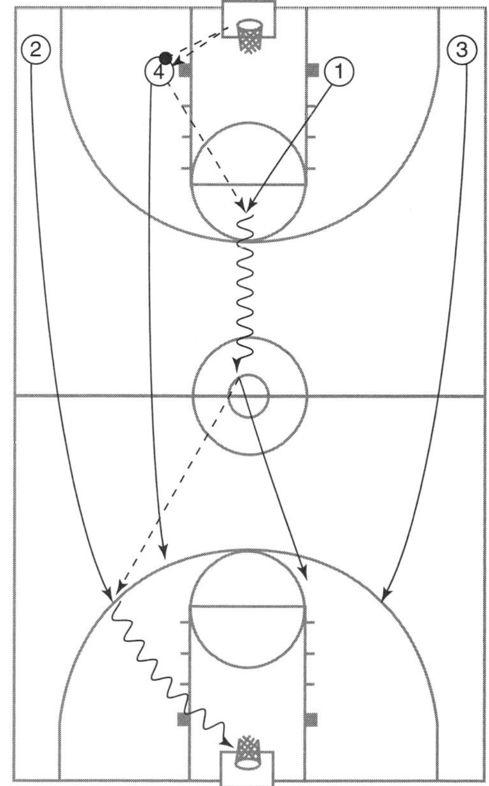

LADY MAGIC TIPS

- The group should try to make 20 shots in 2 minutes.
- Instead of passing to the same player every time or shooting from the same spot, players should mix things up!

Two-Player Fast Break

PURPOSE

To practice passing and moving on the two-on-one fast break.

PROCEDURE

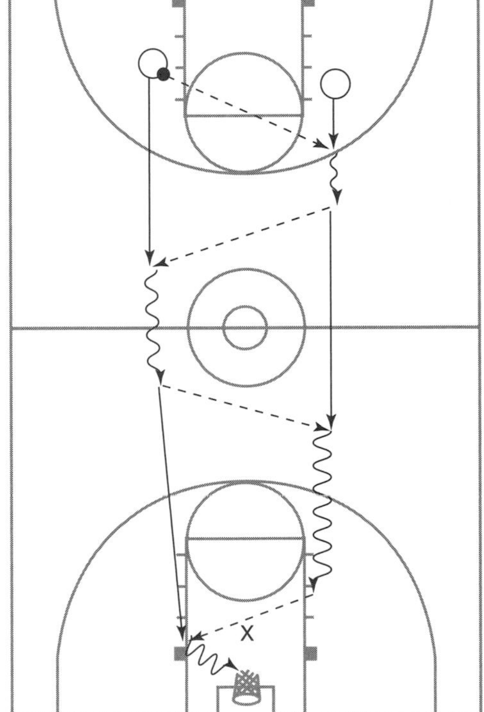

1. Divide players into pairs; one pair will be on the court at a time. Place one defender on the opposite end of the floor.
2. The first pair of players runs down the floor, passing back and forth and trying to score on the other end against the defender.
3. After the pair scores or the defender stops them, the next two players go, and so on. Everyone attempts to score on the fast break against the defender.
4. After every pair has gone, switch defenders and ends, and change up pairs. The drill continues until everyone has played defense.

LADY MAGIC TIPS

- This drill requires good communication between players.
- For added incentive, each defender can count how many defensive stops she has made.

11-Person Break

PURPOSE

To practice rebounding, making good outlet passes, and executing the three-on-two break. This drill requires 11 players.

PROCEDURE

1. Begin with two defensive players on each side of the court; two outlet players are on each sideline. Player 1 has the ball at the top of one key, and players 2 and 3 are on the wings for a three-on-two.
2. Play out the three-on-two situation until the defense gains possession of the ball or the offense scores.

3. The first defensive player to gain control of the ball outlets to one of the two players stepping onto the court. This defensive player and the two outlet players go three on two at the other end.
4. Two of the three offensive players left on the other end of the court claim the now-open defensive positions, while the third offensive player and the remaining defensive player (who didn't gain possession of the ball) replace the outlets on the sideline.
5. The drill continues in this manner until time is up or a designated number of points are scored.

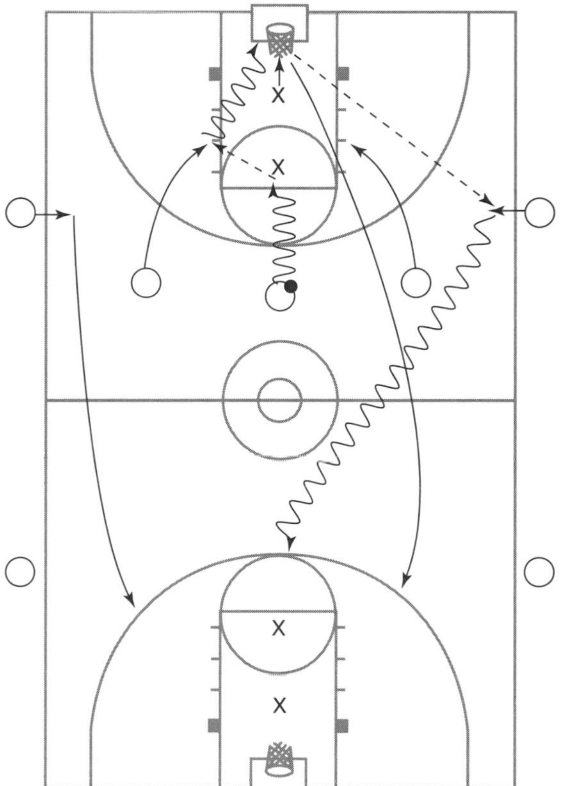

LADY MAGIC TIPS

- The offense has a numbers advantage. They should use this advantage to work the ball around for a good shot.
- The more aggressive the players are in this drill, the better. As a challenge to yourself, try to see how long you can stay on the court!

SUMMARY

Many players think, *I have to have the ball in my hands for my team to score.* That's not necessarily true. Moving without the ball will create many scoring opportunities for you and your team if you know how to get open. This chapter addressed these key areas:

- Moving without the ball and getting open
- Types of fakes you can use
- Setting screens and using angles and cuts to get open
- Inside and outside cuts for post and perimeter players
- Splitting the post and establishing position
- Running the fast break—guards, forwards, and post players

chapter

7

Dribbling—What's Your Handle?

Have you ever thought, *I could have gotten by her if I could have dribbled with my left hand*? If you can go left and right equally well, you will be much tougher to guard. Can you take your opponent by penetrating to the bucket when the defense steps up to help out? Can you play off the bounce? Do you keep your eyes up, and do you see the court? Can you hit your teammate with the sweet pass? The more weapons you have, the more valuable you're going to be to your team. When you have mastered ballhandling, you've given yourself the ability to be a great individual and team player. Besides, you'll be fun to watch.

DRIBBLING OPTIONS

Figure 7.1 Protecting the ball with a right-handed dribble.

Before you can execute the dribbling options we will be talking about, you must be able to protect the basketball at all times (figure 7.1). Stay low, keep your head up, and see the defense. Use your off hand and arm to shield the ball from the defense. As a general rule, you should position your body between the defense and the ball. This means your body, arm, or leg is always between you and the defense. Remember, you should use your arm only to protect the ball. Don't swing it at your opponent. The referees will call you for that.

Your ability to dribble can have a great impact on your team's ability to run its offense. Expanding your ballhandling options can enhance your team's ability to bring the ball up the court, help you get open for a shot, or enable you to get the ball to a teammate for the score. In the following sections, we talk about the seven most common types of dribbles.

Speed Dribble

The speed dribble is used to advance the ball as quickly as possible. You dribble the ball higher so that you can push it out in front of you at a comfortable speed. For this dribble, you use more of a running style as the ball is pushed out in front of your body at the waist to mid-chest area (figure 7.2). Controlling the ball is most important. Find a speed at which you can maintain control. Your head must be up so you can see where the defenders and your teammates are located on the court.

Figure 7.2 Speed dribble.

Hesitation Dribble

The hesitation dribble, a combination of control and change-of-pace dribbles (figure 7.3), is used to freeze your defender. Changing speeds keeps the defender off balance and guessing about your next move. The hesitation dribble forces your defender to react. A quick stutter step might open an opportunity for you to drive by your defender. If the defender backs away and anticipates your drive, you have just created the space needed for a jump shot. The hesitation is a great dribble to use in attacking your defender.

When you combine the hesitation with a head fake, your defender might believe that you are shooting and might rise out of her defensive stance. When she starts to rise, you should stay low and accelerate past her to either side.

This dribble kept me in the men's United States Basketball League for two years. Because the male players were bigger and quicker, I had to attack first. Keeping the defense off balance allowed me to get the ball up the floor without having to turn my back to the action or possibly getting double-teamed.

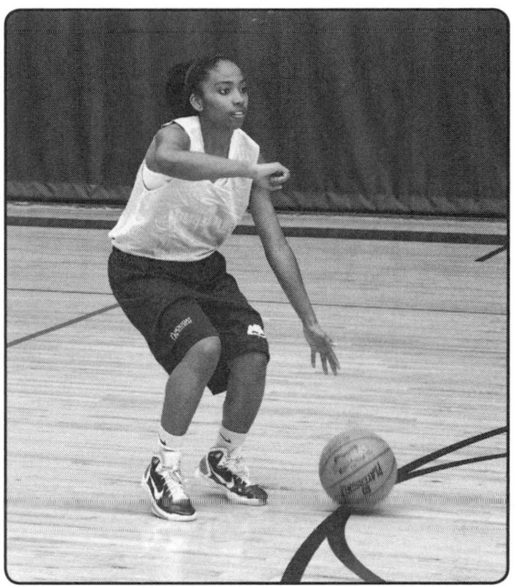

Figure 7.3 Hesitation dribble.

Crossover Dribble

The crossover dribble is used when you are facing your defender. This dribble takes you from one direction to the next. To be effective against the defense, the crossover dribble should be low. Dribble by switching or bouncing the ball from one hand to the other, keeping the ball low and under the defender's hands. Make sure your opposite hand is out, protecting the ball from the defense. Get the defense leaning one way. Then, using a forward angle, cross over and explode in the opposite direction (figure 7.4, page 146).

Proper footwork is necessary once you have accomplished the crossover dribble. You must take your crossover foot and place it as close as possible to the defender's foot. The other leg allows you to push with power for your change in direction. This will help you create a favorable angle to the basket. A favorable angle is a straight line to the basket. For example, if the ball is in your right hand, you want the defender leaning to that side. You quickly cross over, staying low and protecting the ball. As you cross the ball from right to left, your right foot follows. Place your foot directly next to your defender, switch the ball to your left hand, and use your right arm and body to protect the ball. Push the ball out past the hip of the defender; this will make her open up, and you will have the angle to the rim you want. Take forward steps, not lateral ones. Space equals recovery for the defender. The better you position your foot and the more contact you initiate, the easier you will be able to go straight past your defender. If you go straight past the defender, she will be forced to stay behind you because you have the angle on her. Do not look at the ball on your crossover; doing so gives the defense time to slide and recover. Remember to always keep your head up. See the floor.

Figure 7.4 Crossover dribble.

Spin (Reverse) Dribble

If used properly, the spin dribble—also called the reverse dribble—can be extremely helpful. As the ball handler, you change direction by planting your inside foot (figure 7.5*a*). Attempt to split the defender's leg with your planted foot, reverse pivoting quickly as you turn your back toward the defender. As you perform the reverse pivot, the ball changes hands, and your body changes direction (figure 7.5*b*).

Do not leave the ball behind you as you spin. Your defender will try to knock the ball away or steal it. Always keep the ball protected by your body

Figure 7.5 Executing the spin dribble.

as you spin. Spin as close to the defender as you can in order to gain the best angle to move up the floor or toward the basket. You must keep your head up because it is easy for defenses to trap off a spin dribble. If you are aware of everyone on the floor, you can spin or pass the ball as you see the trap developing. Remember that defenses will try to force you to spin on the sideline, using the sideline as a third defensive player. Stay away from the sideline as much as possible.

Drag Dribble

A drag dribble is a backward dribble that you can use to move away from your defender (figure 7.6). The step backward helps create space between you and the defense. It also gives you a better passing lane and a better angle to your teammates, especially to the post area. The maneuver is simple, but effective. When you are dribbling backward, protect the ball with your opposite hand. Whenever you feel pressure from the defender, you should use this dribble to create space instead of picking up your dribble. This will release the immediate pressure you are feeling.

Figure 7.6 Executing the drag dribble.

Behind-the-Back Dribble

As you refine your skills and gain confidence in your ballhandling, the behind-the-back dribble is one you should add to your repertoire. Contrary to what some may say, the behind-the-back dribble can be a valuable option. When used properly, the behind-the-back dribble can help you gain an advantage on your opponent.

If you are dribbling the ball with your left hand and the defense is in front of you, you should lean slightly to your left, making the defense believe that you are headed in that direction. Immediately put the ball behind your back, pushing it all the way to your right side (figure 7.7). The dribble behind your back must occur when your left foot is forward. As you push the ball toward your right hand, move your right foot forward so that it is out of the way. Your right hand controls the ball, and your dribble continues. Your left arm now protects the ball. Remember to push the ball out and go get it as you wrap it around your body. Turn your body slightly and "get skinny," making your body tall and lean.

Figure 7.7 Executing the behind-the-back dribble.

Between-the-Legs Dribble

If you are being guarded closely by your defender and cannot cross over, the between-the-legs dribble is a great technique to use. Similar to the behind-the-back dribble, this dribble is a useful option because it allows you to change direction while moving.

Forward When going to the left, dribble the ball with your left hand. Keep your weight on your left foot as you bounce the ball forward between your legs (figure 7.8*a*) to your right hand (figure 7.8*b*). Use your opposite arm, your body, and your leg to protect the ball as you change direction. Explode as you push off to gain advantage on the defender.

Backward Dribbling between your legs allows you to move in a backward motion while changing direction. Plant your right foot when dribbling to the right side. Pull the ball backward between your legs while your dribble

Figure 7.8 Dribbling forward between the legs.

continues (figure 7.9*a*). The ball is now in your left hand (figure 7.9*b*). Use your right hand, right arm, and body to shield against the defense as it recovers. This backward dribble is also a good way for you (the ball handler) to start another offensive series if your teammates are tightly guarded. You can back off and allow your teammates to reposition themselves.

Figure 7.9 Dribbling backward between the legs.

WARM-UP DRIBBLING DRILLS

Before you practice your dribbling skills, you should warm up with the following drills. These drills will quickly get blood flowing to your fingers, hands, and wrists and will improve your ballhandling skills. Pound each dribble; the harder you dribble, the faster you go.

Ball Slap

PURPOSE

To warm up your hands, quickly getting blood flowing to your fingers, hands, and wrists. Warming up will make it easy for you to grab a pass, rebound, and dribble.

PROCEDURE

1. Hold a basketball in one hand. Slap the ball hard with the opposite hand.
2. Keep moving the ball from right to left while constantly slapping the ball.
3. Slap the ball 10 times with each hand.

LADY MAGIC TIP

Stand up straight when doing this exercise.

Ball Around One Leg

PURPOSE

To build strength in your wrists and hands as well as work on your speed and coordination. Make sure you do not use your arms. Concentrate on using your wrists and hands.

PROCEDURE

1. Stand with your body slightly bent and with your legs apart for balance. Keep your head up and do not look at the ball. Bend slightly at your waist, and bend your knees.
2. Rotate the ball around your left leg as fast as you can for 30 seconds, then reverse the direction for 30 seconds.
3. Do the same around your right leg for 30 seconds.
4. Repeat this drill four times—twice around each leg.

LADY MAGIC TIPS

- Remember to bend your knees, not only your waist.
- Keep your eyes up, and do not look at the ball.

Ball Around Waist and Leg

PURPOSE

To work on your hand speed and coordination. In this drill, you are pushing yourself against a clock to improve your speed.

PROCEDURE

1. Take the ball around your waist, then around both legs in a figure-eight pattern, back around your waist, and then around your legs again. Do this 10 times and use a clock to time how many rotations you can complete in 30 seconds.
2. Reverse the ball and again count how many rotations you can complete in 30 seconds.

VARIATION

Rotate the ball around your waist for 30 seconds, then around just your left leg for 30 seconds, then around your right leg for 30 seconds.

LADY MAGIC TIPS

- Keep your head up.
- Remember that it's OK if you lose the ball. Losing the ball means you are pushing yourself to the limit.

Full-Body Circles

PURPOSE

To improve your ability to dribble with either hand, to help you develop confidence, and to condition your arms for speed and endurance.

PROCEDURE

1. Put the ball above your head, with your hands straight up. Using your fingertips, tap the ball back and forth 20 times. Keep your fingers spread out on the ball.
2. Quickly move the ball clockwise around your head 10 times. Then reverse the direction and move the ball around your head another 10 times. Do the same around your waist.
3. Quickly move the ball around one leg. Keep your knees bent, leaning in the direction of that leg. Your knees should be comfortably apart for balance and space. Go 10 times around one leg, then reverse direction and go around 10 times. Switch legs and repeat the drill.
4. Move the ball in a figure-eight pattern (moving the ball around one leg and then the other). Stay low and balanced. Lean in the direction you are putting the ball around. Go 10 times in one direction, then reverse the figure eight for another 10 times.

LADY MAGIC TIPS

- Stay in a balanced stance with your feet and knees flexed.
- Keep your hands cupped, not stiff.
- Always follow through and control the ball.
- As you feel more comfortable and confident, increase your speed. Challenge yourself.

TECHNIQUE DRIBBLING DRILLS

The following drills will help you work on using proper ballhandling techniques, protecting the ball with your off hand, and improving your weak hand and your overall confidence. In these drills, you will work on your strong hand, on your weak hand, and on protecting the ball. Always start with the ball in your weak hand.

Line Dribble

PURPOSE

The line dribble allows you to practice pure speed. This drill improves your quickness with the ball. Stay low and focus on the quickness of your fingertips.

PROCEDURE

1. Stand behind a line on the court and move the ball from side to side in front of you with one hand. Keep your head up and stay in a balanced stance. Concentrate on moving the ball with your dribble.
2. Switch hands (do the drill for 1 minute with each hand).

Sideline Dribble

PURPOSE

Like the line dribble, the sideline dribble enables you to practice pure speed and helps you improve your quickness with the ball. Again, stay low and focus on the quickness of your fingertips.

PROCEDURE

1. Find a sideline and stand next to it. Dribble the ball to your side, pushing and pulling it front to back. Move it in front and in back of the line on the court.
2. Switch hands (do the drill for 1 minute with each hand).

Figure Eight

PURPOSE

To improve your ability to change direction and move the ball against the defense.

PROCEDURE

1. Keeping the ball low to the ground, use your fingertips to dribble the ball from back to front and through the middle of your legs in a figure-eight motion.
2. Change hands each time the ball goes through your legs. Keep following the figure-eight motion (do this for 1 minute).

VARIATION

Kneel on one knee. If your right knee is down, start with the ball in your right hand in front of your body and dribble around to the left side. When the ball is directly behind your right foot, use your left hand to meet the ball and continue the dribble on your left side. Then push the ball with your left hand through your left leg and start again (do this for 1 minute). Then switch knees and repeat the drill in the opposite direction (for 1 minute).

LADY MAGIC TIP

Work on developing good balance and the ability to dribble with your head up.

High Dribble (Ricochet)

PURPOSE

To work on your coordination, speed, and ability to catch the ball.

PROCEDURE

1. Bounce the ball with two hands from the front through your legs to the back. Quickly move both your hands behind you to catch the ball as it comes through your legs. Start slowly at first.
2. As you get your timing down, start bouncing the ball harder and faster.
3. After the ball goes through your legs, take the ball around your waist to the front. Repeat this 10 times.

LADY MAGIC TIPS

- Bounce the ball through your legs at an angle so it doesn't come straight up.
- Keep your legs slightly more than shoulder-width apart.
- Keep your head straight. Don't look at the ball.

Shooting Off the Dribble

PURPOSE

To develop patience and skill when pulling up for a shot off the seven most common dribbles you'll use in a game: speed, hesitation, crossover, spin (reverse), drag, behind-the-back, and between-the-legs dribbles. The drill will help you learn to pull up in balance and to use the correct form for the jumper.

PROCEDURE

1. Place a chair in the middle of the foul line. Start between half-court and the top of the key with the basketball.
2. Speed-dribble toward the chair. Start to slow down as you approach the key. Use the straight dribble, then pull up for a foul-line jumper. On the shot, look for the offensive rebound.
3. Dribble back to your starting point. Speed-dribble to the opposite side of the chair, pull up, and shoot the jumper. Rebound.
4. Dribble back to the start and repeat—this time using your crossover dribble. Pull up for the jumper. Rebound.
5. Repeat the same drill using all the dribbles mentioned—one time to each side. After all seven types of dribbles have been completed to each side, take 10 one-and-one foul shots.

LADY MAGIC TIPS

- Remember, when you are attacking the defense, you need to read your defenders and your options.
- Stay low as you approach the chair. Keep your head up.
- Make sure that your explosive dribble at the chair takes you near the lane for a short jumper. Don't circle your cuts and fade for long shots.
- Protect the ball with your off hand. When on the left side of the floor, use your left hand; on the right side, use your right hand.

FULL-COURT DRIBBLING DRILLS

I strongly recommend that you do the following drills wearing gloves. Any kind of work gloves will do. You'll find them at any hardware store. If you can dribble the basketball with gloves, after you take them off, you will have a great feel for the ball. You will control the ball better because it will feel smaller and more comfortable in your hands. Start with Down and Back Dribbling. Then move to the succeeding drills to work on numerous types of dribbles.

Down and Back Dribbling

PURPOSE

To improve your skills at dribbling full court in a game. Work on staying low to the ground, getting up and down the court, keeping your head up on the dribble, and seeing the entire court.

PROCEDURE

1. Dribble under control and as fast as you can with your weak hand from one baseline to the other.
2. Touch the baseline with your foot, switch to your other hand, and return.

VARIATIONS

- ***Crab Dribble:*** You are bent over in a crablike position. Run full court with the ball while putting the ball through your legs (one after the other in a figure-eight motion) as you are running. Work on speed, coordination, and balance. Keep the ball moving swiftly through your legs.
- ***Full-Court Zigzag:*** This drill enables you to work on your change of direction. Start on the end line. While staying low, dribble to the sideline, plant your outside foot, pivot, and head in the opposite direction. Take three dribbles and change direction. Explode in that direction. Go full court up and back two times. Remember, while changing directions, you should have some bounce (stay light on your feet) as you push off in the opposite direction.
- ***Crossover Dribble:*** Throw the ball off the backboard and go after it as if it were a rebound. Come down in balance, pivot, and assume a triple-threat position, facing the entire court. Foot-fake in one direction, then zigzag down the court, exploding in the opposite direction as you perform a crossover dribble at the foul line, the half-court line, and the opposite foul line. Go up and back one time.
- ***Jump Stop:*** Follow the same procedure as for the crossover dribble. As you go down the court, jump-stop on balance at the foul line and at half-court. Then, at the opposite foul line, pull up for a jumper. Do the same thing coming back. Go up and back one time.
- ***Spin Dribble:*** Follow the same procedure as for the crossover dribble. Zigzag down the court. At each line, perform a spin dribble, plant your forward foot, and spin in the opposite direction. Move the ball and protect it with your opposite hand. Stay low. Keep your head up. Go up and back one time.
- ***Behind-the-Back Dribble:*** Follow the same procedure as for the crossover dribble, except dribble in a straight line down the court. At each line, dribble behind your back, pushing the ball out to your side. Protect the ball with your opposite hand. Keep your eyes up.
- ***Between-the-Legs Dribble:*** Follow the same procedure as for the behind-the-back dribble. At each line, put the ball through your legs front to back, plant, and change direction. Go up and back one time.

(continued)

Down and Back Dribbling *(continued)*

LADY MAGIC TIPS

- Go full speed in all drills.
- Stay low and balanced as you dribble full court.
- Keep your head and eyes up to get a full view of the court.
- Protect the ball on all dribbles.

Cone Dribbling

PURPOSE

To work on proper technique, sharp cuts, and change of direction by using cones to simulate a defender.

PROCEDURE

1. Set cones every 5 feet (152 cm) from one baseline to the opposite foul line extended. Dribble under control and as fast as you can with your weak hand around each cone.
2. After the last cone, continue down the court for a layup with your weak hand.
3. Perform the same activity with your other hand coming back.

VARIATIONS

- ***Crossover Dribble:*** Dribble full speed toward the first cone. As you approach it, plant your outside foot and change direction as you use a low crossover dribble. Keep the ball waist high as you approach the second cone. Plant with your outside foot and cross over. Continue until you reach the last cone, then make a hard cut to the basket for a layup. Repeat in the opposite direction.
- ***Spin Dribble:*** Dribble full speed toward the first cone. As you approach it, lower your body and plant your inside foot. Start on the right side, spinning in a clockwise direction. Be sure to move the ball from your outside hand on the spin to your left hand, using your body and off hand to protect the ball. Keep your head up to see the defense. Continue to spin at each cone, alternating hands until you approach the last cone. Go in for the layup. Repeat in the opposite direction.
- ***Behind-the-Back Dribble:*** Dribble full speed toward the first cone. As you approach the cone, your body should be forward in front of the ball. Quickly pull the ball with your wrist, fingers, then arm around your back to change direction. The ball should be waist high. As the ball changes direction, use your off hand and body to shield it. Proceed to the next cone and repeat, alternating your behind-the-back dribble from left to right and right to left. Go in for the layup, and repeat the drill in the opposite direction.

LADY MAGIC TIP

Complete each drill twice going full speed at all times.

Combination Drill

PURPOSE

To work on an assortment of gamelike moves, ballhandling, and shooting. This drill simulates gamelike conditions. Work on the layup, power dribble, bank shot, corner shot, and foul-line jumper.

PROCEDURE

1. Start at the baseline. Speed-dribble to the foul line using your left hand on the left side of the court. Then, when you are at the foul line, perform a spin dribble going toward half-court.
2. Perform a crossover dribble at half-court; stutter-step or use the inside-out dribble at the foul line extended.
3. Using a 45-degree angle, make your cut to the basket for the layup.
4. Up and back is one set. Take five foul shots, then go from the right side using the same dribbles and layup.

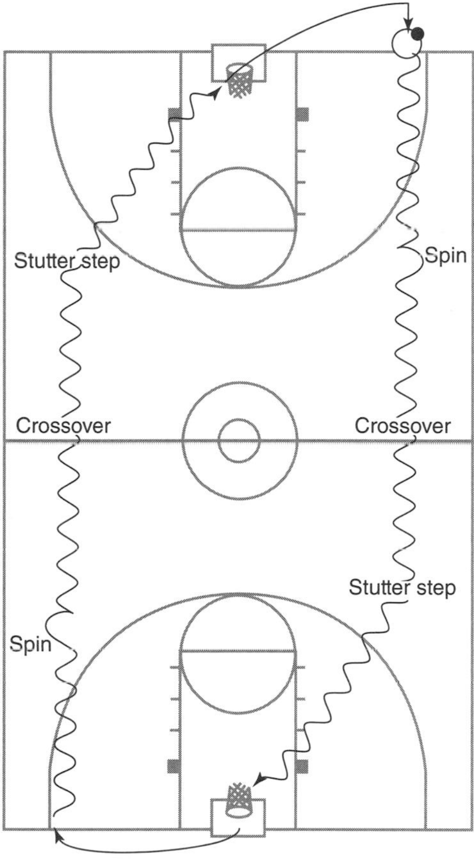

VARIATIONS

- Complete the same drill, this time driving for a two-foot power layup.
- Complete the same drill, this time pulling up for a bank shot from the wing area.

Weak-Hand Drill

PURPOSE

To work on improving your weak hand through repetition and various types of dribbles. Improvement will give you more confidence and more options on the court.

PROCEDURE

1. Start on the left side of the court under the basket (assuming that your left hand is the weaker hand). Start with the speed dribble full court and make a layup on the left side.
2. Rebound your shot and dribble again full court using the speed dribble. Go in for a layup.
3. Continue this drill for 60 seconds. Take 10 foul shots while resting. Begin the drill again. Do five sets total.
4. Push yourself and record how many layups you've made in 60 seconds. Always try to increase the number as you get better conditioned and more confident with your weak hand.

LADY MAGIC TIPS

- Always use your weak hand in order to improve it.
- Dribble the ball waist high. Don't throw the ball out and chase it, but dribble it with control.

Two-Ball Dribbling

PURPOSE

To use high dribbles in the open court while pushing the ball up the floor. The drill will improve your timing, strengthen both hands, and help you develop the confidence to know you can dribble with either hand.

PROCEDURE

1. Walk full court while dribbling two balls. Alternate dribbles (while one ball is up, the other is down).
2. Then, run the full court while dribbling two balls, again alternating dribbles.

VARIATIONS

- Dribble two balls out in front of you and move them from side to side. Dribble the balls together (both balls hit the floor at the same time).
- While standing in place, dribble both balls on your left side, dribbling the balls together. Place your opposite arm across your body. Then dribble the balls on your right side. Your knees should be slightly bent.

LADY MAGIC TIPS

- Keep your head and eyes up.
- Stay under control by alternating dribbles.

ADDITIONAL DRIBBLING DRILLS

Here are some other ballhandling drills you should incorporate into your practice routine. You'll be amazed at the results.

Rhythm Dribble

PURPOSE

To improve your timing, coordination, and hand speed.

PROCEDURE

1. Bend forward slightly from your waist and flex your knees. Your legs should be at least shoulder-width apart.
2. Drop the ball between your legs. Take the ball completely around your right leg, then drop the ball between your legs again. Next, rotate the ball around your left leg. Repeat.
3. Go slow, listening to the beat—the rhythm of the ball—and your hand slapping on the ball. As you improve, use a quicker pace.

LADY MAGIC TIPS

- Work on hearing the ball, as well as on timing, coordination, and hand speed.
- Keep your head up and your eyes looking straight ahead.
- Bend at the knees for proper balance.

Zigzag

PURPOSE

To practice change of direction and control. If you can master this drill, you will be tough to guard.

PROCEDURE

1. Place eight chairs in a zigzag formation on the court. Use the crossover dribble to zigzag through the chairs as fast as you can under control.
2. Pull up and shoot a jumper at the opposite foul line.
3. Come back and do the same at the other end.

LADY MAGIC TIPS

- Stay low and protect the ball on each crossover dribble.
- Keep your head and eyes up. Try not to knock over the chairs, which you should imagine are defenders on the court.

Inside Out

PURPOSE

To work on getting a defender to lean one way and then taking her by going another direction.

PROCEDURE

1. Place eight chairs down the middle of the court. While dribbling to the first chair, act as if you are about to perform a crossover dribble. As you lean in with the ball to cross over, quickly pull it from the inside of the chair to the outside. As you dip your shoulder to go inside, the defense should lean in that direction. Now, go to the outside as quickly as you can.
2. Pull up and shoot a jumper at the foul line, or fan out on your last dribble and take a wing shot.
3. Do this drill up and down the court with your right hand, then repeat the drill with your left hand.

LADY MAGIC TIPS

- Stay low and balanced. Keep your head up.
- Make your inside fake believable.
- Protect the ball—always.

Steal Game

PURPOSE

To improve your ability to concentrate on your dribble while being distracted.

PROCEDURE

1. Two players work against each other while dribbling in a designated area (half-court, key, or foul-line area). Each player must protect her ball while she tries to steal or knock the other player's ball away from her.
2. Protect your ball with your off hand as you dribble it and try to deflect or steal the other person's ball. Try to force the other player out of the circle or area. If you steal or deflect her ball, you win.
3. Switch hands after the drill is over. Then start again.

LADY MAGIC TIPS

- Stay low and protect your ball. Keep your eyes up.
- Use both hands during this drill.
- Be aggressive. Try to deflect or steal the other player's ball.

Two-Minute Tag

PURPOSE

To work on being aware of many players around you. You have to be alert, move the ball, and protect it with your body and arm.

PROCEDURE

1. Use half the court with four or more players. Everyone has a ball. Everyone dribbles left-handed for 2 minutes.
2. One person is "it." That person chases the others, trying to tag someone. Whoever gets tagged must then try to tag someone else.
3. Repeat this drill for 2 minutes with everyone using their right hand.

LADY MAGIC TIPS

- As always, stay low, stay balanced, and protect the ball.
- Be alert so you are not tagged out. Keep moving.

Typewriter

PURPOSE

To strengthen each of your fingers, your hands, and your arms. The drill will build your confidence with both hands as each finger becomes stronger when handling the ball.

PROCEDURE

1. Place a ball in each hand. Crouch and dribble each ball with one finger at a time—as if typing on a typewriter—using both hands simultaneously.
2. Start with your thumbs, then work your index fingers, your middle fingers, your ring fingers, and finally your pinkies. Dribble the balls 10 times low with each hand and then with each finger 10 times.
3. Dribble the balls as hard and as controlled as possible to develop strength in each finger. After you feel comfortable, speed up. Keep your dribble low, about ankle high. Do this drill two times up and down (thumbs to pinkies).

LADY MAGIC TIPS

- Bend down low. You are working to strengthen your fingers.
- Push yourself when you get tired.
- Don't look at the balls.

Low Dribble

PURPOSE

To work both hands dribbling the ball as low as you can with your head up. The confidence you gain by being able to handle the ball with either hand will come in handy in game or practice situations.

PROCEDURE

1. Dribble two balls (one in your left hand and one in your right) very low in front of you for 30 seconds. Stay low, bend your knees, and lower your back to simulate a sitting position.
2. Use your fingertips, not your palm, to keep your dribble alive. Repeat four times for 30 seconds. Each time, count how many dribbles you complete in 30 seconds. Push yourself to increase the number.

VARIATIONS

- With two balls out in front of you, dribble to half-court and back using a low dribble.
- Alternating the two balls in front of you, dribble to half-court and back using a low dribble.
- Dribble low with two balls, one ball on each side. Staying low, keep your head up and eyes focused in front of you. Concentrate. Do the drill for 30 seconds, then rest for 30 seconds. Do this drill four times.
- Dribble low around one leg. Stay low, bending your knees and lowering your back, and keep your feet spread more than shoulder-width apart. With your left hand, start your low dribble around your left leg for 30 seconds. Use your fingertips to push and then pull back the ball on the dribble around your leg. Start by going counterclockwise for 30 seconds, then rest for 30 seconds. Switch hands and legs to the right side. Do this drill four times, two times per leg. Then do the drill four times going clockwise on each leg for 30 seconds.

LADY MAGIC TIPS

- Stay low, bend your knees, and stay balanced.
- Keep your eyes up at all times.
- Work your wrists and fingers as you dribble each ball.

High Dribble

PURPOSE

To work on timing, controlling the rhythm of your dribble, and strengthening your fingers, wrists, and forearms. This drill will get your blood flowing and get your hands and body warm and ready to execute other drills. Pound your dribble!

PROCEDURE

1. Dribble the ball through your legs as you walk to half-court. Keep putting the ball back and forth through your legs. Walk naturally.
2. Go up and back one time.
3. Next, put the ball through your legs back to front instead. Walk up to half-court and back one time. Then, dribble backward, placing the ball through your legs slowly and naturally. Remember to bounce the ball front to back. Walk up to half-court and back one time.
4. Skip, dribbling the ball through your legs front to back. Skip up to half-court and back one time. Then, skip backward while dribbling the ball through your legs front to back. Skip up to half-court and back one time.
5. Dribble behind your back. Lean back slightly with your knees bent. Bounce the ball from side to side (one dribble per side) and waist high behind your back. Look ahead. See the ball in the corner of your eye. Walk slowly full court one time. Then, dribble behind your back while walking backward. Walk slowly full court while bouncing the ball with a good angle in the center of your legs behind you.
6. Dribble behind your back with one dribble. Take one step to the left and bounce the ball with your left hand for one dribble. Push the ball behind you to the opposite (right) side and lean in that direction. Then take one dribble with your right hand as you take one step to the right. Repeat this for a total of 20 times.
7. Perform the scissors jump while dribbling the ball through your legs. Think of yourself as jumping rope down the court. The ball should be dribbled back and forth between your legs from the front. Repeat until you reach the other end of the floor. Next, perform the scissors jump backward while dribbling the ball through your legs. The ball should be dribbled back and forth between your legs from the back. Repeat until you reach the other end of the floor.
8. Dribble the ball low with both hands. Dribble with your fingertips. Stay low and balanced while flexing your knees. Lower your hips until you are in a sitting position. This drill will help improve your hand speed and increase your fingertip control.

LADY MAGIC TIPS

- Keep your dribble at knee to waist height.
- Concentrate on every part of the drill.
- Keep your head up. Try not to look at the ball.
- Feel the timing as you move.
- Keep the ball on your fingertips, not your palm.

High Dribble Wraparound

PURPOSE

To build hand and arm speed while developing coordination, timing, and your ability to catch the ball as it goes through your legs.

PROCEDURE

1. Stand upright with your knees slightly bent. With one hand, wrap the ball from the front around your waist to the back and bounce the ball waist high between your legs.
2. As the ball goes through to the front, catch it with the same hand you wrapped around with.
3. Alternate each side, doing 30 seconds each. Rest for 30 seconds. Complete four sets total, two per side.

LADY MAGIC TIPS

- Concentrate.
- Push yourself as you wrap the ball around your waist.
- Catch the ball with one hand—the hand you start with.

High Dribble Behind the Back

PURPOSE

To help you build confidence and improve your coordination and ball control by not looking at the ball. This drill will help you learn how to dribble behind your back as an added option.

PROCEDURE

1. Stand upright with your knees slightly bent. Take one dribble to the left side with your left hand. Push (bounce) the ball behind your back to the right side. Then, with your right hand, catch the ball on the dribble, take a dribble with your right hand, and push the ball behind your back to your left side.
2. Keep your feet shoulder-width apart for balance, and lean into the direction of your dribble. Repeat this drill 10 times on each side for a total of 20 dribbles behind your back. Do two sets of 20 behind-the-back dribbles.

LADY MAGIC TIPS

- Be balanced.
- Push the ball at a good angle so the ball comes up waist high on your opposite side.
- Keep in mind that your first dribble is more of a rhythm dribble, helping you get ready to push (bounce) the ball to the other side.

Jump Dribble

PURPOSE

To strengthen your arms and fingers as you constantly change how hard you dribble. Work on change of rhythm as you dribble. You need to control the ball while changing from a high, hard dribble to a low dribble.

PROCEDURE

1. Place a ball in each hand and jump as high as you can while dribbling the balls high.
2. Then jump to a medium height while keeping the balls at waist level.
3. Next, jump slightly while bringing the balls to a low dribble.
4. Alternate dribbling high to medium, medium to low.

LADY MAGIC TIPS

- Jump as high as you can off both legs.
- Control both balls simultaneously.
- Keep your head up.

Low Dribble Figure Eight

PURPOSE

To work on the feel and touch you have while dribbling the ball and to improve your ability to move the ball when it's low to the ground.

PROCEDURE

1. Spread your legs slightly more than shoulder-width apart. Bend your knees and lower your back. Start with the ball in your right hand and dribble low with your fingertips around to the outside front of your right leg. Then dribble around the outside (toward the back of your right leg).
2. Push the ball between your legs out to the front of your left leg and continue to fingertip dribble around your left leg to the outside (toward the back of your left leg). Push the ball through your legs to the front of your right leg. Lean in the direction you are dribbling. When you get comfortable, do this 10 times.
3. See how many figure eights you can do in 30 seconds. Then reverse the ball and go in the opposite direction for 30 seconds.

VARIATION

Get into the same position as in the figure eight. Lean in the direction that you are dribbling. Starting with your left leg, dribble a circle around that leg 10 times clockwise, then 10 times counterclockwise. Rest for 30 seconds and repeat the drill, this time using your right leg. As you improve, challenge yourself with a

(continued)

Low Dribble Figure Eight *(continued)*

clock. See how many repetitions you can complete in 30 seconds. Push yourself to the limit. Time how fast you can go.

LADY MAGIC TIPS

- Stay low. Keep your head up and your eyes focused in front. Do not look at the ball.
- Use your fingertips to push and pull the ball around your legs.
- Relax your hands and fingers. The ball will be easier to control.

Spider Dribble

PURPOSE

To increase your hand speed and coordination while dribbling the ball quickly in one spot between your legs.

PROCEDURE

1. Stay low with your legs spread approximately shoulder-width apart. Drop the ball in front of you. You will keep the ball in the same spot as you dribble it.
2. Dribble the ball on top quickly—once with your right hand, once with your left. Swing your arms around to the back. Keep the dribble alive with your hands on top of the ball—right, then left. Keep the ball knee high as you move your hands from front to back.
3. Keep this up for 30 seconds. Keep the ball low and dribble hard. You must remain loose and relaxed for this drill to be effective. This is a superb drill for improving hand speed and coordination.

LADY MAGIC TIPS

- Don't get frustrated and rush—this will cause mistakes.
- Keep your knees flexed.

Low Line Dribble

PURPOSE

To work on dribbling the ball low to the ground while protecting it.

PROCEDURE

1. Find any line on the court. Stay low and dribble with one hand across the line. Using the line, you will be able to see if you are moving the ball enough with both hands.
2. Practice going somewhere while dribbling.
3. Do this 15 times with your left hand and 15 times with your right. Complete two sets of each.

VARIATIONS

- ***Low Sideline Dribble:*** Find another line on the court and set up beside it. Stay low and balanced. You will do the same dribble but with the ball to the side. Move the ball up and down by the side of your foot. If you are dribbling with your right hand, use a line near your right foot. Do the same on your opposite side. Do this 15 times with your left hand and 15 times with your right. Complete two sets of each. Again, this drill allows you to move the ball as you dribble, pushing it out and pulling it back. Do not forget to challenge yourself against the clock. How many dribbles can you complete in 30 seconds?
- ***Low Crossover Dribble:*** Find another line on the court. Start with the ball in your right hand and cross over low in front of you. Use the line to make sure you have moved the ball on your crossover to the left side. Constantly cross the ball from side to side using both hands. Do 50 crossover dribbles, 25 each way. Then push yourself and see how many you can complete in 1 minute.

LADY MAGIC TIPS

- When dribbling with your left hand, make sure that you move the ball left to right.
- Move the ball around instead of staying in one place.
- Stay low when you dribble, keep your head up, and protect the ball with your off hand.
- Use your fingertips to dribble the ball. Don't use your palm.

Machine Gun Low Dribble

PURPOSE

To develop hand speed, quickness, and touch.

PROCEDURE

1. Stay low and balanced. Using both hands at the same time, dribble the ball as low and as hard as you can. Make sure your hands are on top of the ball.
2. Focus on being quick and keeping the ball low. The lower you can keep the ball alive and the quicker you can dribble it with both hands, the more speed and strength you will build in your wrists and arms.
3. Do this for 30 seconds. Complete four sets.

LADY MAGIC TIPS

- Push yourself during this drill to improve coordination.
- Keep your head up and don't look at the ball.
- Think rhythm, not speed.
- Stay very low to the ground.
- Use your fingertips, keeping them round, not stiff.

SUMMARY

No matter what position you play on the court, you will be a greater asset to your team if you can dribble the basketball effectively. Work on the basic dribbles until they become a solid part of your game. Then master the creative dribbles and give your game even more weapons against the defense. This chapter took you through the following areas:

- Dribbles—speed, hesitation, crossover, spin (reverse), drag, behind-the-back, and between-the-legs dribbles
- Ballhandling warm-ups
- Ballhandling drills—half court and full court, one ball and two ball, low dribbles, high dribbles, and no dribbles

chapter

8

Passing and Catching Turnover Free

There's nothing more enjoyable than a great pass. Honestly, it's one of the most rewarding parts of the game because you're setting your teammate up for success. A great pass gets the crowd involved, especially in the women's game, where players don't dunk very often. And if you have great passers on your basketball team, you're going to be good; such teams will get the right shot at the right time. The defense can never catch up with the flight of the ball.

Old Dominion University highlighted passing in the late 1970s and 1980s. We were an exciting team. We were solid passers. More recently, Tennessee and UConn have won championships not in small part because of their great passers.

PASSING FUNDAMENTALS

At every level of the game, players need to know the basic passes. You should know why you're using a certain pass, what its purpose is, and what the result will be. Passing is the thinking player's part of the game. If you know what pass to make in a given situation, you are eliminating potential turnovers. As you improve your passing skills and increase your understanding of situations, you will see the floor in a totally different way.

You must learn how to break down the defense through passing. In addition, you will be even more effective when you have the necessary skills to create easier scoring opportunities for your teammates. As a passer, you have the power to make your teammates look great or terrible by how and where you deliver a pass. In many cases, it's not the defense that takes a shot away from an offensive player—it's the poorly thrown pass by her teammate.

Passing skills can be one of the best parts of your game. Passing can help you confuse the defense and bring your teammates' level of play up.

Understanding the game and having the correct skills have nothing to do with how big or small you are. You need passing lanes against bigger and quicker players, and you need space.

Faking With the Ball

You have to fake a pass to make a pass. The simplest way to create a passing lane is by using a ball fake—an effective tool that is often overlooked. You do not have to be fast, but you must be believable and able to read how the defense is playing you. If you are tightly guarded, use ball fakes to back the defense off (figure 8.1*a*). If your defender moves, you have created your passing lane (figure 8.1*b*). For example, if you want to throw a bounce pass, fake high with an overhead pass. This will cause the defense to react to prevent the overhead pass. While your defenders are reacting and putting their hands up, you can execute the bounce pass. You must stay low and balanced when doing this.

You have to make your fakes believable, which often means you have to overexaggerate. Don't telegraph where you are going to pass the ball. Just because you know you want to pass to the wing doesn't mean the defense has to know this. Be deceptive. Look off the defense in the opposite direction and protect the ball. This takes practice, confidence, and trust in your teammates.

You will be surprised by your success the first time you look off the defense when attempting a key pass. The easiest areas to get a pass by a defender are on either side of her head, under her arm, or close by her body. Think of a hockey goalie trying to stop a puck shot at the side of his head, or under his arm. In the same way, it is difficult for a defender to react to a pass in those areas.

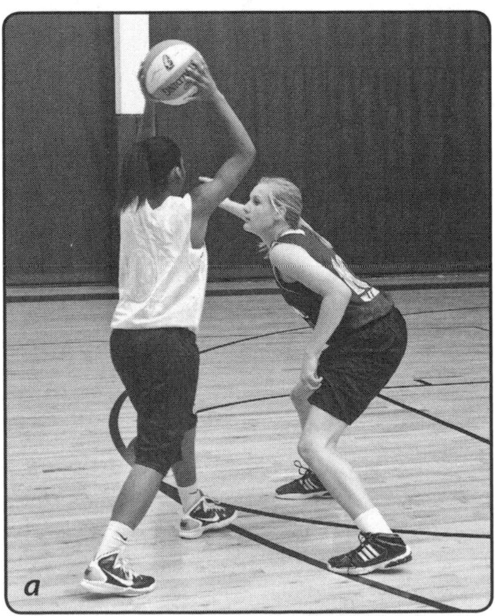

Figure 8.1 Making a fake while looking to pass to a teammate.

If your defender isn't playing you tightly, other passing lanes to your teammates will be open: wing passes, entry passes to the post, and guard-to-guard passes.

By using ball fakes effectively, you can freeze a player for a split second and accomplish your task as a point guard. Until you and your teammates spend quality time together on the court, no-look passes off someone's hands, head, or nose can be common. It may take time for teammates to avoid being faked by your fakes.

Timing

Timing is crucial to good passing. For example, sometimes you'll want so badly to get the ball to your teammates that you'll force the pass. Read the situation. Let the defense make its move. Let your defenders cheat. Know the flow and the angles that are available to you. You might find other players open. For example, you may want to make a lob pass to your post under the bucket, but you have a teammate making a baseline cut. Take your time. Let the area clear out. Then, make the pass. You will be surprised at how effectively you can pass when you add a little patience to your game.

Knowing Your Personnel

Know what your teammates like and don't like. Can a teammate catch a bounce pass and score? Does she have great hands or hands of stone? Does she go get the ball? Find out. You may be making passes to the wrong player in the wrong situation. If you have a great one-on-one teammate, give up the ball early so she can do her thing. If you get the ball to her late down the court, you may be taking away some of her options. Don't give the ball to your low-post player way out on the wing. Give it to her down on the block where she can do damage. Of course, I'm still a big believer in giving your post player the ball early. Give it to her before the defense can get set, allowing her to make a quick move before a double team can materialize. Give her a chance to do what she does well.

Forwards and post players must also know their teammates well. Study how your teammates pass at different positions. You never want to be fooled by a pass from your teammate. Every player has her own style and timing of how she likes to pass. If you receive these passes, pay attention. You never know when a pass is coming your way.

Passing With Either Hand

If you're on the left side of the floor, pass with your left hand. If you're on the right side, pass with your right. This will help keep the defender away from the ball. I always stress options. The defense is trying to limit you. Don't help your defenders.

Placement

Get the ball to the receiver where she wants it. Always find her palms, passing toward the hand she is showing. Put the ball in your teammate's hands away from the defender's arm. If using a bounce pass, bounce the ball in so that it comes up to your teammate's waist and all she has to do is catch and shoot. Lead her to the bucket for the score.

Communication

Successful passing really comes down to communication. The essence is letting your teammate know what to expect. If she knows the options, she will be prepared. Talk to your teammates. Passers are leaders. Be positive. Show confidence in whoever is on the court. Communication also comes in many nonverbal forms: a head fake, eye contact, or a signal with your hands. Today's crowds are noisy. Sometimes you can barely hear the coach in the huddle. That's why all players need to be aware of who has the ball and what scheme is being called.

Keeping in Touch

At Old Dominion my junior and senior years, our crowds at home and on the road were deafening. I would use eye contact or hand signals with my teammates. If Angie Cotman, our off guard, was one on one on the wing and being denied, I would make a fist with my off hand. This meant for her to go backdoor to the basket hard: *Don't stop; there's no weak-side defense.* Bam! Angie has an easy layup. Rhonda Rompola and Jan Trombly, our wings, could always read my eyes. I hardly ever had to say things on the court. We had incredible communication, and it worked.

PASSING OPTIONS

While on offense, you have many options, including a variety of passes. Master all of them and you'll become a more difficult player to stop. Always step into your passes. Get the ball from point A to point B as quickly as possible. Try not to float your passes; this can get you into trouble, and opponents will get easy steals.

Chest Pass

A chest pass is one of the most fundamental passes in basketball. The ball is supported at chest level, primarily by your fingertips on both hands. Your thumbs should be behind the ball with your hands and fingertips spread out toward the sides. Position your elbows close to your body. Place your feet in a triple-threat position with your weight on your back foot. Shift your weight forward as you step into the pass. Extend your arms and rotate your thumbs downward.

For more speed and distance, place emphasis on shifting your body weight quickly and snapping your wrists as your thumbs rotate toward the floor. Follow through to your target and get your weight behind the pass (see figure 8.2). Don't float your pass. Snap it and get it to your receiver. Use the chest pass in the right situation. It's a good, solid short pass that gets the ball from you to the receiver as quickly as possible. It can be used in long situations, but not often. When your team is on a fast break, you can use the chest pass if your teammate is uncontested. Long chest passes slow your break because they tend to float.

Figure 8.2 The chest pass.

Bounce Pass

The bounce pass is often used on the fast break or in a half-court offense by perimeter players who want to get the ball inside. Put some zip on this pass. Get the pass to your teammate quickly.

One or two hands may be used to successfully execute the bounce pass. Either way, the passer places her hands or hand behind the ball, extends her arms, and releases the ball in a downward fashion (figure 8.3, page 174). The ball should strike the floor about two thirds of the way to the receiver so that it can be caught at waist level. Bounce passes can be used to deliver the ball under and away from your defender's hands. In most cases, this type of pass should be made when the defensive player is one pass away from the ball. A bounce pass through traffic is difficult; you must be crafty. Be smart about how you use bounce passes.

The bounce pass is like the chest pass in many ways. In the half-court offense, the bounce pass works well for getting the ball to the post and on backdoor cuts. Most defenders' hands are in the passing lanes, so you should lay a bounce pass under the arm of the defender. The closer the pass is to the body, the more difficult it is for the defender to react.

Figure 8.3 The bounce pass.

Before the defender knows it, your teammate has the ball. Like the chest pass, you can use the bounce pass for distance, but you should pick your spots and put some power behind the pass. If a teammate is open—that is, she is not being guarded tightly or denied—there is no reason to use a bounce pass. You will slow the pass, allow the defense to recover, and take an uncontested shot away from your teammate. Give her a straight-on chest pass instead.

One-Hand Bounce Pass

Passing with one hand is more difficult than passing with two—especially if you are being pressured by a defender. It is also more difficult to disguise this type of pass or to stop it once you have begun throwing it. A good ball fake will clear the defense from your passing lane. When making a one-hand bounce pass, step with your inside leg in the direction of your pass (figure 8.4). If you do not use the crossover step, take a short backswing so you can camouflage your pass. Try not to allow the defense to read which pass you are using. You can be stationary when throwing this pass, or you can throw it coming off the dribble.

Figure 8.4 The one-hand bounce pass.

Using this type of pass helped me when I played in men's leagues. The defense didn't know whether I was keeping my dribble or passing. This gave me a split-second advantage, and I was able to use the bounce pass off my dribble. I know from experience that if you are being guarded by a quick player (such as Tyrone "Muggsy" Bogues), you need time.

In the women's game, quick and speedy players can be found on most teams. So being able to disguise your passing and keep the defense off balance is key.

Baseball Pass

A baseball pass is frequently used by teams that run. This one-hand pass allows the passer to advance the ball a long distance.

Begin the baseball pass by assuming a staggered stance and holding the ball primarily in one hand. Initially, you support the ball with your nonpassing hand. As your weight is shifted backward, you guide the ball with both hands to a position just behind the shoulder of your throwing side (figure 8.5*a*). On the throw, your passing hand extends in a forward and upward motion. The ball is released as your arm straightens (figure 8.5*b*). Step into your pass. Practice with both hands. This is a great pass to use when the defense is caught upcourt or napping.

a

b

Figure 8.5 The baseball pass.

Overhead Pass

The overhead pass can be executed with speed and accuracy over a long distance, which is why it is quickly becoming one of the more popular passes used today. This pass may be used to make an outlet pass to begin a fast break or as a skip pass to swing the ball from one side of the floor to the other.

The ball should be held just above your head with your hands and fingers spread on each side. Do not move the ball behind your head; if you do, the ball can easily be stolen from behind. The palm of each hand should be cupped as the ball is firmly supported by your fingertips. Your elbows are turned to the outside of your body. As you position your feet in a staggered stance, your weight should shift from your rear to forward foot as the ball moves from the top of your head forward. Release the ball out in front of your head as your fingers and wrists snap toward the receiver (figure 8.6). Remember to follow through to your target. On this pass, make yourself a threat on the court. Be big and physical. Being big means taking up space. Your arms are out. You have a wide stance. Many times this is the pass you make off a rebound in traffic. Control the rebound so you can make the overhead pass. Stay big and balanced, and pivot around to keep your defenders away. Swing the ball violently from side to side as you move the ball. This is a legal move. However, you shouldn't try to hit or hurt anyone; just establish your area as you hold the ball. Remember, your area is like your house. Don't let anyone in! This will open up space for you to make the pass.

Figure 8.6 The overhead pass.

Handoff Pass

Figure 8.7 A handoff pass.

Many offenses rely on a simple handoff pass from the point to the wing, from guard to guard, or from a guard into the high-post area. This pass is used when a player cuts closely by a teammate who hands off the ball. As you turn to hand off the ball to your teammate, be sure that you turn your body to shield the ball from the defense. The ball should be handed off waist high and into your teammate's hands (figure 8.7). Be squared up to the defender who is sliding with your teammate. This enables you to set a solid screen on the defender. Don't let her slide by. Be aware if the defense goes with the ball. Roll to the hoop or to an open spot on the floor. Read the situation.

Lob Pass

Known as the alley-oop, this pass works well in fast-break situations that lead to offensive plays. The lob pass is the same as the two-hand overhead pass, except you add a little arch to it (figure 8.8). You can also make the lob pass from the waist if you aren't being guarded and you have enough time. It's not easy to make a proper lob pass on the run. Doing so takes good timing. The lob is also a great pass for entering the ball into the low post.

Figure 8.8 A lob pass.

When you are making a lob pass, your teammate needs to give you a target to shoot for—one or two hands up in the air. A lob pass takes touch, and you must be able to read where and how the defense is guarding your teammate. You do not want this pass to be thrown in a straight line, nor do you want it to be a high pop fly. Give the pass some arch. Remember, touch is vital.

This pass was a key to Old Dominion winning two national titles. With 6-foot-5 Inge Nissen and 6-foot-8 Anne Donovan in the middle, the lob pass led to many easy baskets. They, of course, had to set up the defense by getting solid inside position between the backboard and the defense. They leaned on the defense to create space as the lob was in the air.

Behind-the-Back Pass

Just like dribbling behind your back, a behind-the-back pass can be a valuable asset in your game. It can also be a difficult pass to control because you are passing with one arm. With the ball placed in the palm of your passing hand, swing your arm in a circular motion and follow through around your back (figure 8.9). Snap your wrist in the direction of the intended receiver. This pass can also be a crowd-pleaser when successfully thrown in the right situation.

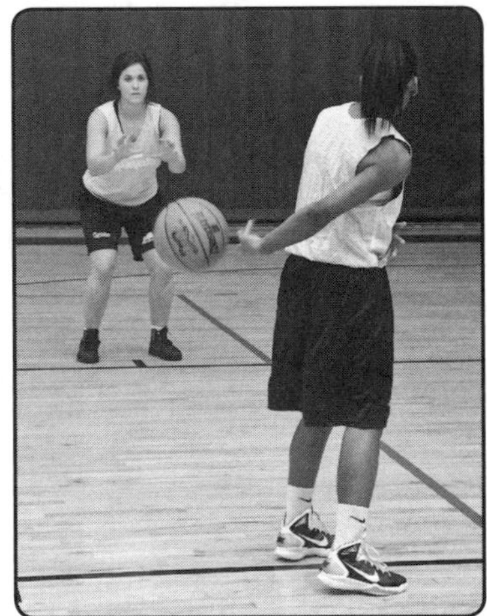

Figure 8.9 A behind-the-back pass.

Tip Pass

I love this pass. With a tip pass, you never truly catch the ball. As you receive the ball, you merely tip it or guide it in a certain direction toward your teammate (figure 8.10). You may even use this type of pass to tip the ball to yourself to gain control. This is a smart and effective maneuver. With this pass, you are thinking one pass ahead of the defense and sometimes your teammates as well, so you must be sure to communicate.

Figure 8.10 A tip pass.

Off-the-Dribble Pass

The better and more proficient you become, the more you can use the off-the-dribble pass. You can make this pass in any direction. It's a great pass for guards because they handle the ball so much. As you are dribbling the ball, you make the pass by quickly moving your dribbling hand from the top of the ball to the back. Instead of taking the next dribble, you push the ball forward, flicking your wrist to pass the ball to your intended receiver (figure 8.11). Having a quick pass is a tremendous advantage. You can pass the ball before the defense realizes it's gone. There's no telegraphing the pass when it's done correctly.

Figure 8.11 Passing off the dribble.

RECEIVING THE PASS

Passing and catching go hand in hand, so to speak. Always keep your eye on the ball and keep your hands up and ready to catch the ball. Great passers are tricky. Whether the receiver is able to catch the ball often depends on the type of pass thrown and the position of the defense.

Always control the ball with your fingertips. It's difficult to catch the ball in your palms. Your fingers give with the ball when it arrives. Keep your fingers spread and relaxed. All passes above the waist should be caught with your fingers up. All passes below the waist should be caught with your fingers down.Meet the ball. Even when making a fake, you should come back to meet the pass. By moving toward the ball, you reduce turnover possibilities. The only time you don't move to the ball is when you are cutting to the basket or making an adjustment to receive the ball.

You worked hard to get the ball, now protect it. Use your arms, legs, and body. Where and how did you receive the ball? How is the defense playing you? Face the hoop. Use your pivoting, faking, passing, shooting, or dribbling to get by the defense.

PASSING DRILLS

With a little dedication and some patience, you can become an expert passer. Use these drills to become better at hitting your teammates for the easy shot or getting the ball downcourt on the move.

Rapid-Fire Drill

PURPOSE

To help you develop three basic types of passes: the two-hand chest pass, overhead outlet pass, and baseball pass. The drill will also help you learn to catch a hard pass and make a quick release. You'll also strengthen your hands and wrists and develop eye–hand coordination.

PROCEDURE

1. Using tape or chalk, mark an area on the wall you are targeting. If you have a toss back (an apparatus that allows players to practice passing without a partner) available, use it. Stand about 2 feet (61 cm) from the wall. Make a hard chest pass against the wall. It should be a rapid-fire pass.
2. As you make each quick, hard chest pass, take one step back, until eventually you are 10 feet (3 m) away. It should take you 10 passes to get 10 feet back.
3. Continue by going back toward the wall, taking 10 steps as you make your chest pass.
4. Repeat this drill with the overhead pass and the baseball pass. On the latter, start by using your left hand. Finish with your right hand.

LADY MAGIC TIPS

- Use correct fundamentals for each pass.
- Step into your passes. Be balanced.
- Focus on your target.
- Look off your pass. Try not to telegraph it, even in a drill, because that will become a habit.

Two-Ball Rapid Fire

PURPOSE

To work on your quick release while not looking at the receiver. You'll learn to see all five players in front of you and learn to catch the ball and pass it quickly.

PROCEDURE

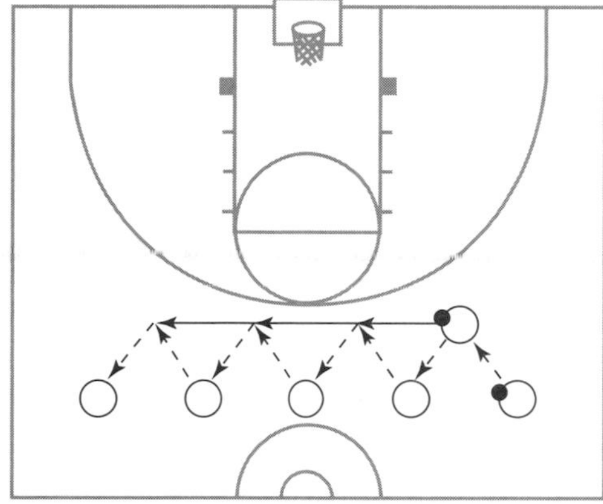

1. Have five players stand in front of you about 5 to 6 feet (152 to 183 cm) away. Your teammates are one arm's distance from each other. You have one ball, and one of the five other players also has a ball.
2. As you pass quickly to one of the players, the other ball will be passed back to you. If you are looking in the direction of your pass, you can expect to get beaned by the other ball.
3. Make as many chest passes as you can in 1 minute. Then, rotate so that everyone eventually becomes the lone passer. Each player should have 3 minutes total of passing.

LADY MAGIC TIPS

- Use a quick release and keep your focus straight ahead. Make your pass as quickly as you can. Quick passes build speed.
- Keep your hands up and be ready to receive the pass.

Monkey in the Middle

PURPOSE

To practice passing to a target (your teammate) while facing pressure from the defense (the player in the middle). This three-person drill includes gamelike pressure and harassment by the defense. You can work on bounce passes, overhead passes, right- or left-handed hook passes, and reverse pivot passes.

PROCEDURE

1. Stand about 15 feet (4.5 m) across from your teammate. The defender (or "monkey") is in the middle. You have the ball; the defender should be contesting your pass and harassing you.
2. Using one of the appropriate passes (reverse pivot, hook pass, overhead, and so on), try to pass to your teammate. On the flight of the ball, the defender should be sprinting over to cover the new passer, who then passes the ball back to you. Do not pass the ball until the defender has arrived.
3. If the defender deflects or steals your pass, you are then in the middle playing defense. If there is not a steal or deflection in 1 minute, rotate and change positions. Everyone should get three chances to be on the outside as a passer.

LADY MAGIC TIPS

- Remember to use a ball fake and look off your pass.
- Use quick passes and be sure to protect the ball.
- Don't telegraph your pass.
- Stay balanced.

Toss Back or Wall Passing Circuit

PURPOSE

To improve your ability to make a variety of passes quicker and with power and accuracy. This drill will improve your strong hand and strengthen your weaker hand.

PROCEDURE

1. Stand 10 feet from the wall or toss back. Pass and catch the ball as quickly as you can, using the chest pass, bounce pass, overhead pass, baseball pass, and behind-the-back pass.
2. Make 25 passes of each type. Take a 1-minute break after you have completed all five types of passes 25 times each. Repeat each set of five three times.

LADY MAGIC TIPS

- Concentrate on the spot where you want your pass to head.
- Keep your hands up and be ready for a return pass.

Passing on the Move

PURPOSE

To increase your confidence and help you learn timing, quickness, power, and accuracy while passing on the move.

PROCEDURE

1. Put tape (your target) on a wall. Then, place tape on one spot on the floor and on another spot 12 feet (3.6 m) from the first spot.
2. Start by standing on the tape on the floor. Pass the ball at an angle to the target on the wall. Slide to the other piece of tape and catch the ball. Then make another pass to the tape on the wall and slide in the other direction to catch the ball.
3. Use a chest pass for this drill. Perform short, quick lateral slides without crossing your feet. Follow through to your target with the proper angle that will get the ball to the opposite side.
4. Do this drill for 30 seconds. Rest for 30 seconds. Repeat three times.

LADY MAGIC TIPS

- Start out in a balanced stance—feet shoulder-width apart.
- Use a proper chest pass. Remember the fundamentals—keep elbows in, lean into the pass, follow through with good rotation on the ball, and keep your thumbs down and palms out.
- Have your hands ready to catch the pass.

SUMMARY

With so much emphasis on scoring and defense, passing and catching don't receive the attention they deserve. To reduce turnovers and have a better chance to win, you must work on the fundamentals of passing and catching. You should work on the following:

- Faking with the ball.
- Timing your pass.
- Knowing your personnel.
- Using either hand to pass. If you can do this, more options will be open to you.
- Communicating.
- Mastering different types of passes.
- Receiving the ball.
- Performing passing drills.

chapter

9

Becoming a Defensive Stopper

Players must have a mentality for defense. On defense, you should play your opponent as if you have no help behind you. The last thing you want to do is allow your opponent to get by you. Most of the time, when your player gets by you, this means that you're not making the commitment—you're not working hard enough.

You'll often see a team with less talent win games because its defense causes turnovers, plays smart, forces the opponent into taking low-percentage shots, and boxes out and rebounds well.

As the saying goes, offense sells tickets, but defense wins championships. Defense takes mental toughness, desire, and spirit. It's you against your opponent. The challenge is there! Make your opponents work for every possession and every point.

DEFENSIVE SKILLS

Let's take a simple test. When coaches are determining whether you are a complete defensive player, they're looking for 10 qualities of a defensive stopper. Can you answer *yes* to the following questions?

1. Are you coachable and defensive minded?
2. Do you have the necessary attributes—mental toughness, hustle, heart, and desire?
3. Do you get good positioning on the floor—on the ball and off? Do you see the ball on the weak side?
4. Do you have the correct defensive stance?
5. Do you jump well?
6. Do you have quick hands and feet?
7. Do you communicate with your teammates?

8. Do you understand how to play defense?
9. Can you play a variety of defenses?
10. Are you a good transition player? Can you switch quickly from offense to defense and vice versa?

These are the basic areas to work on if you want to become a great defensive player. If you can answer *yes* to these questions, you will be great, and you can help your team become great as well. The following principles will help you answer *yes* to questions 3 through 7. They should increase your defensive awareness and make you more coachable. They can also help you overcome any shortcomings caused by your genetics. Training for questions 8 through 10 comes later in the chapter.

Body Positioning

The better defensive position you are in, the better the results. Keep your center of gravity low (figure 9.1). The lower you are to the ground, the quicker you will be. Even if your opponent fakes or changes direction, you can recover. You must condition yourself to stay low and balanced.

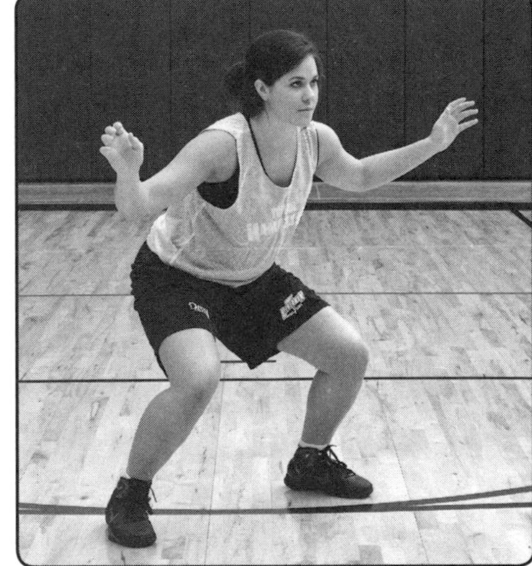

Figure 9.1 Defensive position.

Checkpoints

- ☑ Position yourself where you can see your opponent and the ball.
- ☑ Overplay the baseline at all times to protect it.
- ☑ Turn your opponent into the middle where you have help.

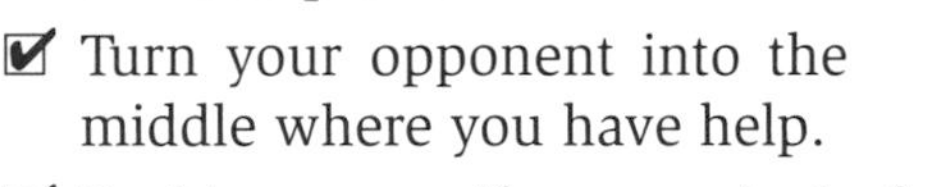

- ☑ Position yourself so your body forces your opponent to go where you want her to go.

Knees and Feet

Your stance is the foundation of good defense. Flex your knees as if you are sitting on a chair, with your head over your knees for balance. Do not bend your back to achieve this position. If you do, it will pull you off balance. Here are some points to remember:

- Turn slightly sideways to your opponent.
- Never get your head and shoulders in front of your waist.

- Keep your weight on your rear foot; you must be ready to go back at all times.
- Try to create mistakes rather than steal the ball. The defense is given more balls than it ever steals.

Hips and Back

You'll generate power if you stay low and explode up. Keeping a balanced, low power base will lead to explosive starts. The stronger your hips and back are, the better your positioning will be. Keep your knees flexed and your back fairly straight, and keep your hips down.

Arms and Hands

Deflections and steals are often the result of proper arm and hand placement. Your arms should be slightly flexed for balance, with your palms open toward the ball for steals. Your hands are always out in the passing lanes.

Proper footwork is important, but active hands can allow the defense to apply immediate pressure on the ball. Be intimidating and harass the ball handler by using your hands. Your palms should be up if you try to steal the ball. Steal it as the dribble is coming up, not going down. The ball is slower on the way up. Also, try not to reach down to steal. This takes away your balance and commits you defensively.

If your opponent begins to shoot, put a hand up to contest the shot. If you're guarding a left-handed shooter, get your right hand up, and vice versa. This way you never cross your body and get off balance.

Head and Eyes

Your head is the heaviest part of your body. Keep it over your knees. If your head is too far forward, you will be off balance. If it is too far back, you will be on your heels. Your head should always be up, and your eyes should be focused on the waist of your opponent, not on the ball. Great ball handlers have great moves, so try not to get faked out by the movement of the ball. A ball handler isn't going anywhere without her hips. You want to watch for the direction her hips are moving.

Footwork

Before you attempt to play solid player-to-player defense, you need to know how to do it correctly. To achieve good defensive play, footwork is essential. The lower you are, the quicker and more explosive you will be. You will be able to change directions more efficiently. Do not bend at the waist. Flex your knees, keep your rear end low, and keep your arms out in the passing lanes. Stay active and pressure the ball. Keep your feet shoulder-width apart with your head over your knees so your weight is equally distributed on both feet for proper balance. Don't get caught flat-footed.

Always keep your feet moving. If your feet are stationary, your footwork is not energy efficient. It takes more time and energy to go from stopping to starting than it does to continue movement. Use your momentum to quickly change position or direction. A defensive player should be cautious while making adjustments. Slide to get to your destination; don't run. Find the angle to beat your opponent to a spot. Of course, there are always exceptions; if your opponent has blown by you in the open court, sprint to the other end. Find the area she's going to and attempt to cut her off. Don't cross your feet or bring them together. Once you do, you lose your balance, along with the proper defensive edge.

As you begin to play defense, you need options for attacking, containing, or recovering from your opponent's moves. The footwork methods you need to work on include step and catch, attack step, drop step, and retreat step.

Step and Catch

As you are guarding the ball handler, she will make a move in either direction. You must be in a low and ready defensive position. Using your outside leg, slide at an angle to a spot where the ball handler is heading (figure 9.2*a*). Never bring your feet together. As you approach the spot, turn the ball handler in the other direction (figure 9.2*b*).

Figure 9.2 Step and catch.

Attack Step

The offense is always attacking you. By using foot fakes, you can be the aggressor. If you attack your opponent, you force her to think and to take time to react. When you are performing the attack step, it's almost as if you are fencing—one foot is slightly ahead of the other. The hand on the side of that foot should be extended toward the offensive player. Push off your back foot and, in a balanced position, go at the ball handler (figure 9.3). Stay low and balanced. You can take a one-step fake or a two-step attack fake at the ball. If done properly, you can make the ball handler use a retreat dribble or pick up and kill her dribble. When you do get her to pick up the dribble, yell "Dead, dead!" This lets your teammates know that the dribble is dead. They can help you deny all passes.

Figure 9.3 Attack step.

Drop Step

The drop step is more of a recovery step that you can use if the offensive player beats you. The offensive player is most likely in a triple-threat position. Boom. She jab-fakes at you, and your front foot is up. By pivoting off your back foot, then opening or swinging your front leg in the direction of her drive, you can slide to an area to recover (figure 9.4).

Figure 9.4 Drop step.

Retreat Step

The offense is always trying to attack and break down the defense. When the offensive player is in her triple-threat position, you must be low and in a good defensive position. If an offensive player goes left or right, you can use the retreat step to push off and slide in that direction. The best way to generate power is by pushing off with your front foot in that direction and taking a retreat step with your back foot (figure 9.5). Then, quickly slide with your front foot. Now, you are back in a balanced stance.

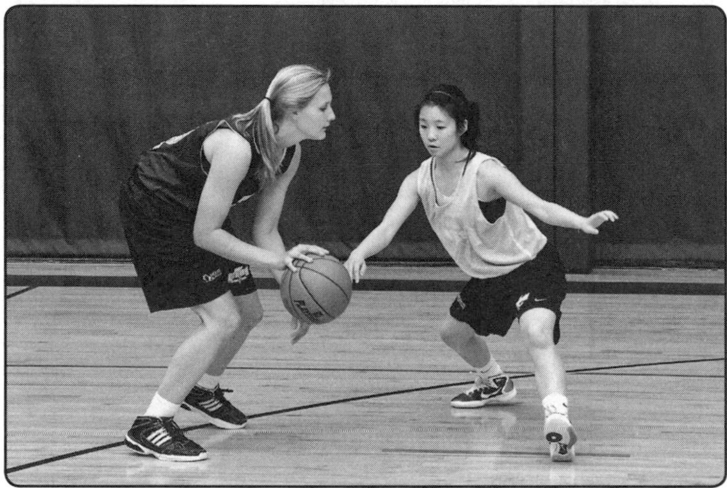

Figure 9.5 Retreat step.

Communication

In competition, many things can distract you: the noisy crowd, loud announcers, other players, lack of concentration, and referees. In spite of all this, you must continually communicate with your teammates. This is especially true on defense. By shouting "help," "screen," "ball," "dead," and so on, you can help a teammate know what's coming at her or what's happening on the court. Communicate to your teammates that the blind screen is coming, or anything else you notice on the floor. On the basketball court, talk is not cheap. It is priceless. It can mean the difference between winning and losing.

DOS AND DON'TS OF DEFENSE

Dos—On Ball

- Stay low and balanced. Keep your feet shoulder-width apart. Keep your hands active in the passing lane.
- Step and catch as you slide, hawking the ball.
- Dictate and try to control where the dribble is going. Pressure and contain the ball.
- Keep your head over the ball. This way you are always in front of the ball.
- Focus on the offensive player's hips.
- Make sure your palms are always open and your thumbs are up.

Don'ts—On Ball

- Don't cross your feet. You'll be off balance.
- Don't bounce while sliding.
- Don't get beat down the floor.
- Don't let the ball handler go side to side to run the offense.
- Don't get nailed by a pick—see it and get over or through it.

Dos—Off Ball

- Focus on the passer's eyes. They don't lie.
- See the ball and the player by using peripheral vision.
- Keep your hands in the passing lanes and keep your knees flexed. Stay one arm's length from the player.
- On backdoor cuts, open up in the lane. See the ball and feel the player cutting behind you.
- Use a fencer's attack and retreat steps.
- See all screens; read and react.

Don'ts—Off Ball

- Don't turn your head to see only the ball or only a player.
- Don't lunge at passes. You will be off balance and get beat.
- Don't have your back to the top of the key when your player is cutting backdoor. See the ball.
- Don't forget to box out.
- Don't get caught too far over if you are weak-side help.
- Don't get screened and fail to communicate that you need help.

TEAM DEFENSE

Defense is hard work, and playing defense as a team is a tough but important challenge. Here are six important reasons for learning to play good team defense:

1. The defense will be consistent night after night, while the offense may be up and down.
2. Having to practice against a tough defense will make your offense better.
3. A good defense helps build mental toughness that will help you win close games.
4. A good defense helps defeat a team mentally. It creates doubt in your opponents' minds about their ability to score and win.
5. In a losing game, a good defense helps ensure that you won't get beaten badly enough to be humiliated.
6. With a good defense, your team will never get so far behind that you can't catch up.

To play good team defense, you must understand your responsibilities. In the following sections, we outline the responsibilities of each position.

Point Guard

The point guard is the communicator between coach and players. Usually the quickest player on the floor, the point guard dictates tempo and pressure on both ends of the floor. On defense, she is the focal person for pressuring the ball handler. If you are a defensive point guard, you should have an attitude to disrupt your opponent. There have been some great defensive point guards in women's basketball. Marianne Stanley, who won two national championships at Immaculata College in the early '70s, would force opponents to take certain angles on the court and force them into the defensive help. Sheryl Swoopes was like a "lockdown corner" in the NFL; you never wanted to pass the ball to her side of the floor for fear that she would shoot into the passing lane, get a steal, and score! Katie Smith can defend and play four positions, from point guard to post. She's a physical defender. Tamika Catchings of the Indiana Fever and Alana Beard of the Washington Mystics have been great defenders since their days at Tennessee and Duke. Not only are they great floor leaders, but also great passers and communicators; they can also play multiple positions. Players respond to point guards who have a take-over attitude. These point guards are like coaches on the floor. A point guard must have self-confidence to gain the respect of the other players on the floor.

Shooting Guard

At the 2 spot, you have different responsibilities than the point guard. You will probably guard your opponent's best shooter. Your speed and quickness should be an asset. You have to be tough on defense. You will be fighting hard through screens as your opponent tries to shake free. See the screens, anticipate, and get help from your teammates. Most of all, get there! After the shot, box out and rebound. As much as you want to fly out on the break, you must remember, first things first. Get the board! Then, it's time to be offensive minded. Many great shooting guards have played in the women's game: hall of famer Cynthia Cooper; Teresa Edwards, a five-time Olympian and widely regarded for years as one of the best players in the world; WNBA stars Deanna Nolan and Becky Hammon; and my former Olympic teammates (both hall of famers) Ann Meyers and Carol Blazejowski—the list goes on and on. They have all been great players and major assets to their teams.

Small Forward

The 3 spot is where the greyhounds live. To play this position, you must be an exceptional athlete—big, strong, and fast. Depending on the matchups, you could guard your opponent's best shooter. Use your quickness to harass the offense. If you are guarding a perimeter player, use your speed; if you're down in the post, use a combination of strength and quickness. You should fight for position, because if you work the offensive boards, you will pick up a ton of points off missed shots. Lynette Woodard of Kansas, Cheryl Miller of USC, Medina Dixon of Old Dominion, Bridgette Gordon of Tennessee, and Clarissa Davis and Andrea Lloyd, both of Texas, were the prototype small forwards. They could get up and down the floor, rebound, shoot, and play defense.

Power Forward

As a power forward, you should be big and physical. You must run the floor well. Your mobility will help you guard the high post and also get down in the trenches with the low post. Be willing to help your teammates by shutting down the lane. Picking up a charge means you saw the play, reacted, and got the job done. You have to be an aggressive, fearless rebounder. You can start a fast break for your team if you clean the glass and get the ball out to a guard. Some of the best players I saw at this position were Pat Roberts of Tennessee, Carolyn Bush-Roddy of Wayland Baptist College, and Lisa Leslie of USC. Leslie could play the power forward position or the post. Katrina McClain might be the best of the bunch. She's a two-time Olympian. She's big, strong, quick, and relentless on both boards. She can score in the half-court offense and can run the floor like a guard.

Post

As the 5 player, you must be the enforcer. You set the tone on defense and in rebounding. Remember, your home is the painted area, and nobody comes into your house without an invitation. You must be physical and willing to fight for inside position, as well as help out on all drives to the basket. Be smart. You don't have to block everything, just contest everything! You have to own the boards and be an intimidator in a variety of ways. Hall of famer Lucy Harris of Delta State University was strong and intimidating; she could block shots and could score at will from the inside. At 6-foot-5, Inge Nissen could take an opponent off the dribble, shoot from 18 feet out, pass the ball, and block shots. On the other hand, Anne Donovan, a 6-foot-8 three-time Olympian, would basically just throw an opponent's shot off its course. No matter how good the opponent's move was to get to the basket, Anne would take the opponent's spirit away and force teams to change their offense to the outside game. The women's game over the years has had some dominating post players with great finesse.

Checkpoints

- ☑ Use a boxer's step or lateral shift on defense. Never cross your legs on defense. When you are getting beat on a drive, resort to a running stride until you recover and return to your boxer step.
- ☑ Study your opponent closely during the early part of the game. Pick out her weaknesses and her strong points. Play her accordingly. If she can only go right, force her to go left. If she isn't a good shooter, play her for the drive.
- ☑ If you are assigned a poor scorer, try to help your teammates anytime it is possible. Sink inside a great deal on the post player and play for interceptions more than usual. Bluff your opponent when she has the ball and fall back quickly for an interception.
- ☑ Force your opponent to take long, hurried shots. Contest every shot with a hand in the shooter's face.
- ☑ Don't ever jump unless you are sure the ball is being shot. Shooters will try to fake you up to get you in the air. Once you leave the floor, the only thing you can do is block the shot or contest the shot.
- ☑ Watch both the ball and your opponent after she passes off, but don't lose your opponent. She is your responsibility until your team has possession.
- ☑ Once your opponent passes off, loosen up on her immediately and sink toward the ball. Never let your opponent pass and break toward the ball. Position yourself quickly so the pass back to your opponent has to be made over you.

- ☑ Keep constant pressure on all offensive players at all times. When you are only one pass away from the ball, extend your ball-side arm out in the passing lane to keep your opponent from receiving a pass. Make her cut behind you, not in front.
- ☑ Remember that a good defensive player never lets her opponent go where she wants to go without a struggle. Jump in front of her, draw charging fouls, and force her from her normal pattern.
- ☑ If you are caught with your back to the ball, throw up one arm in front of your opponent and extend the other arm in the direction of the ball. You may deflect a pass.
- ☑ If you are guarding a player who is two passes away from the ball, you can sink back more than you can if she is only one pass away.
- ☑ Play a post player high, almost in front of her when she doesn't have the ball. Make her go behind you as she crosses the lane. Never let her come over the top and receive a pass. You are then helpless.
- ☑ When double-teaming an opponent, allow at least 3 feet (91 cm) between yourself and your teammate. Keep your arms raised and play in the passing lanes. Approach cautiously to prevent the offensive player from splitting the double team with a dribble.
- ☑ Do not bat the ball under the defensive basket. Catch all balls coming off the board, and pass the ball to outlet zones as quickly as possible.
- ☑ Regardless of how easy a shot may appear, always get yourself in position to rebound in case it misses. Never take a basket for granted. Your teammates will miss rebounds more often than you think.

PLAYER-TO-PLAYER DEFENSE

In basketball, defense is broken into two main kinds—player-to-player, where you guard an opponent individually, and zone, where you cover an area of the court, forcing teams away from penetration and into a perimeter game. In this section, we concentrate on the skills you need to become a terrific player-to-player defender.

Great defense can turn on a crowd and inspire your team. The best defense is an aggressive, harassing type, especially if you are trying to force teams into mistakes and turnovers, though other types of defenses can also work. It depends on the team's strategy and how your coach decides to play a particular team.

Aggressiveness demands hard work, determination, pride, and the ability to read situations. Good teams and players keep an enormous amount of pressure on the ball from the start to the end of the game. This style of pressure can wear down opponents mentally and physically. Many opponents get frustrated, and then you have them—they'll turn the ball over, miss their shots, and lose their spirit. But, remember, there is a difference between playing solid, aggressive defense and making mistakes and committing unnecessary fouls.

The first point to remember about player-to-player defense is that you should position yourself an arm's length away from your opponent as you defend against the triple-threat position. Remember to keep your knees bent and your feet shoulder-width apart. Do not bend at the waist. Keep your head over your knees and do not stand flat-footed.

As the ball handler is dribbling, you should be directly in front of her—unless you are overplaying and forcing the ball to her weak side or to one side of the floor. Your head should be over the ball; wherever the ball is, that's where your head should be. This technique keeps you centered on the ball.

Watch and study your opponents on film or in pregame warm-ups. Know if they are good ball handlers and quick, good passers. If they are quicker than you, back off a step and play good position defense, forcing them to a particular area of the floor.

Use everything you can to distract the offense, applying constant pressure. Stay low with one hand up and the other hand in the passing lane. Keep yourself on the ball. Follow the ball with your hands as it is being passed. If the ball handler passes to a wing or the post, you should always jump in the direction of the pass. Get in front of the cutter, make her go behind you, and deny the return pass. If the ball handler shoots, you must get a hand in her face. Turn toward the shooter, perform a reverse pivot, and box her off the boards.

Here are the three main aspects of player-to-player defense:

1. Containing the ball handler. Keep the offense from the basket.
2. Channeling or forcing the ball handler to one side of the court to limit her options.
3. Going one on one (player to player) with the ball handler.

Advantages of Player-to-Player Defense

Today, most coaches employ player-to-player defense for ball pressure and more aggressiveness on defense. They also use it to force a quicker tempo. Coaches will dictate what type of defense is used depending on the talent and ability of their opponents. Player-to-player defense is great against teams that shoot well from the outside. It forces more passing and movement. Good player-to-player defense can also force the offense to use up the shot clock and take shots with little time on the clock. Zones can be effective as well; however, although zone defenses take away the dribble penetration, they encourage the outside shot.

Weaknesses of Player-to-Player Defense

Player-to-player is a high-intensity defense. The defenders are depending on each other to contain and attack the offense. Teams that have great ball handlers can break down a good defensive team with penetration and can draw the defense by shooting or passing off. This type of defense also extends the floor so there are more gaps for teams to cut into. In this defense, players are also taken away from the boards. To play pressure player-to-player defense, you and your teammates have to be superbly conditioned.

Other Aspects of Player-to-Player Defense

To have a well-rounded defensive game, you have to understand why you are being asked to play a certain way. You must know how to play the passing lanes on the ball, how and when to switch, and how to get over a screen. This is all part of understanding how to play defense.

Overplaying the Pass

Overplaying a pass is one way that defensive players get an edge. If you have done a solid job of forcing the ball handler to pick up her dribble or overplaying her to one side, you must now read her remaining options. Get in the passing lane by keeping your arms up and ready (figure 9.6). You can deflect a lot of passes and prevent the offensive player from passing to the open spot on the floor. Overplaying can be used as a surprise tactic, but it can be risky. If you deny hard and overpursue your opponent, the player may be left open as you scramble to get back into the play, or your teammates may have to rotate to cover for you. You'll reduce the risk if you have made the ball handler pick up her dribble first. Never give your opponent an easy passing lane. Make her work to get a good pass off.

Figure 9.6 Denying the passing lanes by overplaying the pass.

Off-the-Ball Defense

Off-the-ball defense means that you are at least one pass away from the ball. I always found off-the-ball defense to be fun and challenging. It's still a pressure defense, but it's a different type of pressure. It's cat and mouse. You're reading the ball handler and seeing the player you are guarding at the same time (figure 9.7). Are you going to allow her to get the ball? Heck no! But if she does, it will be in an area where she's not ready to shoot. The key here is simple: See the ball; see the player. If you do that, you're in control.

Figure 9.7 Keeping an eye on the ball and your player with off-the-ball defense.

One Pass Away (Denial) If you are using player-to-player defense and your teammate is putting considerable pressure on the ball handler, you should be denying one pass away when the ball is on the strong side. Denial positions add pressure for the ball handler trying to pass to a teammate. Position yourself with your back to the ball, but keeping the ball in your peripheral vision, and your arms extended, denying the pass to the receiver. You want to be as big as possible. You should be an arm's length from the receiver, and your head should be positioned over the shoulder on the side of your front foot. This foot should be positioned between the feet of the receiver. Your arm on the same side is extended into the passing lane. While keeping your head over the shoulder, look straight ahead. You should be able to see both the ball and the offensive player by using your peripheral vision. As the receiver fakes toward the ball, you can use the defensive slide to cover your opponent. Stay balanced and do not lunge for the ball. Do not bring your feet together.

Always be flexible. You know that the receiver is going to try to fake you. Read the situation. If the offensive player receives the ball, you should quickly retreat back to your on-the-ball defensive position. If you are doing a great job of denying and the receiver goes backdoor, quickly open your position to the ball by performing a reverse pivot with your outside foot. Keep your arms in the passing lanes and slightly feel your opponent as she cuts through the free-throw area. Make sure you always see the ball. If the ball is not passed inside and the receiver goes to the opposite wing, you should continue in a one-pass-away denial position.

The closeout on the wing can be very effective if you are properly balanced. Stay low when you are running toward the receiver as she catches the ball. Slow down into a balanced jump stop. Keep your hands active and in the passing lane. Keep your head up and your feet shoulder-width apart. Now you can force the receiver to the inside baseline side. If you are standing straight up, the receiver can go by you.

Let the offensive player know that she is going to have to work hard for the ball. You'll be surprised how many players aren't willing to work for it. Even a good player, if pressured by good denial defense, can be taken right out of the flow of the game.

Two Passes Away (Weak Side) Two-passes-away defense requires an altogether different mentality. If you play it right, your team will be successful. If you gamble often, you will put added pressure on your teammates to cover for you. The weak side is weak because, in many cases, it is the last line of defense if the ball is moved quickly by the offense.

If you are the weak-side player, read the passer's eyes. Many times the passer won't look off her pass, and you can step in for the steal. If the ball is reversed quickly to the weak side, you can get there and play good defense until your teammates have rotated into position.

The defender can use several methods to play an opponent two passes away. If the ball is on one side and you are on the weak side, you should be in an open stance, with one hand toward your opponent and one hand toward the ball. Use peripheral vision so you can see both. If you turn your head either way, you will lose sight of the ball or your opponent. Also, you must be prepared to defend the lob pass or skip pass over the top of the defense. The farther your opponent is from the ball, the farther you can drop off from her. Cheat ball side or help side. Help means just that: You help defend against any cutters. If an opponent is cutting through the lane, make her change her route by stepping in front of her. Take away dribble penetration if a teammate needs help by sliding over and forcing the ball handler to pick up her dribble. Also, be willing to take the charge when rotating over. Boxing out on the weak-side boards is a must.

Players who help must be aware of ball movement and where their opponent is so that they can adjust accordingly. In addition, a weak-side player must talk and call out the screens. You are in a perfect position to see the play develop, so it is your responsibility to communicate with your teammates.

Defense Against Screens

When playing defense, one of the toughest challenges is having a screen set on you—whether you see it coming or not. A blind pick hurts. You should constantly be looking left and right and checking where the offensive players are. The key to getting through screens is making your move before your opponents set the screen.

When you are playing defense, you must be aware of screens that the offense will set to free a teammate. You can use various options to get through or over a screen. Switching can also be very difficult for offenses to work against. The key is communicating with one another. Most important, you need to yell "screen" or "pick" to a teammate if she is being screened. Let her know left side or right side. One of the worst situations in basketball is being screened by a blind pick and getting nailed when a teammate could have warned you.

Get Over the Screen Know the opposing team's personnel. If the opponent you are guarding is a great shooter, you need to get over the top of the screen. See the screen coming, belly up to the offensive player, and stay between her and the screener. This is also referred to as jumping to the ball. Slide through the screen (figure 9.8). You must communicate with your teammates so that they allow you to go between them and over the screener.

Figure 9.8 Getting over the screen.

Figure 9.9 Sliding behind the screen.

Slide Behind the Screen If the player you are guarding isn't a great shooter, you can slide behind the screener and your teammate (figure 9.9). For this option to work, you must have help or hedging from your teammate. Help means your teammate will pick up your player until you can recover. When your teammate hedges, she is stepping out and forcing the ball handler to go wide, preventing her from turning the corner to go to the basket. When your teammate forces the ball handler wide, you can recover from the screen and slide over to guard the ball handler again.

Switch Your first option should be to slide over the screen and stick with your player. Sometimes, though, the screens are solid, and you have to switch with a teammate to help you out. If you can't get past the screen, (figure 9.10*a*) you must communicate this to your teammate. This is usually done by yelling "Switch!" Switch means you stay with the player who has screened you, while your teammate picks up your player (figure 9.10*b*). Defenders switching on screens can be very frustrating for offenses.

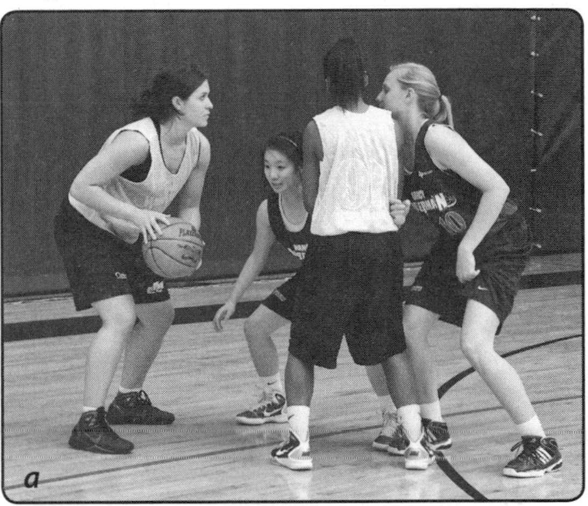

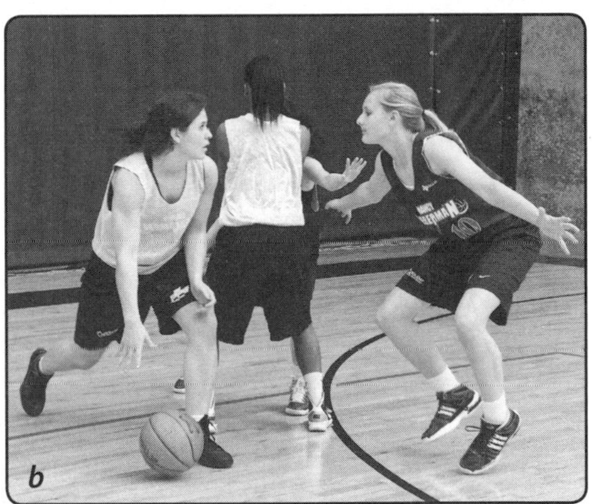

Figure 9.10 Switch.

Some coaches will tell players to automatically switch on all screens 18 to 20 feet away from the basket or on those close to the basket. The key is to do so. You must be committed to calling the switch and doing it. Sometimes, a player will think, *I can get through it*. The players don't switch, and they get beat.

Screen on the Ball When guarding the ball, you should check both sides and listen for your teammates to call out a screen. Good defensive players can put a lot of pressure on the screener if they are alert and active. If you sense a screen coming, jump to the player who has the ball and get as tight as you can to the ball handler so you can fight over the screen. The more active you are, the more likely you will be able to draw the screener out of position or even get an illegal screen called by the officials. When you are using this over-the-top technique in a nonswitching situation, your teammate who is guarding the screener needs to hedge out as the ball handler attempts to turn the corner around the pick. This gives you the chance to recover and catch up to the ball. Once your teammate has hedged, she jumps back to defending the screener. If the screener rolls to the basket, you must get between the ball and the screener. Make the offense use a lob pass over the top—this is a tough pass to make. If you are guarding the ball, do not commit yourself until the ball handler starts her dribble or until the screen is set.

Screen off the Ball If you are off the ball, you should be opened up and able to see who is cutting and screening. You should not be screened two passes away. By being in a sagging position, you have the ability to anticipate a screen coming. Slide through the screen. Make sure you communicate with your teammates. Find your opponent and recover to defend her. You will know if you can or cannot get through or over a screen. This is when a decision to switch must be made. Situations change quickly during a game. That's why communication is key to being successful.

Guarding the Post

Because many teams try to get the ball inside to score, defending the post is one of the most challenging aspects of half-court defense. If the post player has good position, the defender must constantly be moving and reading where the ball is. This will determine how to effectively defend the low-post player. Your options are playing in front of the post, playing behind the post, or using three-quarters denial—either baseline side or inside. Guarding the post takes pride, intelligence, and the ability to be physical.

Fronting the Post Fronting the post means getting in front of the post player with your hands up high and making yourself big and active (figure 9.11). You are encouraging the passer to make a pinpoint lob over her defender, who should be applying ball pressure, and you. You are in the passing lane and should expect weak-side help on the lob pass. If there is no weak-side help, the offense gains the better offensive rebounding position.

Figure 9.11 Fronting the post.

Figure 9.12 Playing behind the post.

Playing Behind the Post If you are playing behind the post (figure 9.12), you allow the post player to receive the entry pass. As she turns to shoot or make a move, you should take a step back and play straight-up defense with your arms up to defend the shot. If the post player puts the ball on the floor, the guards should be dropping. You have inside position; when the shot goes up, box out and the rebound is yours.

Using Three-Quarters Denial If your opponent is on the low post, position yourself three-quarters to her baseline side, with your outside hand in the passing lane as you are splitting her side (figure 9.13). Force your opponent toward your help, which will come from the weak-side guard. This type of defense makes the post appear not to be open. If your guard is pressuring the ball, the entry pass will be tough for her opponent to make.

If the post player has gone to the high post and the ball is up top, you can deny high side. You should have weak-side help under the goal. If the ball is passed to the wing, jump to the ball in front of the post on the flight of the ball. This way, as the post player goes back down low, you are already in baseline three-quarters denial defense.

Figure 9.13 Denying the post with three-quarters denial.

TRANSITION DEFENSE

Run, run, run. An up-tempo style is what today's coaches want. The key is having better and quicker athletes who are able to play the transition game. You might be a great running team, but you must know how to get back against a team with a similar style. Transition is simply reacting and moving quickly from offense to defense and vice versa. This is where real conditioning pays off. It takes a lot of precious energy to turn and sprint as a team in order to get back and set your defense. You need to slow down the ball or force the ball handler to pick up her dribble. This effort allows your teammates to recover down the floor. When you have stopped the ball, you should recover and find your player or help out a teammate if someone is open. In player-to-player defense, you find the open player. In a zone, you go to your assigned area. In both cases, players need to hustle and communicate with each other. Here are some basic rules for transition defense:

- In transition, turn and sprint. Always know where the ball is.
- Try to contain or stop the ball handler from advancing.
- Get the ball out of the middle of the court. Force the ball handler to commit to a side.
- Play your half-court defense, whether it is player-to-player or zone defense. Get back and into your defense.
- Remember that nothing beats communication. Talk to each other.

FOOTWORK DRILLS

There's no better way to improve your defense than by using your feet, not your hands. These drills will help you increase your foot speed in different directions.

Lane Slides

PURPOSE

To improve foot speed, balance, and defensive sliding.

PROCEDURE

1. Start on one side of the foul lane in a proper defensive position. Slide from one side to the other. Stay down in your defensive position. Try not to rise up.
2. Touch the lane line with your outside hand and slide in the other direction—once again using your outside hand to touch the lane line. Continue sliding back and forth for 30 seconds.

LADY MAGIC TIPS

- Stay low, keep your head up, and stay in a proper defensive stance. You'll be quicker and more effective in the drill.
- Think *step and catch* when you are sliding. Don't bounce. Step with your outside leg and catch up with your inside leg.
- Do not cross your feet or bring them together. If your feet are together, you'll be off balance and slow.

Triangle Slide

PURPOSE

To work on all three areas of defensive movement: lateral slides, the closeout and attack, and retreat steps. The drill will also help you improve your balance and enable you to practice quick drop steps.

PROCEDURE

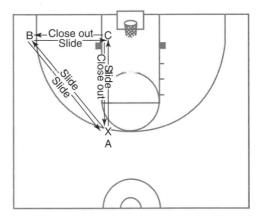

1. Start at point A (top of the triangle) in a defensive stance, with one hand in the shooter's face and one hand in the passing lane. Slide laterally to point B, open to the corner, and slide laterally to point C, denying the low post. Close out to (run at) point A, quickly and in balance.
2. Touch point A and change direction. Perform a retreat slide back to point C, open toward point B, and close out to point B. Then, slide laterally from point B to point A.
3. Repeat this drill three times. Take 30 seconds for each rep. Rest for 60 seconds.
4. Always start your next repetition at a different point so you are using your lateral slide, closeout movement, and retreat step in all areas.

LADY MAGIC TIPS

- Stay low and in your proper defensive stance.
- Think *ball pressure*. Slide quickly for success. On the closeout, you are running at the imaginary player with the ball. As you approach, slow down and stay balanced.
- Use short, quick steps. Keep your head steady and your knees flexed.
- Change directions quickly.
- Always lead with the outside leg when making your defensive slide.

Diagonal Slide

PURPOSE

To help you develop defensive quickness and balance while moving in a diagonal slide backward; to improve your ability to change direction quickly; to work on transition for offense and defense.

PROCEDURE

1. Use the low blocks and foul-lane area for this drill. Start on the left block at the baseline, facing the basket. Stay low and in your proper balanced defensive stance.
2. With your right foot, slide back at a 45-degree angle to the opposite lane line. Use short, quick retreat steps. Stay on the balls of your feet as you move in a diagonal direction. Touch the line with your feet.
3. Quickly drop-step with your left foot and pivot with your right. Slide to the other side of the lane. Make three lane slides at a diagonal angle until you reach the foul-line elbow.
4. Facing half-court, slide across the foul line to the opposite side. Then, repeat the three diagonal slides backward until you reach the low block. See if you can complete the slides up and down in 30 seconds. Rest for 60 seconds, then repeat the drill three times.

LADY MAGIC TIPS

- Use short, quick retreat steps, stay balanced, and never cross your feet.
- Push off with your inside leg and always use your outside leg to slide in that direction.
- Always work hard in all defensive drills. Maintain an attitude of pride. This is also a great one-on-one drill.

Mirror Drill

PURPOSE

To work on sliding, running, attacking, and performing retreat steps. This drill also allows you to work on quick footfire and ball fakes. (You can do this drill with a teammate acting as a mirror, or you can use your own imagination.)

PROCEDURE

1. Start in the middle of the court in the proper defensive stance. If you have a partner, take turns mirroring each other. If you are doing this drill alone, that's fine. It's a great time to use your imagination and determination on defense.

2. Start by using a quick stutter step or footfire. Then, slide in all directions, retreat, attack, and close out. Add a fake as you are doing the footfire or stutter step.
3. At first, do this sliding drill hard for 2 minutes each day. Add 1 minute until you can slide continuously for 20 minutes. That's right—one half of a game.

LADY MAGIC TIPS

- Stay in your stance and stay balanced. Don't cross your feet when you are sliding at angles. Remember to stay low.
- On attacks or closeouts, put your hand to the imaginary ball to contend the shot. Your hands are always in the passing lane.
- Slide quickly in all directions on all changes of direction. Drop-step quickly with either foot.
- On footfire or stutter steps, keep your feet moving quickly as you fake at the imaginary ball. Make it believable.
- Concentrate as you get fired up. Have pride. Don't get sloppy. Do all drills with 100 percent intensity.

Tube Slide

PURPOSE

To help you increase strength and speed and improve conditioning, as well as better footwork technique so that you can learn to stay down in the proper defensive stance and slide without crossing your feet.

PROCEDURE

1. Using a resistance band (or an old inner tube or a piece of plastic), tie the ends together to make a circle—anywhere from 2 to 4 inches (5.1 to 10.2 cm) wide and about 24 inches (61.0 cm) long. Slip the tube around your legs, above your ankles. You should feel the tube tightly on your ankles about shoulder-width apart.
2. Start on either side of the foul line and get into a proper defensive position. Slide to the opposite side of the line. Keep the tube tight as you slide across the lane. This will force you to concentrate on keeping the tube tight and not bringing your feet together.
3. Return to the other side using the same technique. To build your conditioning and strength, do this drill for 10 minutes.

MAGIC TIPS

Do this drill slowly so that you can feel the pull of the tube on your legs.

Half-Court Shuffle and Slide

PURPOSE

To work on several aspects of player-to-player defense and conditioning.

PROCEDURE

1. Start under the basket and face the baseline. Be sure you're in the proper defensive position. Shuffle backward to the middle of the foul line.
2. Slide right until you reach the sideline.
3. Shuffle backward to half-court.
4. Slide across half-court to the opposite side. Turn around.
5. Shuffle backward to the foul line extended.
6. Slide across to the foul line and finish the drill by shuffling backward until you are out of bounds.
7. Do this drill continuously for 5 minutes.

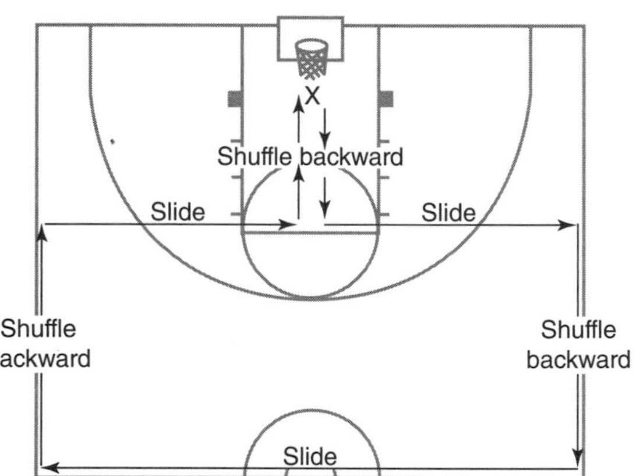

LADY MAGIC TIPS

- Use the proper stance; don't cross your feet. Stay balanced.
- Keep your hands in the passing lane. Keep your head up and straight.

Block-to-Block Medicine Ball

PURPOSE

To condition and develop your strength and quickness when sliding in either direction.

PROCEDURE

1. Start at the left foul-lane block with a medicine ball. Face the sideline in the proper defensive position. Pick up the medicine ball, holding it waist high.
2. Slide left until you reach the foul line. Put the ball down and quickly slide to the right and back to the block without the ball.
3. Touch the block with your outside hand and slide back to the medicine ball. Pick it up and slide across the foul line, facing half-court.

4. When you reach the opposite lane line, put the ball down and slide right, moving back across the foul line until you reach the lane line. Touch it with your outside hand.
5. Then, slide back the other way to the medicine ball. Pick it up and slide down the lane line, facing the sideline. When you reach the low block, put the ball down and slide back to the right, touching the foul line and then sliding back to the ball.
6. Do this drill six times, three in each direction.

LADY MAGIC TIPS

- Stay low and balanced. You will have more speed and quickness.
- Place the medicine ball on the court. Don't drop it or throw it.
- Work hard on the change of direction once you have put the medicine ball down.

Lane Slide and Closeout Drill

PURPOSE

To work on various types of slides and to practice being ready to guard the shooter. When on defense, you often have to slide to stay with your opponent. Sometimes, you have to slide and then quickly close out, aggressively pursuing your opponent while staying balanced. Without lunging or losing balance, you need to close out (sprint) under control and be ready to guard the shooter.

PROCEDURE

1. Start under the basket on the left side, facing the foul line. Close out to the foul line with one hand up to the imaginary shooter and one hand in the passing lane. As you approach the foul line, start to slow down. Touch the foul lane with your foot and backpedal to the baseline with your hands above your head.
2. Again, close out to the foul line. This time, pivot (turn) and sprint to the backboard. As you approach it, touch the backboard with two hands if you can. (If not, touch the net.)
3. Once more, close out to the foul line, sprinting up the foul lane. Then perform the retreat step and diagonal slide, back and forth, across the lane to the baseline.
4. Repeat this drill three times, with 60 seconds of rest between each set.

LADY MAGIC TIPS

- Stay low on your slides. Don't cross your feet.
- As you get ready to close out, lower yourself and stay balanced. Don't lunge and get beat. Closeout means containment.
- This is a great conditioner. It will pay off.

SPEED AND QUICKNESS DRILLS

Good defense starts with foot speed, quickness, and knowledge of angles. These drills will condition you to improve your defense.

Defensive Turns

PURPOSE

To improve your foot speed, anticipation, and quickness. This drill will be easier if you have good conditioning and if you keep your feet moving, not planted. It takes energy to stop and start.

PROCEDURE

1. Start out in the proper defensive stance. Run in place, stutter-stepping as fast as you can. Do a one-quarter turn to the right and then return quickly to your starting point. Do this for 30 seconds. Rest for 30 seconds.
2. With the same stance, stutter-step your feet once more. Do a one-half turn to the right and then return quickly to your starting point. Do this for 30 seconds. Rest for 30 seconds.
3. Do the same drill, but with three-quarter turns. Do this for 30 seconds. Rest for 30 seconds.
4. Repeat, but with full turns. Do this for 30 seconds. Rest for 30 seconds.
5. After you have completed all four turns, take a 1-minute rest and then repeat all four turns to the left side.

LADY MAGIC TIPS

- You need to keep your feet moving quickly. Keep your head and arms up, with your thumbs pointing to your shoulders. You are using your legs, not your arms, to turn.
- You should do as many turns as you can in 30 seconds.
- On the half, three-quarter, and full turns, you really need to explode and almost jump around in place. Then jump back just as quickly.
- This is a great drill for developing quick reaction and explosiveness in different directions.

Rapid-Fire Foot Drill With Jab Fake

PURPOSE

To work on playing good, solid defense on the ball by keeping your feet constantly moving up and down, like pistons; to learn to attack, jab at the ball handler, and cause her to react; to practice applying pressure and killing the ball handler's dribble.

PROCEDURE

1. Start out in a proper defensive position. Quickly move your legs up and down in a stutter or rapid-fire motion.
2. As you are doing this drill for 30 seconds, jab four or five times at the imaginary ball handler, alternating with your right and left hand.
3. Then, quickly return to your rapid-fire stance and footwork.
4. Do three sets, each 30 seconds long. Rest for 30 seconds. Repeat.

LADY MAGIC TIPS

- Stay low and keep pumping your legs.
- Stay on the balls of your feet, with your arms up by your sides for balance.
- Attack quickly with your jab fake. This should be done with your right hand and right foot, or with your left hand and left foot.

Line Jump

PURPOSE

To increase foot speed and quickness in front-to-back and side-to-side jumping.

PROCEDURE

1. While facing the baseline, stand next to the sideline (or any line). Keep your arms out at your sides for balance. Jump from side to side, clearing the line completely. Jump for 30 seconds. Rest for 30 seconds.
2. While facing the baseline, stand behind the half-court line (or any line). Jump over the line and back, clearing the line completely. Jump for 30 seconds. Rest for 30 seconds.
3. See how many jumps you can do in 30 seconds. Record the number and use that figure to improve your speed and quickness. Complete three sets of 30 seconds each. Rest for 30 seconds.

LADY MAGIC TIPS

- Slightly flex your knees. Keep your arms out and at your sides for balance and momentum.
- Stay on the balls of your feet as you hit the floor. Explode in the opposite direction.

Wing Denial Drill

PURPOSE

To learn to play tight denial defense and to see the ball and the player you are guarding without getting beat. Like anything else, this takes practice.

PROCEDURE

1. Start on the left low block, in a proper denial stance, with your outside (left) arm in the passing lane. Keep your head looking forward, seeing the ball and your imaginary opponent. Keep your knees slightly flexed, and keep your inside arm out in the passing lane behind you. By having that arm out, you look bigger and the space around you looks smaller.
2. Using a fencing step, slide to the wing area as fast and as balanced as you can. When you get to the foul line extended, quickly use your retreat step to return to the left low block, maintaining the same form. Try not to cross your feet when sliding. Slide to the wing and back five times.
3. As you come back to the lane, quickly open to the imaginary ball when your inside foot hits the painted area (low block).
4. Next, go through the lane and hit the opposite block with your inside foot. Pivot and then slide as you deny out to the foul line extended. Go up and back five times.
5. Complete three sets. Take a 60-second rest between each. Repeat.

LADY MAGIC TIPS

- Maintain a good angle while denying to the wing. Your arm should be in the passing lane and should be active to discourage the pass.
- As you get to the wing, stay low and balanced. Don't lunge at the ball. Contain.
- Use a retreat step. Try not to cross your feet.
- In the lane, never lose track of your player. Feel her behind you as you move across the lane.
- Pivot quickly and deny the other side. Work hard to react and explode up and back.

Deny Drill

PURPOSE

To work on playing denial defense on the wing, concentrating on keeping your arms up at all times, and seeing the ball and your opponent. This drill is also good for conditioning.

PROCEDURE

1. Use lightweight dumbbells; the weight should depend on how big or strong you are (it could be 2, 4, 6, 8, or 10 pounds). One dumbbell will be on the block, one at the foul line extended, and one in your hand. Start on the low block in the proper denial position. See the ball and your imaginary opponent. Your outside arm is out in the passing lane with a dumbbell in that hand.
2. Slide to the wing area, put down your dumbbell, and pick up the one on the floor.
3. Slide two or three steps back and open quickly by pivoting on your left leg as if you are protecting against the backdoor cut. Then, slide to the low block.
4. Put your dumbbell down and pick up the one on the block.
5. Repeat the denial drill for 30 seconds. Rest for 30 seconds. Do two sets, one on each side.

LADY MAGIC TIPS

- Stay low and balanced. Bend your knees as you put the dumbbell down. Don't bend at your waist.
- See the whole court by using your peripheral vision. Don't cross your feet.
- Have your elbow slightly bent to take pressure off the joint.
- Remember to keep your palm to the ball—your thumbs are down when holding the dumbbell.

Additional Defensive Drills

These drills round out your defensive training by working on upper- and lower-body quickness and strength. They will also help you improve your full-court defensive skills.

Boxing Drill

PURPOSE

To work on hand speed and endurance. This drill is more difficult than it looks or sounds.

PROCEDURE

1. Place boxing gloves on both hands and shadowbox for 2 minutes without dropping your hands below shoulder height. Eventually, your arms will start getting tired. At this point, concentrate and focus on conditioning and hand speed.
2. Rest for 2 minutes. Do three sets of 2 minutes each. When you take the gloves off, you'll be surprised by how light and fast your hands feel.

LADY MAGIC TIPS

- Be quick and have fun.
- Remember that intensity and imagination are keys to this drill.

Vertical Jump (Tracking)

PURPOSE

To work on a takeoff with one foot or two.

PROCEDURE

1. Go to any wall and measure how high you can touch while standing straight up and reaching your hands high above your head. Mark it or have someone else mark it.
2. Do the same as you jump as high as you can off two feet. Use two hands to touch the wall. Mark it.
3. Standing sideways next to the wall, jump as high as you can again using two feet. This time, use your inside hand to touch the wall. Mark it.
4. Now you have starting points, and you will be able to track your improvement. Measure your jumping every few weeks.

LADY MAGIC TIPS

- On all jumps, flex your knees at 60- to 90-degree angles depending on your leg strength. Explode up, not out. Use your arms to create more upward power.
- Be positive and always give your best effort.
- Jump quickly.
- Remember, you are working on a gradual, steady improvement of two feet.

One-on-One (Full Court—Individually)

PURPOSE

To improve your skills in the full court.

PROCEDURE

1. Playing by yourself, start at the baseline, directly under the bucket. Use your imagination. Pretend that you're guarding a player in the backcourt. Turn the imaginary ball handler a minimum of three times, sliding at an angle to a spot. Then, overplay the ball and slide again at an angle to the opposite side.
2. As the ball handler gets to half-court, force her to one side of the floor. Now overplay slightly; don't allow the ball to reverse.
3. As you funnel the ball to near the key area, the ball handler passes to the wing. You must jump to the ball and make the ball handler cut behind you as you deny any possible pass.
4. If the passer stays and doesn't cut, you need to deny the pass back to her from the wing.
5. Slide to the baseline, turn around, and repeat the drill.
6. Shoot 10 foul shots while resting.
7. Repeat three sets (up and back is one set). Take a total of 30 foul shots.

LADY MAGIC TIPS

- Use your imagination. You've been on the court before, dogging the ball handler. Work her, turn her.
- Move your feet quickly. Don't cross them. Turn them.
- Stay low and balanced. Keep your hands active as if you're hawking the ball.
- Once you have the ball over to one side of the floor, keep it there.
- On all passes to the wing, jump to the ball and deny any return pass to the guard.
- Be aggressive and work hard.

Horizontal Rope

PURPOSE

To help you develop leg strength and quickness. This drill will also improve your vertical jump and balance.

PROCEDURE

1. Have a 12-inch (30.5 cm) rope connected to two chairs about 2 feet (61 cm) apart. The rope should be about 6 inches (15.2 cm) above the ground. As you improve, raise the height of the rope to a maximum of 12 inches.
2. Jump back and forth with both feet for 30 seconds. Rest for 30 seconds. Repeat three sets for 30 seconds each. Take 10 foul shots.
3. Stand on the side of the rope. Jump from side to side for 30 seconds. Rest for 30 seconds. Repeat three times for 30 seconds each. Take 10 foul shots.

LADY MAGIC TIPS

- Keep your arms at your sides for balance, but use them to swing upward for momentum as you jump.
- Bring your knees up high to clear the rope.
- Hit the soles of your feet and explode in the opposite direction.
- Keep your head straight and work on your focus and concentration.

Net Touch off One Leg

PURPOSE

To work on your explosiveness and maximum potential; to steadily increase your vertical leap.

PROCEDURE

1. Start at the foul line. Sprint to the left side of the basket. As you approach the basket, leap off your left leg. Use your left hand to touch the net, rim, or backboard (whichever you can touch) on the left side.
2. Sprint back to the foul line (the right side of the foul line). Then turn, sprint to the right side of the basket, and jump as high as you can off your right leg, using your right hand to touch the net, rim, or backboard on the right side.
3. Do five backboard touches on each side. Shoot 10 foul shots while you are resting. Repeat three sets—30 jumps total, 30 foul shots.

LADY MAGIC TIPS

- As you approach the backboard, jump up, not out.
- Dip your knees and drive up as quickly as you can, extending your ankles, knees, and hips.
- Remember, you must have the attitude to want to touch the rim, backboard, or net. Go for it.
- Use your arms for balance and momentum. Drive them upward as you jump.

Two-Hand Alternate Touch

PURPOSE

To work on developing your strength, speed, and endurance; to learn to keep your hands up so you will build arm and shoulder strength.

PROCEDURE

1. Standing under the rim, backboard, or net—whichever is appropriate—jump as high as you can. First, use your left hand to touch the net. Then, go right back up with your right hand.
2. Alternate touches, five on each side. Take 10 foul shots while resting. Repeat for a total of 30 touches and 30 foul shots.

LADY MAGIC TIPS

- Flex your knees at a 60- to 90-degree angle, according to your leg strength.
- Extend your lead arm as fast and as high as possible.
- Use your opposite leg to help. Drive up high to your target.
- Come down on the balls of your feet.
- As you land, be ready to use your momentum to explode back up with the other hand.

SUMMARY

There is no greater challenge on the court than being a defensive stopper. In this chapter, we covered several areas that can help you become one of those stoppers:

- Defensive positioning: knees, arms, hands, head, and eyes
- Communication and footwork
- Defensive tips for improvement
- The advantages and weaknesses of player-to-player defense
- Knowing how to overplay the pass, play off the ball, and deny the wing (one pass away)
- Getting through screens, knowing when to switch, and guarding the post player
- Defensive drills that can be used to improve overall defense

chapter

10

Owning the Boards

The importance of rebounding is reflected in this very profound statement: "The completion of defense is rebounding." Rebounding is one of the greatest tests of determination, desire, and fundamentals. It doesn't matter if you are 6-foot-5 or 5-foot-5; proper technique enables you to box out much taller players. If you keep your opponents off the ball, they won't get easy put-backs or fast-break chances. In other words, if you can outrebound the other team, you have a chance to win the game.

In basketball games at every level, one of the biggest factors in determining the outcome is which team wins the battle of the boards. The team that does often controls the game. No team has ever hit all of its shots in a game. That's why defensive rebounding is such a major part of the game. Rebounding is rewarding, and it will help your team win.

KEYS TO REBOUNDING

The three keys to rebounding are positioning, boxing out, and using your leverage. Don't be afraid to "hit" your opponent—to make contact with her (your buttocks to her knees). Don't hesitate to, in basketball slang, "lay a body" on someone under the boards while you are jockeying for position. Let your opponent know that this is your area and your rebound.

Positioning

Work hard to keep your body between the opposing player and the basket. Keep this position as you contest the shot, putting a hand in the shooter's face to distract her (figure 10.1*a*, on page 220). If she is right-handed, put your left hand up. If she's a lefty, your right hand goes up. You never want to cross your body; this will cause you to be off balance and out of position. After the shot, maintain your position between your opponent and the basket by turning and pivoting. Create some contact so you feel where

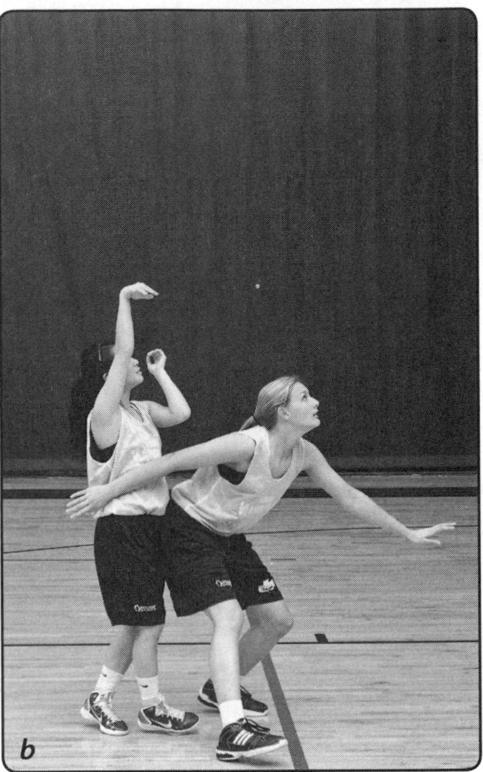

Figure 10.1 Contesting the shot.

that player is (figure 10.1*b*). Box her out for 2 or 3 seconds (we'll talk about this next). Then, go for the rebound and keep her behind you. Be physical and aggressive on both boards. Jumping ability is important, but not more important than good positioning.

Boxing Out

If you are on defense, you should have the advantage because of your rebounding position. Defensive rebounding means boxing (or blocking) out. This is accomplished properly when the defensive rebounder uses a front or reverse pivot to box out a player. There must be contact. After pivoting, use your rear end to make contact with your opponent(figure 10.2*a*), which prevents her from going forward to rebound the ball. Move quickly to release from the contact and go to the ball (figure 10.2*b*).

In player-to-player defense, each player is responsible for boxing out the person she is guarding. In a zone, players are responsible for boxing out the offensive player in a specific area. Remember to position yourself between the offensive player and the basket. Don't let players push you too far under the basket. This will take you out of good rebounding position.

Figure 10.2 Boxing out on the shot.

When covering a shooter after a long-range shot, you should turn and follow the shot with your eyes. Pivot and feel where the shooter is. Once you have boxed her out, go for the rebound. If you rebound too quickly, the shooter can go around you without any contact. Also, on outside shots, if the rebound comes out long and you have rushed to the basket too quickly, the ball can carom over your head.

If you're facing a great offensive rebounder, forget about the rebound. Turn around and guard her, playing her numbers to numbers to keep her off the board.

Using Leverage

To have leverage, you must get low and have good balance. Your feet should be shoulder-width apart. Assume a "sitting" position, and box out your opponent at her knees. This allows you to be quicker and to explode to the basket, or it enables you to continue boxing out your opponent. You can avoid being pushed out of your rebounding position by staying low. The lower you are, the better.

Checkpoints

- ☑ Pursue the ball. Have determination and desire. Great rebounders think that every miss is their rebound.
- ☑ Box out. Establish your ground and get position quickly. Getting position takes hard work and anticipation. Have your hands ready. Know the angles and percentages from where shots are taken. Positioning is a function of savvy and hard work. Don't let players push you too far under the hoop.
- ☑ Have balance and be big. Keep your knees flexed, arms out, and feet shoulder-width apart. Putting your rear end out creates space. Someone might be called for going over your back because of this.
- ☑ Remember that timing is everything. If you jump for the rebound and the ball is still hitting the rim, all your hard work won't pay off.
- ☑ Work on having good hands. Be strong and relaxed. Fingertip control can help you get a rebound that you didn't think you could get. Great rebounders can give themselves a second chance by tipping the ball to an open area.
- ☑ Use everything you have to protect the ball. That's why we have elbows, knees, and bodies. Most important, when you do grab the ball, keep it high. Don't bring it down for opponents to steal. Be aware that players will be slapping at it.
- ☑ Be strong and aggressive. This is a great combination. Great rebounders have a special desire and determination. They have an attitude and mental toughness. If you're going to rebound, come strong into the paint or don't come at all.

REBOUNDING FUNDAMENTALS

Becoming a good rebounder requires you to react in many ways before and after the shot. In this section, we briefly look at some ways to do this. We also give you some pointers on offensive rebounding (including tip-ins) and rebounding foul shots.

Reading the Shooter's Shot

Reading a shot is a matter of judgment. Is the shot going to fall short or go long? Did the shooter have good rotation on the ball? If the shot is a three-pointer, the rebound should be longer. If the shot is from the corner, chances are it will rebound to the weak side. Observing a shot can help you get in the correct area for the rebound. You can anticipate where the rebound might go, and you can start to establish your position under the basket or start to maneuver from the perimeter.

Rebounding Foul Shots

To prevent the offense from scoring an easy basket, the defense must get the rebound off a foul shot. The defense has inside position on both sides of the basket. Those defenders must move to box out the offensive players who occupy the second position on each side. The third player (defensive spot) on one side should box out the fourth spot (offensive player), while the other third-spot defensive player boxes out the shooter. You should communicate with your teammates regarding which player or area you are boxing out.

Offensive Rebounding

Offensive rebounding is an often overlooked aspect of basketball. With all the work on offensive and defensive schemes, not enough attention is paid to being able to get position for second and third shots off the offensive glass.

When you or your teammates shoot the ball and miss, and the ball comes off the rim just slightly in one direction or another, you should try to tip the ball back to the basket. If successful, you'll not only get the field goal, but you'll be credited with a rebound as well.

Having good rebounding position will definitely help when you are trying to tip the ball in. Control is important if you are going to be successful. Jump as high as you can. Your knees, hips, and ankles should be flexed. Your hands must be up and ready to tip the ball. The quicker you get to the ball, the better your chances of beating your opponent to it and getting a clean chance to tip it in. Cradle the ball on your fingertips and tap it back with control. Make sure your fingers are flexed slightly. This will eliminate the potential for jammed fingers.

Otherwise, when shots are missed, this is a perfect time—especially if you play close to the basket—to pick up easy points on hustle and desire. Keeping the following four points in mind will help you recognize where missed shots may fall:

1. Perimeter shots usually rebound long because the ball comes off the rim with more power.
2. Corner shots tend to rebound long to the weak side.
3. Bank shots usually rebound closer to the basket.
4. You must follow your own shot. You should have a feel for how it came off your hand. Were you too strong? Did you have good rotation? Were your arc and follow-through high enough?

Be active and get around the person boxing you out.

REBOUNDING DRILLS

Rebounding is the part of the game that allows you to win or lose. Good rebounders are never stationary. They are always moving and closing in on the basket, and they are aggressive on both ends of the court.

Superman

PURPOSE

To help you develop aggressiveness and desire. This drill will also improve your jumping ability and endurance. The drill enables you to work on footwork, passing, catching, rebounding, and protecting the rebound.

PROCEDURE

1. Start by standing on the block outside the foul lane. Face the basket.
2. Toss the ball over the rim to the opposite side of the backboard. The pass needs to be a two-hand chest pass; you should aim high over the backboard. Then go get the ball. Be quick and explosive.
3. Rebound the ball with authority using two hands. Take one step in the lane and catch the ball outside the lane on the other side. Start again outside the lane, tossing the ball to the side you started on.
4. Do this drill for 30 seconds. Be intense. Rest for 1 minute. Then go for another 30 seconds, followed again by a 1-minute rest period. Complete three sets with a 1-minute rest after each. Shoot 10 foul shots during each rest period.

LADY MAGIC TIPS

- Maintain balance. Land on the balls of your feet, with your elbows out.
- Keep your head up. Look at the ball. Keep your hands up high, and be ready to rebound.

Rebound and Power Move

PURPOSE

To increase your endurance and strength while you practice using pump fakes to draw fouls and complete the play off a rebound. A solid rebounder never changes her mental attitude and desire to be aggressive.

PROCEDURE

1. Begin this drill by facing the basket. Start in front of the backboard on the right side. Hold the ball over your head with both hands. Jump five times with the ball in this position, touching the backboard if you can.

2. On your last jump, pull the ball down and make a hard ball fake. Make it believable. Then, go up strong for a power move off both feet. Shoot the ball with two hands.
3. Do the same drill on the left side. Remember to jump quickly and explode to the backboard. Be balanced and land on the balls of your feet.
4. Complete two sets of 10 on each side. Rest for 2 minutes between each set. Shoot 10 foul shots while resting each time.

LADY MAGIC TIPS

- There's no substitute for being fierce and aggressive.
- When you have good position, balance is important. On rebounds, you are going to be hammered. Stay strong and have a solid base.
- You need to go up strong after the ball fake. Don't anticipate the foul; finish strong.

Offensive Rebounding Against Pressure

PURPOSE

To work on rebounding and scoring when you know that there will be pressure from a defender.

PROCEDURE

1. Starting at the foul line, toss the ball underhand to the left side of the backboard using your left hand. Explode to the ball and grab the rebound with both hands. Perform a pump fake, then make the layup.
2. Alternate sides. Go back to the foul line and toss the ball off the right side with your right hand. Get the rebound with two hands and make a pump fake. Then make your layup.
3. Be intense. Hustle back after each shot. Make five from the left side and five from the right. Repeat this three times. Take a 1-minute rest between sets.

LADY MAGIC TIPS

- Make sure you are balanced as you grab the rebound.
- Pump-fake violently as if you are faking the defense.

Tip Drill

PURPOSE

To work on tipping the ball on the rebound. Tipping the ball is a great way to gain control of the rebound—maybe not on the first attempt, but on the second or third. In games, you will sometimes be able to tip the ball in cleanly or tip it to yourself or a teammate.

PROCEDURE

1. Start at the foul line. Toss the ball underhand off the right side of the backboard with your right hand. Tip the ball with one hand to an open area on the same side. Then, grab the rebounded tip and sprint back to the foul line.
2. Now, toss the ball off the left side with your left hand. Tip the ball with one hand to an open area on the left side.
3. Hustle back to the foul line after you rebound each tip. Tip five times on each side. Repeat three times. Take a 1-minute rest between sets.

LADY MAGIC TIPS

- Tip the ball to an open area. Go get it.
- Be aggressive.

SUMMARY

Rebounding can be one of the most challenging skills to learn and to execute effectively. It takes a player who is willing to hustle and get positioning. To own the boards, a player must have heart and desire. This chapter took you through these areas:

- Positioning, boxing out, and using leverage
- Defensive and offensive rebounding
- Checkpoints for rebounding
- Tip-ins, reading the shooter's shot, and anticipation
- Rebounding drills

chapter

11

Becoming the Complete Player

To get to the level of being great, you must make the game your passion. You must devote endless hours, days, and years to developing your game, both mentally and physically. Being able to identify your own strengths and weaknesses is very important. Coaches are looking for the all-purpose player who can perform at a moment's notice in a variety of roles. Three areas of the game can spell out a winner:

- Having a love for the game
- Being in great physical condition
- Accepting all challenges

Most rosters have as many as 15 players—all wanting their chance. All of these players are important, and each plays a role in the team's success. That's why you must blend your skills with those of your teammates to better your team.

If you happen to be the standout on your team, you should make the commitment to lead by example. Set the tone for each practice and game. If you're not the star but have worked hard enough to be one of the starting five, you've earned your position. Make sure you keep it by hustling and pushing yourself to be the best team player you can be. If you are coming off the bench, that's fine. All players should watch games on TV and study the teams that play well. Emulate the players you love and try to do their moves. When I was younger, I watched Dr. J and tried his moves.

In this chapter, we discuss a variety of issues that pertain to your growth as a basketball player. This information will provide you with the foundation you need to blend your skills with those of your teammates in order to become the most complete player you can be. Let's begin by looking at 10 steps that can help you achieve and handle the success that will come with your hard work and dedication.

10 Steps to Stardom

1. ***Competitive greatness:*** Always compete. This requires having the proper mental attitude. You need to have patience, faith, determination, and fight.
2. ***Coachability:*** Be hardworking, loyal, and enthusiastic. Listen well. Have the ability to adapt to different systems. Be a leader.
3. ***Skill development:*** Have a will to work at the basics, giving attention to all details. Strive for perfection. Use repetition to achieve success.
4. ***Conditioning:*** Adopt the proper mental, physical, and emotional training habits. This also includes the proper diet, prevention of injuries, and the ability to take on all challenges.
5. ***Confidence:*** Lead by example. Respect all, fear no one.
6. ***Practice habits:*** Be the first one on the court and the last to leave. Be cooperative, have discipline, be alert, and have enthusiasm and team spirit.
7. ***Loyalty:*** Be loyal not only to yourself, but also to your school, coaches, and teammates. There's nothing more important than this.
8. ***Goal setting:*** Plan your improvement. Achieve each level of your goals, little by little, until you reach where you want to be.
9. ***Ambition:*** Have the confidence and desire to be the best. Work hard. Be better than others. Make your dreams a reality.
10. ***Being a good sport:*** Show respect, integrity, and good judgment in how you treat teammates, opponents, coaches, and officials. Have self-control.

PRACTICE, PRACTICE, PRACTICE

Obviously, to be a solid basketball player, you must practice. Taking a positive approach to practice, your teammates, and your coaches is necessary right from the start. Never say the dreaded words "I can't." Always say "I'll strive."

Other players can't give you confidence. They can encourage you, but you're the only one who knows if you have put in the hard work. When you have been dedicated to your work on the court, being self-confident is much easier!

Self-confidence creates enthusiasm, and you play with an attitude. Attitude is what builds winners. Have you ever noticed that the great ones always come through? They make things happen instead of waiting for things to happen. It's called producing results. Results start in practice.

I have six rules that apply to practice on the court. If these principles could be used to describe you and your team, you're on your way.

1. Self-confidence comes from experiencing success. Winning builds an attitude and belief that you can and will always win.

2. Desire means focusing on self-improvement, welcoming all challenges, and having a will to do what it takes to win.
3. Leadership is a quality you earn from your teammates. If you show you can lead, others will follow.
4. Aggressiveness means being tough, physical, and assertive. Your actions will force others to play hard.
5. Determination is a special characteristic. It means you want to succeed. You don't accept defeat. You always strive to be better.
6. Responsibility is being accountable. You don't point fingers.

Preparing for Practice

Look forward to practice. This is where questions will be answered and where your knowledge and skills will be developed. You need a proper mental attitude before you even walk into the gym. Be competitive and focused. If you don't understand something, ask questions. You will be more open to trying things your coach's way if you understand what's expected. Respect the older players. Learn from someone you respect as a good role model.

I always used practice to challenge myself and to work on my weaknesses: my left hand and outside shot. Being good wasn't enough; I had an insatiable appetite to be the best.

Your practices have been well planned by your coaches. You have a lot to learn in a short amount of time. The most important thing is being organized and getting from drill to drill, while making sure you give your best effort each time.

Start thinking about how you want to improve during these sessions. Is there a teammate who is difficult to guard or an offense you don't quite understand? Remember, preparation and mental readiness can help you physically. I was always the first player in the gym. Get to practice early enough to get taped, warm up, stretch, shoot, and work on a few weaknesses.

Ready, Let's Go

When the whistle blows, you should sprint to your coach to show that you're eager and ready to get started. Most often, the beginning of practice is running—not at full speed, but to loosen up—followed by stretching. Getting loose is important. The last thing you want is to pull a muscle going through a three-person weave. You really can prevent annoying, nagging injuries.

Have Fun, but Stay Tough

Even though you are working hard and concentrating, you can still have a good time. Talk, laugh, have fun, and enjoy being with your teammates and coaches. Help keep practices loose and spirited. Never lose sight that basketball is only a game. And if you are working hard, concentrating, and staying relaxed, you will be able to give your best effort. If you're unhappy or if you're fighting with your teammates, this will take away from your ability to give your best effort.

Keep in mind, however, that even though you're having fun, you still must compete with your teammates. Be tough physically and strong mentally. Occasionally, teammates will take it easy against one another because they don't want to get hurt or make a teammate look bad. That's very nice, but these teammates are not making each other better. Teammates should challenge each other to the best of their ability. They should make each other work hard and play hard. This is the only way to improve.

Push your teammates to be better. Don't expect anything less. At times, the action can get so physical that tempers or emotions flare. So be it. It's part of the game. The most important thing is not to carry a grudge off the court. If you get knocked down or picked too hard, deal with it in practice. Don't take it off the court and divide your team. This will cause more problems than you can imagine.

Ask Questions, Then Listen Up

We all have questions during practices or games. Understanding your coach's system is very important. If you are not sure about something, ask the coach. It could make the difference in whether you and your team succeed or fall short.

When your coach is talking or a teammate has asked a question, you should listen! You may have had the same question but didn't ask. If you listen, you might even be able to follow up with another thought that could help someone else on the team understand. And most of all, remember that it's disrespectful to talk when someone else is talking.

Set Minigoals

Practices can seem as if they go on for an eternity, so you should break them down in your mind. Here's an example: *Just 11 practices until the first preseason scrimmage. Then, just 6 practices until we tip it off for the season opener.* In addition, you should establish minigoals within each practice: *I'll work to my maximum effort in the first drill. Then, I'll rest.* While resting after that drill is finished, think, *I'll give the same effort and intensity in this next drill.* You'll get the most out of each aspect of practice if you break things down and concentrate on every part. Practices will also move quickly. It's difficult when you look at 2 hours and think, *Man, I've got to concentrate for* that *long?* If your concentration is in short, snappy bursts, practice can be fun, and you will be able to give it your all.

PLACES TO PLAY

Today, young players have many opportunities to refine their game. How much you practice and play is entirely up to you. Don't limit yourself to playing only when your team officially opens practice. Play as much as possible, and play year-round. When the weather is nice during the summer, you'll find numerous opportunities for practicing. In this section, we talk about some places to play.

Summer Practices

Even though coaches can't always be in attendance—because of rules that limit the amount of practice time that coaches can have with their athletes in the off-season (such rules vary depending on where you live)—teams usually have their own open-gym time and coach-free schedule throughout the summer. Use this time with your teammates to your advantage.

Summer Leagues

Somewhere in your town or area, there's a summer league. Usually games take place once or twice a week. You are mixed with players you don't know. The games are competitive, but they take place in a more relaxed environment. These leagues keep you in shape mentally and physically throughout the summertime. You form friendships with players you didn't know. Ask your friends and coaches if they know of any such leagues. If not, call your local YMCA or park and recreation department.

Basketball Camps

Basketball camps are a great investment in your future. They give you the opportunity to compete, to be pushed, and to challenge yourself against different types of players. There is nothing better than drilling on the fundamentals of the game. Improvement comes with repetition. That's exactly what camps offer. They also allow you to compete with kids outside your area to see how good you really are.

I use my camp in Dallas to promote skill development and provide an arena to develop self-esteem and confidence. My campers receive instruction in the following areas:

- Fundamental skills
- Promotion of physical abilities
- Discipline, leadership, and responsibility
- Game situations
- Being good sports
- Drug awareness: "Drug free, the way to be"
- Positive reinforcement, confidence, and self-esteem

Basketball camps can be fun and challenging, not to mention great places to make longtime friends. Plus, many camps across the nation are scouted by college coaches. It's a great opportunity to get noticed.

When selecting a basketball camp, you should think about your objectives. Are you already a good basketball player? Do you want to improve the skills you already have? Or do you want to learn the basic skills of the game? Here are some factors you should consider:

- ***Cost:*** This may or may not be a factor in selecting the camp of your choice.
- ***Staff:*** What coaches or players will be there to teach and demonstrate?
- ***Enrollment:*** Find out the size of the camp and the number of instructors per camper. The ratio should be around 8:1, players to coaches.
- ***Sleep or day camp?*** Do you want to go to a weeklong sleepover camp or a weeklong day camp? Maybe you are more interested in a three-day mini-day camp. You have a variety to choose from.
- ***Individual all-skill camp:*** This is where you can work on both ends of your game, offense and defense.
- ***Individual position camp:*** This type of camp is terrific for working specifically on your position—guard, forward, post.
- ***Recruiting camp:*** You can get a lot of exposure at many of these camps. During the proper time period, coaches can evaluate talent at these camps.
- ***Team camp:*** This is a chance to work together in the off-season. Team camps can be both fun and beneficial to you and your team.
- ***Girls-only or coed camp?*** Both have benefits. Competition versus guys is a good workout and improves your game. However, you can see your overall improvement better when playing against girls.

Playing Against Guys

Before puberty, females and males can play on the same team in any sport, provided they have had the same skill training. In early adolescence, some girls have the ability to physically dominate boys. Therefore, matching by size, weight, and skill rather than by sex may be necessary. The evidence seems to indicate that grouping athletes into competitive categories based on skill level or size—not on sex—provides the greatest opportunity for growth and development for members of both sexes.

However, at this age boys and girls are very sensitive to their perceived inadequacies, such as lack of size or skills. Coaches need to help males and females believe that they can compete—win, lose, or draw—without having their masculinity or femininity questioned.

The physical changes in size and strength manifest themselves at about 11 years in females and 13 years in males. After these ages, males are generally taller and heavier, and they show greater speed, strength, and power because of the influence of testosterone. In many sports, this is not a major problem for females competing with males because skill, agility, and coordination are primary determinants of success.

After puberty, there may be questions about whether females should play against males in contact or collision sports. If you are comfortable playing against males, it is a great way to improve your game. Their size, strength, and quickness will truly challenge you. However, you can challenge them with your court sense, finesse, and fundamental skills. Take advantage of your strengths. Playing against guys can only help you improve. Here are some tips for competing against guys:

- Play hard.
- Use the opportunity to improve.
- Don't ever quit. Concentrate and stay focused.
- Don't back down physically.
- Don't worry about the opponents; worry about your game.
- Be confident.
- Earn the respect of the other players. Once you have, they have helped you improve.

Getting Into Pickup Games

Finding pickup games is easy. Go to the local park, YMCA, or health club. My son, TJ, loves to go to the local recreation center with his friends. Go to your school or play in your driveway. Take a bunch of friends to the park and play. You will usually meet other people there. Mix it up. Try to play against people who push you. Play hard, be physical, and work on areas of your game that you usually neglect in your team's practices. Expand your creativity on the court. Remember, it's street ball. Don't call every little foul. Take it and move on. Here are some tips for getting into a game:

- Take your own ball.
- Yell "Next!"
- If you lose, get to the sign-up board first so you get in the next available game. Whenever I lost, I made a beeline for the board for another chance!
- If you're shooting to see who plays, make it. That way you won't have to rely on being picked.
- When picking teams, pick to win.
- Compete against the best players you can find. This will raise your level of play and make the game more enjoyable.
- Be confident and play hard.

Basketball Tournaments

Every summer, thousands of male and female players of all ages and abilities compete against others of similar age, height, and experience in tournaments. Depending on the event, you might also find three-point shooting competitions or free-throw contests. Three-on-three tournaments, including Hoop It Up and Gus Macker tournaments, are held on an ongoing basis in the summer. Pay attention to announcements in your area to sign up and participate. In addition, you may get an opportunity to raise money for local charities. Most hoop events these days are tied to a charitable component. You have fun playing ball, competing for a T-shirt (yes, a T-shirt!) and pride, and a local charity can benefit. Serve others. That, my friend, is doing things the right way.

GAME TIME

Now it's time for all the hard work and practices you've been through to be put into action. Game time is about results and giving your best effort. What a great feeling it is to run out onto the court for pregame warm-ups, having family, friends, and fans cheer you and your teammates on. You're pumped. Your adrenaline is flowing. You're breaking a sweat in layup lines, getting loose and relaxed. You should also be staying focused.

So many things can affect you during the game. Maybe the outcome has critical implications for postseason play, maybe you're matched up against your archrival, or maybe there are factors surrounding a teammate or coach that cause a lot of external eyes to focus on your game. Whatever the situation, you must concentrate on playing your best and must ignore the hype. Here are some tips that might help you keep your focus before, during, and after the game, even when you are facing special circumstances.

Pregame

Everyone has her own way of preparing for the game. I always wanted to be at my locker early so I could relax and take my time. I would put on a T-shirt and shorts and then go out and shoot around, loosen up, and think about the game and my responsibilities. By arriving early, I was able to do this without a lot of people around. I usually returned to the locker room as my teammates were first arriving for the game.

Usually, coaches want you in the locker room ready to change and get taped 90 minutes before game time. After you get dressed (and taped if necessary), you should warm up your body and stretch a little. Players like to go out to the court and do their own shooting routine in order to get loose and get focused on the upcoming game. In many cases, coaches then put the team through about 20 minutes of player development (what we call PD) before players are left to loosen up, stretch, and focus once more on their own. About 35 minutes before the game, players should be in the locker room waiting for the coach. Remember, it's now time to give the coach your full attention. At this time, all technology should be turned off, and there should be no distractions. This is a nonnegotiable area! Usually, your coach will have matchups and plays listed on the chalkboard. This is the time to think about what your matchup or responsibility will be. Your coach is setting the offense and defense. Concentrate on what's being said. If you have any questions, be sure to ask. Now is the time. This is a very positive moment for you and your teammates and coaches. As a team, you are preparing to do battle with your opponent. If the game plan is carried out and executed, you have a good chance for victory.

After the information is given, it's time to get ready. Some players are loud and some are quiet as they head out of the locker room toward the court. This is a very emotional time, and you should be getting pumped up—high-fiving, talking, and listening to music in the locker room and on the court. Once you hit the court, you should have this incredible desire to meet all challenges. Think about everything your coach said in the locker room. Your coach may have told you that number 10 is your player. She likes to drive, and her weakness is that she can't shoot with her left hand. Think about what that means to you. If you understand your responsibility, you can produce results by running plays correctly, shutting down offenses, and rebounding. That all comes from the constant practices and through communication between you, your coach, and your teammates. Play for today and take it one game at a time.

Halftime

Halftime is a time to reflect on what has happened in the first half. If your team is ahead, try not to be too satisfied. Games can turn around quickly. If you're behind, let your coaches map out what they think has taken place. The stat sheet usually doesn't lie. It will reflect key areas: shooting, rebounding (offensive and defensive), and turnovers. Your coach will give suggestions or make adjustments for the second half. Once you have the information, talk it over with your teammates. Always be positive. Then relax. Stretch. Try not to get stiff. Keep your warm-ups on if you're cool. Then, get back to the court and warm up for the second half. To give your best effort in the game, you must stay focused and have concentration throughout halftime.

Postgame

When the game is over, you want to feel as if you left everything you had on the court. After all your hustle and effort, you should be drained.

Whether you win or lose, after the buzzer sounds, you should shake hands with your opponents and the referees and then head to the locker room. Of course, the mood will reflect whether you won or lost. If you won, enjoy it.

Many times you will learn more about your team and yourself from losses. Losses expose weaknesses. Winning sometimes disguises them. Your coach will probably gather the players in the locker room for his or her final thoughts about the game. After that, you should shower, change, and relax. It's over. There will be another game.

Revenge Isn't Always Sweet

During my freshman year at Old Dominion, our team had a tumultuous relationship with our coach, Pam Parsons. She left after the season and went on to become the head coach at South Carolina. Heading into my junior year, we eyed the South Carolina matchup, which would be played in Columbia.

Old Dominion was 23-0 heading into the game. Our confidence and play were at an all-time high, although our All-American center, Inge Nissen, twisted her ankle and didn't make the trip. Nothing meant more to us than revenge. We'd show her. Have you ever heard of trying too hard? We got spanked by 25 points. Our focus was Coach Parsons, not her team. I had a glorious game—6 for 25 from the floor. To make matters worse, a fight broke out at center court. I think our poor play and the tension of the game got to us. I tried to break up the fight and got tossed from the game. The showers didn't seem like a bad idea at that point. Revenge doesn't mean a lot; just play the game that you prepared for in practice.

Don't Believe the Hype

Hype is for the media, fans, and people selling tickets and merchandise. When two teams play, there's no way around it: Someone is going to win, and someone is going to lose. Keep your focus on what you have to do to win. Never get caught up in trashing your opponent to the media. What you or your teammates think in private is your business. The games are emotional enough. Don't give your opponents extra incentive. It's common for coaches to put up articles in the locker room to get their teams fired up. Don't give anyone more incentive with your words.

The Marquee Matchup

Certain matchups can become part of the hype—star versus star, all-state versus all-state. TV, radio, and newspapers are becoming more involved with covering sports. If you are a great player, an All-American, or a Gatorade Player of the Year, that's great. You will have other great players to compete against. The biggest problem is thinking you have something to prove. Don't fall into that trap. You will prove your point by following the game plan. The most important thing is to give your best effort as a team.

The Big One

The big game can refer to a crosstown rivalry, a game between conference or district rivals to determine which team gets to the next level, or the championship game. In this situation, you need to be relaxed so you can perform at your highest level of play. Again, the media and big crowds seem to change how important a game is. You should stick to your routine. Don't overdo it. Your coaches will help you prepare mentally and physically. Don't put added pressure on yourself. Think of big games as opportunities—ones that other players and schools would love to have. During my senior year in college, the world champion Soviet Union team was touring the states, routinely beating our best collegiate teams by 30 to 40 points. Our arena downtown, Norfolk's Scope arena, was sold out: 10,000 plus for the game. National champs versus world champions. Our coach, Marianne Stanley, told us to relax, play hard, and enjoy the game. We did and loved every minute of it. We were so pumped when the game started. The excitement carried us to a tie game at the half. Unfortunately, foul trouble for me, Inge Nissen, and Anne Donovan—along with a great Soviet attack—led to the world-champion Soviets winning by 10.

Some Simple Advice

At the 1993 women's basketball Final Four in Atlanta, Texas Tech All-American Sheryl Swoopes and I were talking during practice. (I was covering the tournament for CBS radio.) We talked about the pressure of playing in the finals against the other heralded player in the tournament, Ohio State's Katie Smith. I shared a few words of advice with Sheryl: "Remember, Sheryl, it's just another game. Get caught up in the hype and you'll be fighting more opponents than just Ohio State. Katie and Ohio State are great. Don't worry about them. Concentrate on what your job is." I think Sheryl was relaxed. She set an NCAA tournament record—47 points—as Texas Tech beat Ohio State, 84-82, for the NCAA title.

COACHABILITY, ATTITUDE, AND BEHAVIOR

More than anything, you need to respect your coach. Your coach wouldn't be in that position if he or she wasn't qualified for the job. Be coachable. Don't get stuck with being labeled "uncoachable." Many players who aren't as good will get a chance to play if they can be described as follows: "She's very coachable, a team player, and willing to learn."

Being coachable is what I call ART:

A = **Attitude.** Have a willingness to listen and learn. Always give your best effort to show that you're a good sport. Attitude is how you handle yourself in all situations.

Acceptance. Be willing to learn your coach's style and system. Believe in that system.

R = **Respect.** Show respect in a variety of ways: by practicing hard, by listening to your coach's philosophies for the team, and by treating your coach with consideration. Respect also means never talking negatively about your coach or team. Stick up for the team.

T = **Trust.** Know that the things your coach is telling you will lead to improvement as a team and individually.

Team. Remember that winning as a team is more important than achieving individual goals.

Taking criticism. Handle criticism and make it a positive message. Use criticism of your game, practice habits, and attitude to improve your overall performance on and off the court.

Accepting a Role

If you think you're not important because you're a reserve, you're dead wrong. Reserves are vital to a team's success. You provide daily competition for the starters. You push them to be better. You will continue to improve if you see your role as a positive one. You have to be sharp and ready to enter a game at any time. You must know every phase of the game. In addition, by cheering your teammates on, you can give them positive energy. It doesn't matter if you play 1 minute or 25. You have a role to play; do it to the best of your ability. You are essential to your team's success, attitude, and character. Role players make the team a winner. They, above all, ensure the success of a team.

The Bench

Back in 1975, when I was on the Pan-American and Olympic teams, I was a sub, a reserve, a benchwarmer. My pride would frequently get hurt when I didn't play in games. You see, I practiced every day and put in just as many hours of sweat and pain as the others. But my teammates were more experienced and better skilled in many areas. Each night I couldn't wait to get to the next practice. I was going to play hard and get better. My attitude and desire pushed my teammates as well as myself. My competitiveness almost made them want to kill me. No, I wasn't a star, but I can tell you this: Anytime you want to look at my gold medal or Olympic silver medal, I'll share it with you. Being a reserve built my character and incentive. Hard work, desire, and luck did the rest.

Showing Dedication

Coaches are looking for players who have talent, especially physical talent. But they are also looking for players who are hard workers, who love the game of basketball, and who are dedicating themselves to constant improvement. Coaches also try to find players who want to win—players who want to win more than they want to have the highest scoring average. Coaches want players who can make other players on their team better. They want players who display good attitudes and are willing to be positive in order to help teammates. What you say and do to a teammate goes a long way in the overall success of your team.

Coaches also want student-athletes who are willing to work to excel in the classroom. You need to be well balanced in terms of your studies and how you perform on the court.

On-Court Demeanor

Being a good sport counts. These days, negative types of behavior seem to be out of control, such as trash talking, taunting, showboating, and abusing the officials. The game you play should be spirited, and teams should give all out effort. But whatever happened to being a good sport? It's OK to talk and have confidence. You may even use talking as a psychological tactic on the court: "When you guard me, I own the three-point line. Come out at me and I'll take the jumper." Or, "Are you going to guard me or what?" But it shouldn't involve cursing or degrading talk. Remember that this may lead to payback. Chances are someone will be talking trash to you one day. Keep it in the spirit it was intended.

Many players believe that being a good sport relates only to how they treat their teammates. It has to go beyond that. Athletes often don't realize how they behaved in a game until later. Just think for a minute how you want to be treated. If you're guarding a player who blows by and makes a shot, you don't want her to come back in your face, talking trash and taunting you. How would you feel? If you make a great play (or if someone on your team does), you can celebrate; just don't degrade your opponent.

Think about it. If you trash-talk or taunt your opponents, you are likely to get into a fight, which proves nothing. You and your team may receive technical fouls. This could take you out of the game mentally so that you can't perform at your best level. You may even get tossed from the game. If you get thrown out, you are of no help to your team. You've let your teammates down. If you're looking to go to college, coaches will notice your attitude and behavior on the court. Your own coach could also discipline you for this type of behavior.

If you abuse the officials, you're a marked player. When you have a question about a call, you can ask the referees. How you ask the question will determine how you're dealt with. Respect the referees. They often have to make judgment calls, and it's a tough job. Believe me, the calls will even out. How many times have you hacked someone without the ref seeing it? Just because you see fights, trash talking, and showboating on television doesn't mean you have to do it. Be your own person.

Being a Role Model

There's no greater feeling than being respected for how you conduct yourself. Being a role model causes others to look up to you for what you have achieved. Just think of all the positive qualities you can project as a solid role model: being a good sport; being hardworking, reliable, and encouraging; keeping your teammates up; having a good attitude; being responsible, competitive, and trustworthy. Now that's something to strive for.

What makes a good leader? If you apply the following points, you will be a leader or be well on your way to becoming one. A leader is a person who has authority or influence over other people. A leader is

- someone who takes charge,
- someone who is willing to make decisions,
- someone who stands by her words,
- someone who is flexible and willing to accept suggestions from others,
- someone who is consistent and understanding, and
- someone who is hardworking.

Promoting Yourself and Your School

Your coaches will likely encourage you to make yourself available to the media and to the community in which you play. Be positive and personable. When you make an appearance, speak with enthusiasm about your team, your coach, and the prospect for success. Don't underestimate how much this rallying of the community can mean to a team.

Look at the magic that Texas Tech's Sheryl Swoopes created not only with her skills, but also with her personality during her team's championship run in '93. Sheryl was like a magnet, attracting hordes of fans and media. She was accessible, engaging, and warm and humble at the same time. That blend of personality has been a terrific way for Sheryl to promote herself and women's basketball. And who has received more publicity in her college and WNBA career than UConn grad Diana Taurasi? She is a three-time national champion, two-time Olympian, and two-time WNBA champion. She has done a terrific job garnering national attention with her extraordinary skill, winning ways, and infectious personality. Fans have always been drawn to style and game, and Diana has both.

The media can bring your team or program a great deal of exposure. The members of the media have a responsibility to provide news and information to the public. As a player, you should be accessible. Remember, you need to fulfill your responsibilities to the media whether you win or lose. If you don't talk to the media when you lose, why should they want to hear from you when you win? Help make their job easier, and good things can happen.

Many college sport programs have radio and television packages. Even high school games are being carried on cable television. Your sports information office can be invaluable in sharing interesting facts about you. The office can arrange interviews with the media and serve as the liaison. This is proper promotion that allows you and your team to get noticed.

Working Through Problems With Coaches

This is a very important area because there will, undoubtedly, be times when you don't see eye to eye with your coach. Remember, you are playing for your coach in his or her system. Try to be flexible and understanding about what is required of you. Small problems tend to become larger problems when there is a communication breakdown between player and coach. This type of problem can affect not only you and your performance, but the team's performance as well.

Let's say something is bothering you about your coach. The first thing you should do is go talk to the coach. Express your concerns, whether they are related to a personality problem or a problem with your playing. Share your thoughts in an adult manner. This might help your coach understand a problem that he or she didn't know existed. If you keep it to yourself, it can't be solved. The bottom line is that you must try to work out any and all problems in a player–coach relationship. This will definitely help you in all other relationships you have in the future. You should always try to find common ground. Don't assume that coaches know there's a problem. Tell them. If you are not ready to talk to the head coach, one of the assistant coaches would be a good start. The assistant coaches might be able to be a buffer between you and the head coach. They can also share insight into how you should handle a situation. Basically, assistant coaches can help solve a minor problem before it becomes a major one. Rely on their friendship and advice.

Finally, remember that you can make a player–coach relationship work. You might not always agree with your coaches, but no matter what, you should show them the courtesy and respect they deserve. They are there to help make you a better student, athlete, and person.

Working Through Problems With Teammates

Dealing with teammates is similar to dealing with coaches. It can be more difficult because you're working with many personalities.

If you have a problem with someone on your team, you should take her to the side and discuss it. Again, use the same behavior you would want someone to use with you. Try not to embarrass her in front of your other teammates or coaches. Don't fight with her; that would not solve anything and could result in injury to you or her. Express your points, then listen to what she has to say in response. Make some compromises if necessary. Many times the problem is a simple misunderstanding between two people. The main thing is to work it out before it disrupts the focus of the team. You're never going to agree with everyone; it's a matter of how you choose to handle your relationships with others.

A rift between two teammates can split a team. Friends of the two teammates have a natural tendency to take sides. If you are not involved in the problem, stay out of it. Working on what you have to do for the team is more important than getting in the middle of another person's situation.

BEING RECRUITED

Every athlete has her own story of how she was recruited—what she looked for and what her objectives were in selecting a school. Let me tell you, when you are 16 or 17 years old, it is tough to make a decision that will affect you for the rest of your life.

With so many choices available, this has become a tough and tedious process. You need to research all areas of each university that you might be interested in. You are determining where you will spend the next 4 or 5 years of your life. You may be attending a local college or one that is far away from friends and family. Being recruited can be very exciting and can be a confidence builder, but it can also be frightening—frightening because you have to make such an important decision, usually with guidance only from coaches and family.

Getting Ready for Recruiting

Very strict rules exist regarding recruitment, allowing college coaches to contact players only in specific ways at specific times of the year. During *dead periods,* college coaches must not have any in-person contact with prospective players or their parents whatsoever. (Note, however, that coaches may contact a prospective athlete who is enrolled in the college's summer term and has signed a National Letter of Intent or other written commitment to attend the college.) However, coaches may write or call. During *quiet periods,* college coaches cannot watch players practice or play. They also cannot speak in person with any prospective players or their parents off their college campus. However, they may again write or call any prospective players. During *evaluation periods,* college coaches can watch prospective players play, but they cannot speak to them in person. Again, though, they may write or call the players, and the players may visit their campus. Finally, during *contact periods,* college coaches can have person-to-person contact with prospective players and their parents both on and off their campus. In addition, coaches may visit the prospective players' high schools and watch them play. They may also write or call any prospective players.

In women's basketball, a recruiting-person day is defined as a single coach engaged in a one-day (12:01 a.m. to midnight) off-campus recruiting activity of a prospective student-athlete, including a prospective student-athlete who has signed a National Letter of Intent (or the institution's written offer of admission or financial aid). Two coaches engaged in recruiting activities on the same day must use 2 recruiting-person days. The coaching staff must not use more than 100 recruiting-person days during the contact and evaluation periods for the academic year.

Recently, the NCAA has also set up rules regarding social media. Division I and II rules do not allow coaches to contact prospective athletes through any form of social media, including text messaging. Rules do allow coaches to set up social media pages; however, they cannot use such outlets to directly contact recruits, nor can they discuss possible recruits on them. For more information on recruiting rules and regulations, visit www.ncaa.org.

Your high school coach has an important role in the recruiting process. The high school coach is the direct link to the college coach. If you are an athlete who wants to play basketball in college, your high school coach has a responsibility to become familiar with the Xs and Os of recruiting. The coach will have to put in extra time, paperwork, and effort in selling you, the athlete. But the benefits for your coach, the community, the school, and you are worth the effort.

During the summer, your coach should help you get involved in a local summer league or an AAU team. Many teams also hold team open gyms or camps so the players can work on their teamwork, timing, and friendships. I like the idea of keeping teams together so they can build trust and can compete together. Summer is also the time for your coach to talk to you about the NCAA Clearinghouse and make sure you have started the process. The NCAA requires all seniors to complete an NCAA Initial-Eligibility Clearinghouse form. Most high school counselors have these packets in their offices. If you have any questions about the certification process, contact the NCAA Clearinghouse at P.O. Box 7136, Indianapolis, Indiana 46207, or call 877-262-1492 (or fax 317-968-5100). Remember, you will not be able to set up visits without completing this process. These rules apply to Division I and Division II schools only.

In the preseason, you should send out fall schedules with a cover letter containing your vital statistics, conference period, athletic period, and so on. Juniors should sign up for the PSAT. Seniors should have already taken the test in the summer. If you are a senior and you haven't taken the PSAT, you should do so as soon as possible. The preseason is the time when colleges will be setting up their school, campus, and home visits. This is also a good time for you to sit down with your coach and set up a calendar for all of the visits. Most college programs will work through your high school coach, as well as work with you, the athlete.

Follow all rules established by the NCAA regarding visits. Your high school coach should be present at your home visits. High school coaches should encourage their athletes to have a list of questions for the college coach. It is also a good idea to limit the home visit to 2 hours. Be prepared with your questions and expectations. You can also see whether you feel a connection. Your coach should encourage you to narrow your choices to a top five. The campus visits can become confusing and time consuming. This is a nerve-racking time; get what you need and assess your options. By narrowing your choices, you have a better chance of picking the university that is best for you.

The NCAA allows you to sign a letter of intent before your senior season. This has both advantages and disadvantages. One advantage is that it allows the athlete to focus on her senior season and not be bothered by recruiters all season. In addition, the athlete is guaranteed of having a scholarship even before the season starts, and she knows that she is the university's top choice. A disadvantage is that the athlete may settle for a university that she might not have truly wanted. She might have a terrific senior year and increase her value to a top Division I program.

The best way for you to handle recruiting is to ensure that you get exposure. Do anything you can to help get a scholarship. Send letters. Get to know the college coaches in your state. Work summer camps and attend college clinics.

Making Your Decision

There is nothing more precious in the world than one's honor and loyalty. When you finally narrow your choices and select a school, be proud. The school is making a financial and educational commitment to you, and that commitment is a two-way street. I see too many athletes transfer for reasons such as these: "I'm not getting enough playing time"; "I hate my teammates"; "It's too far away from home." These are situations that the athlete should have thought about before signing.

Remember, nobody owes you anything. Show humility, not arrogance. Give, do not take. Just because you are a high school star does not mean you are a college starter. Yes, some players will adjust more quickly than others. Be receptive to learning. Do not announce to a coach that you deserve to start. Earn that right. Show the coach in practice how much you want to start. That is more satisfying. It annoys me that some recruits ask, "Will I start?" or "How many minutes will you play me?"

Do not ask or expect a coach to break the rules regarding recruiting. Although it happens repeatedly, it is wrong. Have a sense of honor. Know what you can have and ask for it—nothing more, nothing less. I'm always amazed when I hear about athletes who have been taken care of by schools, coaches, or boosters later reveal wrongdoings that create major problems for that institution. The athletes are now gone so it does not affect them; it affects only the current and future athletes of the school. Why do that to your alma mater?

As corny as it sounds, you are in charge of your own destiny. Allow friends and family members to offer you advice on what school to attend, but make the ultimate decision yourself. You are the one who has to live with your decision, playing ball, going to school, and making the necessary adjustments for the next 4 years at the selected college. Your parents and coach are not going to school with you. They may not like the same things you do. This is your chance to make a good, solid independent decision. Weigh all the factors, make your choice, and stick with it.

In reaching this important decision, here are some questions that student-athletes should ask themselves:

- Does the school meet my academic needs?
- Is this the right school for all my personal needs?
- Is the coach a good person and a good coach as well?
- Does my game fit the system?
- What are my teammates like?

Academics

Academics should be at the top of your list of topics when asking questions of coaches, academic advisers, and school officials. You are being awarded a scholarship because of your athletic ability, but you must take your opportunity for education seriously. Your letter of intent is a contract. For 4 or 5 years, you will receive a paid education in exchange for your time, commitment, loyalty, and hard work in representing your institution. Think about what field interests you. No matter what it is, give it plenty of thought. As with anything you do, you should have an organized plan for the classroom, specifying where you want to be and how to achieve it.

You should find out the graduation rate of the athletes at your institution. This gives you insight into the commitment that the school has to its student-athletes. It will also give you an indication of how many years it has taken for other athletes to receive their diplomas. Many coaches will tell you that accurate graduation rates cannot be calculated because transfers and dropouts, for example, count as nongraduates. Tell them you understand that, and ask for a breakdown. If the school has numerous transfers and dropouts, this could tell you something about the program.

Things to Ask

1. What is the coach's graduation rate as coach at this school?
2. What is the team grade point average?
3. Is a study table required? How many hours or days does it meet?
4. Is tutoring available? If so, from whom and at what cost?
5. Considering my high school grades, reading ability, and college admission test scores, can I compete academically at this institution?
6. Does the school offer a complete program in my field of study? Or will I be offered softer courses designed to keep me eligible?
7. Does the school have an academic athletic advisor?
8. If a player has a conflict between a class and practice, how is the situation handled?
9. How much class time is missed during the year because of basketball?
10. What happens if I can't maintain the GPA required?

Personal Needs

Examine your personal preferences. In what area of the country would you like to attend college? Going far away from home can be scary. Do you want friends and relatives to be able to watch you play? Or, do you want to break those apron strings and see how you develop away from the security of home? Do you prefer a warm or cold climate? Do you want to attend a big school or a small school? Some athletes love the big-time schools, complete with nationally recognized football programs and a host of other sports. Others are more suited for a smaller city, nestled in the country. The number of students and other factors should help you decide what environment will ultimately make you happy.

Things to Ask

1. Do I want to spend the next 4 to 5 years of my life in this college environment?
2. Given my ethnic background and recreational interests, can this college and its surrounding community provide for my social needs?
3. Do the athletes live separately from other students, or do they mix with the school socially and academically?
4. Can my parents, relatives, and friends come to see me play? Do I want to attend a college that is close to home? How important is this to me?
5. Exactly what does the scholarship cover and what does it not cover?
6. Will the school find me a well-paying summer job that conforms to my career plans?
7. If I become injured and am unable to play, will the school continue to honor my scholarship and continue to help me obtain a degree?

8. Does the institution have an active organization of alumni and boosters who help athletes with career planning?
9. Are other athletes at the school who come from my environment and background happy with the social structure?
10. Will my scholarship cover a fifth year if I need it to get my degree?
11. How many days do I get off for Thanksgiving and Christmas?
12. What happens to my scholarship if I sign a National Letter of Intent, then get injured during my senior year of high school?
13. What major cities and airports are near the school?
14. How safe is the campus?

The Coach

Decide what type of coach you want to play for. Examine whether your skills fit the coach's philosophy. If not, are you willing to make adjustments? If the coach stresses defense and you're good at that, you could have a good match. If you're a half-court player and the coach has a run-and-gun philosophy, you're probably not going to be happy. Also look at the coach as a person. Many terrific coaches have never won national titles. Look for qualities in a coach that you value: loyalty, honesty, integrity, dedication, and so on.

Things to Ask

1. Is the head coach the kind of person whom I want to be the most important person in my life for the next 4 years?
2. Is the coaching staff really willing to treat academic demands as a higher priority than athletic demands?
3. Is the coach respected by his or her peers and players (current and former)? Is the coach respected by the fans, the media, and the community?
4. What is the coach's game philosophy? Practice philosophy?
5. How long has the coach been coaching, and what are his or her successes?
6. What is the coach's philosophy on conditioning and strength training? Is there a strength coach?
7. What is the coach's experience? Who are the assistants and what are their strengths?

The Program

Do you want to go to an established winning team and be one of the many great athletes who came through that program? Or, do you want to go to a lesser-known school and be part of building a tradition?

What about exposure? Are you interested in national recognition? Can you handle the limelight? Are your skills good enough to play at a major college program? Do not let anyone kid you. Combining basketball and academics is a full-time job. A scholarship means commitment, not convenience. Some young athletes who are extremely talented in high school find it difficult to handle the demands of a college program.

Things to Ask

1. How many other players are being recruited at my position?
2. Do I have the quickness, strength, and skills to play regularly at this level of competition?
3. Do my skills and playing experience fit with the style and tempo of this program?
4. Does the school have a "revolving door" reputation with players coming and going? How many players have left and why?
5. What is the breakdown of the team by class?
6. Where does the team practice? Are the games played there?
7. How long are the team's practices?
8. Who is in the team's conference?
9. Does the conference have a postseason tournament?
10. Does the conference receive an automatic bid to the NCAA tournament?
11. What was the team's record over the last few seasons? Where has the team consistently finished in the conference, region, and national championships?
12. How does the team travel?
13. Is the program supported by the president of the university, the athletic director, the professors and faculty, and the community?
14. What is the game schedule for the coming years? Is the team playing top-ranked opponents?

What College Coaches Look for in a Recruit

Coaches look at many things when recruiting. Mainly, they want to put together a team of individuals that can achieve success both on the court and off. In general, college coaches are looking for athletes who have a commitment to excellence—people who are self-motivated, have positive attitudes, and exhibit above-average skills and abilities. Coaches want to know if you're coachable and if you are receptive to instruction.

You'll be a strong candidate if you've taken and met academic requirements, which include test scores, core courses, GPA, and so on. Obviously, coaches want to know if you have an interest in their institutions, and if so, if you will sign early or late, and why. Here are some other questions that coaches may have:

1. What kind of individual are you? Will you fit in with my program and philosophy? What's your background?
2. Are you participating in AAUs, BCI, and so on?
3. Who is helping you with the recruiting process (e.g., family, coach)?
4. Is our school in your top five?
5. Do you have the total package?

SUMMARY

Learning the fundamentals of basketball is just the beginning for you. The complete game is physical, mental, and emotional. To become a complete player, you should keep the following points in mind:

- Be ready for game time. Game time is what you have been waiting for. It's a time to learn what is going right and wrong and how to improve.
- Try not to get caught up in the hype of a game. Keep your focus.
- Accept your role on the team—whatever it might be.
- Never taunt your opponent. A true athlete lets her play do her talking.
- Find out where to play. Get involved in pickup games.
- Promote yourself and your school.
- Be prepared for recruiting. You have homework to do.

Index

Note: The italicized *f* and *t* following page numbers refer to figures and tables, respectively.

T

About the Author

Courtesy of Nancy Lieberman

On November 5, 2009, basketball hall of famer **Nancy Lieberman** added an accomplishment to her already illustrious career when she became head coach of the newly formed Texas Legends, making her the first female head coach of an NBA or NBA D-League team. She has since been named assistant general manager of the team.

Before earning a full athletic scholarship to Old Dominion University in Norfolk, Virginia, Lieberman set another landmark by becoming the youngest basketball player in Olympic history (male or female) at 18 years old; she earned a silver medal at the 1976 Summer Olympics in Montreal. She exploded onto the college scene and drove the Lady Monarchs to two consecutive National Championships and a WNIT Championship. Lieberman became the first-ever two-time winner of the prestigious Wade Trophy, which recognizes the player of the year in women's college basketball. Lieberman was selected as the Broderick Award winner as the top women's basketball player in America, and she received three consecutive Kodak All-American honors during her collegiate career, making her one of the most decorated female athletes in the United States.

Lieberman went on to shape the landscape and future of women's professional basketball as player, coach, and renowned analyst. Beginning her professional career with the Dallas Diamonds of the Women's Basketball League in 1981, she quickly led her team in 1984 to the WABA Championship while also capturing the title of league MVP. More remarkably, Lieberman is recognized as the only woman to play in an all-male league—the United States Basketball League—with the Springfield Fame (1986) and Long Island Knights (1987). In 1988, Lieberman toured the world with the acclaimed Harlem Globetrotters as a member of the Washington Generals.

In 1997, Lieberman came out of retirement and was drafted by the Phoenix Mercury during the inaugural season of the WNBA. During her time as a professional player, Lieberman hit several milestones, including an induction into both the Naismith Memorial Basketball Hall of Fame and the Hampton Roads Hall of Fame as a player in 1996. In 1999, she was inducted into the Women's Basketball Hall of Fame, the New York City Basketball Hall of Fame, and the Virginia Sports Hall of Fame.

After playing in the WNBA, Lieberman was named general manager and head coach of the WNBA's Detroit Shock in 1998, where she helped the team to the highest winning percentage of any expansion team in professional sports and was runner-up for Coach of the Year. Lieberman served as president of the Women's Sports Foundation for two years. Thereafter, she was named head coach of the Dallas Fury of the NWBL in 2004, when she guided the team to a championship title and runner-up in 2005.

Lieberman again made history on July 24, 2008, by coming out of retirement once again to play for the Detroit Shock of the WNBA. She became the oldest player in the history of the league at the age of 50. She broke the previous record of 39 years old, which Nancy herself established as a member of the Phoenix Mercury in 1997.

Lieberman has served as an analyst for ESPN/ABC for the NBA, WNBA, and NCAA Women's Basketball. She has provided commentary for NBA-TV, NBC, and the NFL Network and has written for the *Dallas Morning News, New York Times,* and *USA Today.* Lieberman is an accomplished author, having written an autobiography titled *Lady Magic* (1991), *Playbook for Success* (2010), and several instructional videos for aspiring basketball players.

Lieberman's success as an athlete and leader is based on her boldness and ability to take positive action. She has a passion for educating athletes and business leaders to improve efficiency and attain peak performance. Lieberman's in-depth experience in industry is unparalleled; for this reason she is recognized as a prolific motivational speaker for Fortune 500 companies. Nancy travels around the United States for speaking engagements for private and public corporations, not-for-profit organizations, and basketball camps. Her speeches cover myriad topics, such as business and sports, image and self-esteem, teamwork, and parenting.

Guiding youngsters and helping the disadvantaged have always been passions of Lieberman and are reflected in her involvement with the Special Olympics, the Jimmy V. Foundation (named for the late Jim Valvano), the Susan G. Komen Breast Cancer Foundation, and recently her work with the National Multiple Sclerosis Society Lone Star Chapter. Lieberman hosts and coaches basketball clinics and camps for girls and boys in Dallas, Detroit, and Phoenix, hoping that through positive guidance and instruction she can facilitate success in the next generation of student-athletes.

It is only fitting that awards are given in her honor, such as the Nancy Lieberman Award, which is bestowed on the most outstanding female point guard in NCAA Division I Basketball. It has been presented to the likes of Sue Bird, Diana Taurasi, Temeka Johnson, Ivory Latta, and Lindsey Harding. Nancy Lieberman's legacy as a mom, basketball player, hall of famer, coach, general manager, Olympian, writer, broadcaster, and motivator will endure.

SPECIAL CONTRIBUTION

Rob Parker, who once lost to Nancy in a one-on-one basketball game broadcast on radio in Detroit, is an award-winning sports columnist. He writes for both ESPNNewYork.com and ClickOnDetroit.com. Parker is also a regular debater on ESPN's "1st and 10" with Skip Bayless. Parker has previously written for *The Detroit News, Newsday,* the *Detroit Free Press, The Cincinnati Enquirer,* the *Daily News* (New York), and *The Times Leader* (Wilkes-Barre, Pennsylvania). Parker—from Jamaica, Queens, New York—lives in Downtown Detroit.

An Essential Part
of Nancy's Playbook...
Life doesn't stop for timeouts. Just ask pro-mom and Basketball Hall of Famer Nancy Lieberman. That's why PhytoBurst Nutritional Chews are the perfect way to get nutrition on the go, all packed into convenient, bite-sized squares.
Mannatech.
PhytoBurst™
Nutritional Chews
Dietary Supplement
60 SOFT CHEWS
It's the little chew that packs a huge health punch for your busy lifestyle.
Mannatech.
Live for Real.
To learn more, visit Mannatech.com or contact your Independent Mannatech Associate.